QUANTUM LEAPS
and
LOST SOCKS

Your Playful Guide to Transformation

I0458635

IMAN KAMEL

ISBN: 978-1-964619-80-4

Cover Art by Lincoln Gardner
Author Photo Credit to Ute Freund

To Klaus, my anchor in the storm, my co-captain on this wild voyage of life. Through laughter and tears, through calm seas and tempestuous waves, your love has been my compass, guiding me home to myself.

A Quantum Dance Through Hidden Gardens

When a young girl climbs a forbidden lemon tree in her grandmother's Cairo garden, she has no idea she's taking the first step on an extraordinary journey that will span continents and consciousness itself. Now acclaimed filmmaker and wisdom keeper Iman Kamel invites you to follow her path of unexpected awakening - from dancing with dolphins in the Red Sea to fever dreams in China's remote temples, from Berlin's underground art scene to sacred ceremonies beneath desert stars.

Let her wild adventures and hard-won wisdom become the springboard for your own transformation through the five phases of the Lotus-Born Heart Process. Join thirteen women on a Nile journey where ancient Egyptian deities emerge as living forces of creation. Navigate the fertile darkness of Primal Mud wearing mismatched socks that spark quantum revelations. Discover how Sekhmet's fierce grace can turn your greatest challenges into fuel for breakthrough innovation.

This is where science meets soul in the most delightful ways - where your morning coffee ritual becomes a dance with Hathor's creative joy, where quantum physics confirms what temple priestesses always knew, and where even your sock drawer holds keys to cosmic awakening. Through immersive stories, practical rituals, and playful practices, you'll discover how the extraordinary hides within your most ordinary moments.

Whether you're a visionary leader bridging worlds, an artist expanding horizons, or a seeker weaving science and spirit, this journey will transform how you experience reality itself. Each page is an invitation to remember your infinite nature - while keeping both feet joyfully planted in the fertile soil of everyday magic.

Welcome to a revolution of consciousness that begins with a single climb up a lemon tree. Your journey into unlimited possibility awaits.

TABLE OF CONTENTS

PART I
OPENING GATEWAYS

PREFACE: THE OCEAN IN A DROP

"You are not a drop in the ocean.
You are the entire ocean in a drop."
—Rumi

At dawn by the Nile, as the rising sun painted the ancient waters in hues of gold and rose, Rumi's words echoed through my contemplation. Watching my reflection ripple and dance on the river's surface, I felt the depth of his truth resonate within me. Each wavelet contained the entire universe, just as we each contain the infinite potential of the cosmos.

This book emerges from a life lived as a cosmic nomad, wandering this precious blue dot and beyond in full, passionate embrace of adventure and transformation. My path has led me from the mystical peaks of Japan's Yamagata mountains to the ancient wisdom of California's redwood forests, from the wild beauty of Madagascar to the futuristic visions of Astana, Kazakhstan. Each destination has added its unique note to the symphony of understanding that resonates through these pages.

I have danced through life wearing many forms - filmmaker capturing untold stories, keynote speaker igniting minds with visions of possibility, healer channeling divine energies, artist mentor awakening creative fire, producer weaving dreams into reality. In sacred ceremonies and homeopathic triturations I've explored the power of the blue lotus, merging with the vibrant presence of Egypt's divine forces. My films have carried messages of hope and awakening across the globe, touching hearts and opening minds to new possibilities.

After passing through times of profound darkness and illness, I emerged transformed, like Hathor the divine milk-giver, carrying within me the nourishing waters of rebirth. This understanding arose through direct experience, from filming on winding roads to facilitating workshops across continents, from diving deep into healing practices to soaring high with artistic vision. Each moment revealed we are far more vast and magnificent than we imagine. I have played in this world, truly played, discovering that life's greatest mysteries often reveal themselves through joy and wonder.

The Neteru pulse through our world as living, breathing presences - divine forces expressing through every aspect of existence. Sekhmet's fierce compassion burns in the hearts of healers and activists. Hathor's creative joy dances through artists and lovers. Tehuti's brilliance sparks in scientific breakthroughs and cosmic discoveries. Their temples serve as living portals to higher consciousness, where past, present and future merge in eternal dance. Each human being embodies a hologram of the universe itself, containing all the power and creative force of existence within their own heart.

You hold in your hands a journey of awakening, a pathway of transformation, a guide to discovering your infinite nature. Through the phases of the Lotus-Born Heart process - from the fertile darkness of Primal Mud, through the quest of Seeking Light, the challenges of Luminous Ascent, the joy of Radiant Blossoming, to the creative power of Sacred Seeding - you will discover the vastness within.

As you journey through these pages, you will find yourself transformed, shocked, irritated, inspired, moved, enlightened - often all at once. This is natural, for transformation spirals through existence itself. Let yourself be guided by your intuition, trust the wisdom of your heart, and dance with the countless fellow travelers walking these pathways.

My deepest hope is that this book serves as a mirror, reflecting back to you your own infinite nature. That it awakens within you the remembrance of who you truly are - the light itself seeking expression through your unique form. That it empowers you to embrace your role as a conscious co-creator of reality, a sacred vessel through which the universe experiences itself.

For this remains the greatest truth I have discovered through all my travels and transformations: we exist as pure consciousness, expressing through millions of unique forms, each one precious, each one perfect, each one containing the whole within itself. I am an emanation of the Holographic Being, as are you, as is every particle of existence.

Every time you lose yourself in creative flow, every moment when time bends and shifts, every instance of spontaneous knowing - you touch this living wisdom. These practices offer direct gateways to embody these transformative energies, to dance with these divine forces as intimate partners in creation.

Welcome, beloved fellow traveler, to the journey of embodying your true nature. Welcome to the adventure of discovering the infinite within. Let us play together in these boundless realms of possibility.

With love and gratitude,
Autumn 2024

Incantation to Isis
Isis, Lady of Healing, your hands hold the balm
That soothes all wounds, a gentle, mending calm.
Grant my touch your grace, on leaf and heart so frail,
With healing for myself, with healing that won't fail.
Isis, Mistress of Nature, with every breath I take,
Merge my spirit with creation's pulse, for my soul's sake.
From dewdrop's gleam to the sun's golden ray,
May the rhythm of life guide me on my way.
Isis, Mother of Courage, awaken the lioness within,
Burn away fear, let boldness begin.
Not for dominance, but to face the unknown,
May my spirit soar, where seeds of strength are sown.
In the bird's joyous song, my spirit takes flight,
Beyond the bounds of Earth, bathed in cosmic light.
Isis, hear my plea, guide my journey true,
In unity with all worlds, with all I ever knew.

Through the Looking Glass: Your Journey Begins

Like Alice stepping through the looking glass, you're about to enter a world where ordinary boundaries dissolve and wonder awaits around every corner. Find your favorite reading nook, perhaps by a window where morning light spills across the pages. This book opens as a doorway, a companion for dreamers, a treasure map to your own inner realms.

As you open these pages, worlds unfold before you. Some days you might find yourself walking alongside a young girl climbing a lemon tree in Cairo, the scent of citrus sharp and sweet in the air. Other afternoons, you'll float down the Nile under a canopy of stars, their ancient light reflecting in the sacred waters below. Like Alice discovering she can grow tall as a house or small as a mouse, you'll find these stories and immersions invite you to expand beyond ordinary horizons - one moment vast as the cosmos, touching infinite wisdom, the next intimate as a whispered secret between friends.

These stories yearn to be savored, like honey dissolving slowly on your tongue. Read them aloud in the quiet hours before dawn, letting your voice dance with the rhythms of ancient temples and modern adventures. Carry a single image with you through your day - the flash of a kingfisher's wing, the cool touch of temple stones, the way sunlight fractures through mosque windows into rainbow geometries. Let your voice become an instrument of transformation. Record yourself reading the immersions or passages that call to you, then listen with closed eyes. Notice how your tone shifts naturally - perhaps growing fierce with warrior tales, soft with temple prayers, playful with trickster gods. Each telling brings these stories to life in new ways.

Let time flow naturally around these stories and immersions- some might stay with you for a season, others might transform you in a single afternoon. Like the Nile itself, your journey through these pages follows its own rhythm. Dip in and out, linger where your heart calls, rush forward with the current when it moves you. A single phase might unfold over months, or several might dance together in a week's time.

When questions flutter in your heart like restless birds, let this book become your oracle. Hold it in your hands, feeling its weight, its presence. Whisper your question into its pages, then let them fall open where they will. The first words that catch your eye might offer unexpected wisdom - perhaps a description of temple incense awakening your intuition, or a shamanic journey illuminating your strength.

Your intuition will guide you perfectly through these pages. Begin wherever you feel called - perhaps with the fierce flames of Luminous

Ascent, or in the nurturing depths of Primal Mud. Each phase offers its own invitation. One morning you might dance with Sekhmet's power, the next float in Isis's embrace. Trust the wisdom of your wandering.

Create a sanctuary for your reading. Light candles scented with temple offerings - frankincense, myrrh, sacred lotus. Wrap yourself in soft fabrics that feel like embracing clouds. Play music that stirs ancient memories - drumbeats echoing heartbeats, melodies winding like the Nile through your dreams. Let your environment become part of the unfolding tale. Personally, I love total silence when engaging with these inner journeyings. I listen to my inner music so to speak!

Let music and movement carry you deeper. Create playlists that match each chapter's essence - thundering drums for power tales, ethereal flutes for moon mysteries. When stories stir your soul, let your body respond. Dance "inner abundance" through your limbs, feel "Seeking Light " ripple up your spine. Every movement becomes part of the story.

Take these stories into nature's embrace. Let birdsong harmonize with temple chants, watch leaf-shadows dance like ancient priestesses across your pages. Read to flowers and trees, who listen with timeless patience and share their own silent wisdom. A butterfly's emergence might illuminate a passage about transformation, while a slowly unfurling leaf reflects teachings about patience.

Turn reading into playful exploration. Gather friends for cosmic storytelling - Create a wonder circle - gather with fellow explorers to read aloud, share dreams, make art inspired by the stories. Each person discovers different treasures, and together your perspectives expand like desert horizons at dawn.

Weave random phrases into wild new tales, act out scenes with scarves and candlelight, create collages from images that mirror the themes. Wonder multiplies when shared. These stories yearn to spark your own tales, your own healing journeys, your own sacred adventures. Challenge them, question them, argue with them in the margins. Let them be springboards for your own discoveries, portals opening onto your unique path - weave phrases into new stories, create collaborative tales, let laughter and creativity spark unexpected insights.

Before sleep, read a passage and let it sink into your dreams like stones dropping into still water. See what ripples return with the dawn. Share favorite passages with kindred spirits who speak the language of wonder. Let these stories become bridges between hearts, weaving new connections.

Some days, simply let yourself be carried by the current of adventure - following a filmmaker through Berlin's underground art scene, or holding your breath as she navigates her first storm at sea. Each tale becomes a mirror, reflecting facets of your own unfolding journey.

Let your journal become a book of wonders. Make choosing it a ritual - perhaps awakening a notebook that's been waiting for this moment, or following synchronicity to find the perfect companion for your journey. Fill it with pressed flowers that echo temple gardens, sketches of patterns in morning tea leaves, poems inspired by ancient chants. Create your own sacred text alongside these stories. Your journal becomes a living map of this meandering. Fill its pages not just with words, doodle the landscapes of your imagination - sketch the temples that appear in your dreams, draw spiraling paths through your own inner wilderness, create constellations from connecting ideas. Let your pen wander into unexpected territories, creating visual echoes of your journey.

Keep a dream journal by your bedside. Dreams continue the conversation these stories begin, weaving new patterns in your sleeping mind. Record your night flights over pyramids, dances with lioness goddesses, discoveries of hidden doorways in familiar walls. Draw the symbols that appear, even the ones that defy ordinary logic. Your dreaming mind speaks in images and metaphors, just like these tales.

This book lives and breathes - revealing new secrets with each reading, responding to the season of your soul, offering exactly what you need in each moment. Let it accompany you through joy and challenge, illuminating the extraordinary that dwells within ordinary moments.

Remember childhood's infinite possibility? When worlds nested within worlds, and meaning shimmered just beneath the surface of things? These pages invite you to reclaim that clear-seeing heart, not to escape reality, but to engage it more deeply.

Watch for synchronicities as they arise. A random page might offer exactly the wisdom you seek. A friend's chance comment might illuminate a story in a new way. These moments of alignment weave a tapestry of meaning, showing how these ancient tales live in our present moment.

And so, like Alice, prepare to step through the looking glass. Find your comfortable chair, brew your favorite tea, light a candle or simply let your heart's light guide you. What story will speak to you today? Where will these tales lead? Your journey of wonder begins the moment you open these pages.

You're living these stories, breathing them, dancing them into being through your unique way of experiencing them. Let them transform you, surprise you, awaken you to the extraordinary flowing through your own remarkable life.

Now open the book anywhere and begin. Through the looking glass, wonder awaits.

The Unraveling: A Holographic Being Fable

There is a city where time moves like honey dripping from a forgotten comb - sweet, languid, predictable. The ancient marketplace pulses with life, yet something essential sleeps beneath its rhythms. Above the spice merchants' stalls, ibis birds circle in mysterious patterns, their wings writing messages few remember how to read. The sun paints the cobbled streets gold, but the people's eyes have forgotten how to catch its magic.

This is a place where everyone knows their role, their path, their small piece of the great pattern. But like a tapestry viewed too close, they've lost sight of the greater image they're part of. Their movements follow the precision of clockwork, yet lack the wild dance of stars.

Then, like a mischievous wink from the universe, a single, impossibly green sock tumbles across the cobblestones. Its surface ripples with swirling hieroglyphs that seem to shift and change when no one is looking directly at them. A startled ibis takes flight, its shadow forming the shape of a crescent moon against the stones. And in the hush that follows, the ordinary world tilts on its axis, whispering, change is coming.

Into this scene steps the Traveler, perched atop a sturdy donkey laden with bulging saddlebags. His fingers are stained with ink, and a worn scribe's satchel bounces against his hip, filled with gleaming pebbles and fragments of ancient scrolls. A silver feather gleams at his throat, catching the light in impossible ways. His eyes hold the depth of millennia, though his smile speaks of eternal youth. A whisper ripples through the crowd: "Perhaps this is no ordinary visitor."

Elara, the weaver, feels her heart skip a beat. A thread of midnight blue, the color of wisdom's deepest waters, snakes through her fingers, awakening a longing for mysteries half-remembered in dreams. Little Mara, a sprite of a girl usually lost in the market's whirlwind, finds her gaze locked with the Traveler's, a silent recognition passing between them. For a moment, she thinks she sees the flutter of wings behind his shoulders, but surely that's just a trick of the light.

The Traveler's presence sends ripples through the city's careful routines. Jars of spices begin to dance to unheard melodies, filling the air with a symphony of clinking glass and exotic aromas. Children chasing cats find themselves on rooftops, the city spread before them like a living tapestry, its hidden corners revealed. Laughter, the kind that bubbles up from the belly and spills over like stardust, begins to sprinkle the marketplace.

In Elara's workshop, her loom pulses with newfound energy. Threads of sapphire blue, reminiscent of moonlit nights under desert skies, entwine with fiery orange, the color of a shaman's laughter at dawn. Silver ibis feathers appear mysteriously among her threads, and sometimes, in the quiet hours before dawn, her tapestries seem to whisper ancient songs. Her work, once a reflection of the city's slumber, now sings with stories of forgotten dreams and reawakened possibilities.

Little Mara, her heart buzzing with a melody only she can hear, finds herself drawn to the edges of the familiar. She follows trails of hieroglyphs that appear and disappear in the dust, led by the scent of lotus and myrrh that grows stronger with each step. One afternoon, the trail leads her to a hidden garden tucked away in a forgotten corner of the city.

Beneath a crumbling archway, veiled by sun-bleached walls and wild vines, three magnificent statues stand sentinel. The first, a jackal-headed figure with eyes that seem to peer into souls, stands guard at the entrance. The second, a majestic falcon crowned with a solar disk, spreads its wings as if ready to take flight. Between them stands a woman of indescribable beauty, her arms outstretched in welcome, her stone face holding all the mystery of the moon. Black lotuses bloom impossibly from cracks in the dry earth, their petals drinking in shadows and transforming them into light.

Though Mara doesn't know their names - doesn't yet understand that she stands in the presence of Anubis, Horus, and Isis - their energy fills her with a sense of coming home. Beneath the woman's outstretched hand, she finds a small carved flute. Its notes, when she dares to play them, weave through the city's streets like tendrils of dawn light, awakening something long dormant in those who hear them.

The garden's discovery spreads through the city like ripples in a dream pool. People begin to find their way there, first in ones and twos, then in steady streams. They come bearing simple gifts - colored ribbons, smooth stones etched with hopes, wild flowers picked from between cobblestones. Each offering a seed of transformation planted in fertile soil.

At her loom, Elara's hands move with newfound purpose. Each thread she weaves hums with the energy of rediscovery. The Traveler watches from the shadows as people gather, not to buy or sell, but to witness the emergence of something profound in her work. Between the falcon's wings and the jackal's knowing gaze, images of transformation take shape - seeds sprouting, lotuses blooming, stars dancing in human form.

The city's rhythm shifts, deepens, expands. Conversations in the marketplace flow like rivers finding new channels. Dreams long forgotten rise to the surface like pearls. Even the stones of the streets seem to pulse with renewed life, each cobble a mirror reflecting fragments of a greater whole.

The final tapestry on Elara's loom reveals what some have already begun to suspect. The Traveler stands revealed as Tehuti, divine scribe and keeper of wisdom, his ibis head crowned with the moon's crescents. Beside him, the stone woman from the garden glows with the light of countless stars - Isis herself, whose love reweaves the fragments of what was broken. Their forms intertwine not in romantic embrace, but in the sacred dance of wisdom and love, masculine and feminine energies in perfect balance. Between them blooms a lotus of pure light, its petals containing entire universes.

The Traveler slips away as quietly as he arrived. His donkey bears him toward new horizons, saddlebags now filled with the stories of awakening he has witnessed. But his departure is not an ending. In the garden, new flowers continue to bloom from ancient soil. At Elara's loom, threads weave themselves into ever-expanding patterns. And little Mara's flute song carries on the wind, calling to others who are ready to remember that divinity dwells in the heart of the ordinary, waiting to be discovered anew.

The people of the city, gazing upon these wonders, feel something stir in their own hearts - a recognition of the magnificent dance they've always been part of, an awakening to the truth that every small moment contains the seeds of infinite possibility. They begin to see themselves as living threads in a tapestry that stretches from the depths of the Primal Mud to the heights of the stars, each one a hologram containing the pattern of the whole.

And so the city continues to unfold, each day a new discovery, each person a thread in an ever-expanding tapestry. The pattern grows more beautiful for having been forgotten and remembered again, like a lotus rising from the mud to touch the light of infinite stars.

What forgotten divinity sleeps in your own heart, beloved? What sacred mysteries wait to be rediscovered? The garden gates stand open, and the song of Isis and Tehuti still echoes through the ages. Will you answer?

The Honeycomb and the Lotus: A Cosmic Dance of Unfolding

The golden cells of a honeycomb glow with inner light. You are here, in one of these cells, going about your daily life. Some days feel small, confined by the walls of routine and responsibility. Yet within these very walls, magic stirs.

Feel the subtle vibration humming through your cell. This is the song of life itself, connecting you to countless others, each living their own stories, each contributing to a pattern more beautiful than any single cell could create alone. Like ripples in a pond, your smallest actions send waves through the entire honeycomb.

Reach into the heart of your cell. Here, nestled in sweet darkness, lies a seed - your lotus-born heart. It pulses with timeless wisdom, with dreams waiting to emerge, with the power to transform your entire world. This seed holds a magnificent secret: within you lives the same force that turns mud into flowers, darkness into light, ordinary moments into glimpses of the divine.

From the quantum dance of subatomic particles to the vast spiral of galaxies, the universe pulses with this endless potential for unfolding. Every atom in your body whirls in an eternal dance of possibility. Each breath draws you deeper into life's grand choreography. You exist as both particle and wave, fixed and flowing, singular and infinite.

The Lotus-Born Heart Process mirrors these profound patterns of transformation. Like a lotus rising through murky waters, we begin in the fertile depths of being - the Primal Mud phase. Here in the rich soil of unexamined patterns and hidden truths, infinite possibilities exist in divine superposition. Your potential lies dreaming in the darkness, waiting to awaken.

From these depths, an inner light calls you upward into the Seeking Light phase, where curiosity becomes your compass. Like a lotus stem pushing through murky waters, you navigate the space between what is and what could be. Every question opens a doorway. Every challenge invites expansion. Your consciousness stretches toward the surface of greater understanding.

As you rise, your movement gains purpose and power in Luminous Ascent. The walls around you become translucent. Your consciousness expands like petals opening to the sun. The honeycomb cell reveals itself as a microcosm of the universe - every boundary a doorway, every limitation an invitation to grow.

In Radiant Blossoming, your petals unfold to embrace the light. This phase brings both personal transformation and contribution to life's greater beauty. Each petal that opens reveals a new facet of consciousness, a new way of seeing and being in the world. Your individual blossoming intertwines with the unfolding of life itself.

The journey spirals outward through Sacred Seeding. Like a lotus releasing its seeds upon the water, you become a source of inspiration and renewal for others. Your awakening ripples through the honeycomb of existence. Your presence calls forth the sleeping potential in everyone you meet.

You embody the holographic nature of reality - each part containing the whole. The mud holds the promise of blossoming. The blossom carries the memory of the mud. Every phase of the journey exists within every other, an infinite dance of becoming.

Ancient forces await to guide you - some fierce like desert winds, others gentle as dawn light on water. These forces live within you, ready to help transform your ordinary cell into a gateway to the extraordinary. They pulse in your blood, whisper in your dreams, and dance in the spaces between your thoughts.

Every heartbeat drums a call to awaken. Every breath invites unfolding. The cosmic waters await your touch. The lotus of your heart yearns to open.

Will you accept this invitation to discover the honeycomb of your being, to awaken the lotus seed of your heart? Will you let these walls become the structure that supports your blossoming? Your journey begins with a single choice: to see yourself as both bee and lotus, quantum dancer and sacred seed, ready to illuminate the entire hive with your unique and radiant light.

The path unfolds before you, rich with possibility. Take this first step. The universe yearns to dance with you.

The Living Presence of the Neteru: The Vibrant Dance of Being

The Neteru pulse through our world like cosmic rhythms, as alive today as the force that turns seeds into forests and stars into galaxies. They are the living currents of creation, flowing through every heartbeat, every transformation, every moment of awakening.

When lightning splits the sky, Sekhmet's fierce clarity illuminates our path. Her power flows through us when we stand up for truth, when we protect what we love, when we transform obstacles into opportunities for growth. That same force shape-shifts into Hathor's nurturing radiance in moments of joy and connection, then playfully morphs into Bast's sensual delight in life's simple pleasures. They are not three separate goddesses but facets of the same divine light, reflecting different aspects of our own luminous nature.

In the sleek glass and steel of our modern cities, Tehuti's wisdom still writes itself in synchronicities and sudden insights. Horus soars through our highest aspirations, while Anubis guides us through the depths of transformation. Isis weaves through every act of healing and rebirth, while Osiris teaches us that every ending contains the seeds of a new beginning.

The Neteru are not confined to ancient temple walls - they are the living forces of nature herself, expressing through every facet of existence. They dance through our dreams, spark our innovations, and pulse through our creative expressions. When we tap into our intuition, we're touching Isis's knowing. When we break through limitations, we're channeling Sekhmet's strength. When we create beauty, we're expressing Hathor's artistry.

This book is an activation key, awakening these divine forces within you. Each page is a mirror reflecting different aspects of your own infinite potential. Through stories, practices, and explorations, you'll discover how these cosmic energies express themselves uniquely through your being.

The journey unfolds like a lotus opening to the sun - from the fertile mud of potential, through the waters of transformation, into the full radiance of awakened being. It spirals in holographic magnificence, each part containing the whole, each practice awakening multiple aspects of your divine nature.

The Neteru await in the beating of your own heart, in the pulse of your dreams, in the power of your becoming. They live as dynamic presences ready for embodiment. Through them, we remember our own divine nature - infinite, multifaceted, ever-evolving.

Are you ready to awaken these forces within you? To discover how Sekhmet's fire ignites your spirit? How Aset Isis's magic flows through your hands? How Hathor's love opens your heart? All these cosmic powers pulse through your being, here and now, in the sacred space of your own unfolding life.

Welcome to the dance of unfolding.

Perceiving the Unseen Realms of Existence: A Multi-dimensional Perspective

Dawn breaks over Cairo. My pen glides across the journal page, capturing wisdom flowing from unseen realms as vendors set up their stalls below. Pigeons wheel overhead, their wings cutting through dimensions. The scent of baking bread mingles with star-fire and ancient incense as my consciousness soars through cosmic libraries where the Neteru share their secrets. My physical form anchors to the scratch of pen on paper while my awareness traverses temples of light. The worlds dance together - insights from subtle realms flowing into written word, each sensory detail of physical reality enriching the journey.

A dove's call pierces the veil. Following its flight, my vision shifts to encompass both beating wings and the shimmering threads of light trailing in their wake. My hand sketches these patterns of energy, translating light into symbol, air into story. In the market square, a lotus blossom catches sunlight. Its geometry unfolds galaxies, each petal a doorway to deeper knowing. Later, in a café corner, my laptop hums with transcribed visions while mint tea warms my hands. To passing eyes, I appear absorbed in work. Yet my consciousness spans vast libraries of light, each keystroke bridging heaven and earth. A nearby cat's purr grounds the surging energies.

This art of journeying transforms every space. Practice brings fluidity. Like a musician simultaneously reading notes, playing strings, and channeling emotion, we learn to dance between worlds. Our physical senses stay sharp while multidimensional perceiving and vision expands. Safety demands full presence when driving or operating machinery, yet even professional spaces welcome subtle wisdom woven naturally into practical action.

We receive messages from the Neteru, and insights from the Akashic Records, all while remaining present in physical reality. Our senses expand beyond the traditional five, encompassing a spectrum of subtle perceptions – the whispers of intuition, the tingling of energy fields, the resonance of shared consciousness. We cultivate the ability to journey with open eyes, to be present in both the physical world and the unseen realms simultaneously. It's a dance, a merging of the mundane and the magical, a recognition that the boundaries between these realms are fluid and permeable.

Shamanic circles create vessels for collective journeying. Sacred drums pulse heartbeats of ancient worlds. Each participant travels unique spirit paths while shared energy weaves us into a luminous field of exploration. Our journals capture maps of realms beyond ordinary sight - crystalline cities, wisdom councils, healing sanctuaries spanning multiple dimensions.

Through devoted practice, perception opens to subtle layers gracing everyday moments. Morning light through leaves reveals sacred geometry. A garden path becomes a threshold between worlds. Each breath draws awareness through veils of reality - physical form, energy bodies, soul essence, cosmic mind flowing as one river of experience. You perceive the subtle energies that surround you – the auras of people passing, the spirits of trees lining sidewalks, ancient whispers from the land beneath your feet.

In quiet meditation, breath slowing, mind still, awareness expands to embrace the vast cosmos. Stars and galaxies dance, infinite possibilities shimmering within the quantum field. A flower unfolds its petals in exquisite beauty, revealing intricate geometry, Fibonacci spirals, golden ratios - the mathematical language of the universe made visible. Fingers trace these patterns in air, a silent choreography mirroring creation's dance, while mind weaves insights connecting microcosm to macrocosm.

Yet this awareness rises from proper practice. Sacred space holds the gateway. Protection and preparation create clear channels. Like a prism splitting light into rainbow streams, consciousness expands through multiple dimensions while remaining grounded in embodied wisdom. The worlds weave together - matter and spirit, seen and unseen, known and mystery - each enriching the others in an infinite dance.

Trust these stirrings of expanded perception. Begin in sacred space, with proper preparation. From seeds planted in sacred soil, awareness blooms through all dimensions of being. The journey unfolds, eternal and ever-new, as we open to the magnificent multiplicity of existence.

The Holographic Being: An Invitation to Wholeness

Your life unfolds as a magnificent, multifaceted gem. Each facet – your passions, skills, experiences, and challenges – reflects light in its own unique way. Every surface, whether brilliant and polished or textured with experience, contributes to the dazzling, ever-evolving whole. This is the essence of your Holographic Being.

The first seeds of this understanding sprouted during my early days as a filmmaker in Berlin. Living between cultures, I titled my first short film "Hologram," weaving together the rich tapestry of my Egyptian heritage with my emerging European life. Each world enhanced the other, creating something entirely new.

My path led me to embrace an expansive way of being. The call to dance, make films, practice Japanese calligraphy – these seemingly diverse passions revealed themselves as perfect expressions of my wholeness. Many souls today share this natural inclination toward multiplicity, yearning to weave together their various interests, talents, and professional paths into a life that rings true to their deepest nature.

The Holographic Being celebrates this multidimensional nature! Every facet of our experience contributes to the brilliant, unique gem we each embody. Modern science now echoes what ancient wisdom traditions have always known: the profound interconnectedness of the universe and the remarkable capacity of human consciousness to shape reality.

Quantum physics reveals particles existing in multiple states simultaneously. Neuroplasticity shows our brain's constant ability to rewire and adapt. The placebo effect demonstrates how belief creates tangible changes in the body. These discoveries point to a universe far more responsive and fluid than previously understood.

The Holographic Being manifests as lived reality. I embody the filmmaker, the shaman, the healer, the Akashic records reader, the cultural diplomat, the entrepreneur, the author, and the mentor. These expressions flow together as facets of one Holographic Being, each enriching and informing the others. Through years of exploration and integration, this understanding has crystallized into clear pathways of transformation.

This book opens as a fertile field for your journey of self-discovery and transformation. We'll explore your unique experiences, your cultivated skills, and the sacred aspects of yourself waiting to shine. Here you'll find tools to polish every facet, to embrace your full brilliance, and to weave your multifaceted nature into a life of purpose, passion, and ever-unfolding potential.

As you embrace your Holographic Being, your transformation ripples outward. Your unfolding touches those around you, shapes communities, and contributes to the evolution of our world.

The Uncreated Potential

Within you, beloved traveler, lies a universe of untapped possibility. Just as a seed holds the complete blueprint of a magnificent blossom, your Holographic Being carries an infinite wellspring of transformative power, waiting to unfold.

This potential speaks in many voices. Sometimes it comes as a gentle whisper, a creative impulse seeking expression. Other times it stirs like a cosmic force, a profound sense of purpose yearning to manifest. You might feel it as the urge to write, to heal, to create, to transform the world - or simply as a deep longing for a life overflowing with authenticity and joy.

The very restlessness you feel signals this vast energy seeking its path into form. Each moment of divine discontent, each dream that won't stay silent, each intuitive flash points toward the extraordinary possibilities awaiting their birth through you.

The Lotus-Born Heart process reveals itself as a sacred technology for awakening these dormant seeds. Through immersive journeys into both shadow and light, through practices that honor both ancient wisdom and quantum possibility, you'll learn to recognize and nurture the infinite potential dwelling in your depths.

Begin by creating spaces of sacred silence in your daily life. Let your mind grow still, like the surface of an undisturbed pool. Watch what rises from these depths - memories of childhood dreams, visions of possible futures, subtle knowings that transcend ordinary thought. These glimpses reveal fragments of your vast, uncreated potential.

Open your journal and let your pen dance with the question: "What wants to emerge through me?" Write without censoring, without limiting. Let your soul speak through symbols, stories, drawings - whatever form your truth desires to take. The act of witnessing these longings begins their journey into manifestation.

Listen for the voice of your inner child, who knew no bounds to possibility. What adventures did they dream of? What magic did they know was real? Their wisdom holds keys to doors you may have forgotten existed.

This exploration of uncreated potential forms the foundation for your journey through the five phases ahead. Like rich soil preparing to receive precious seeds, this recognition of your infinite nature creates the perfect conditions for transformation.

Your uncreated potential is both a gift and a responsibility - a sacred trust between your soul and the universe itself. As you step into the Lotus-Born Heart process, you begin the magnificent adventure of bringing heaven to earth through the unique expression of your Holographic Being.

The journey awaits. The seeds stir. The time for unfolding is now.

PART II
LOTUS-BORN HEART PROCESS

I. PRIMAL MUD

Isis, Voice of Compassion, may your song take flight,
Whispering hope where sorrow shrouds the light.
Through my being, let its healing echo ring,
Soothing distant worlds, where hearts take wing.

Isis, Lady of Plenty, by your bountiful hand,
Guide me through the market, across this vibrant land.
Each morsel touched by starlight's gentle gleam,
To nourish bodies, and ignite a radiant dream.

The Vase: A Sanctuary in the Mud

The world buzzed and whirred, a symphony of sensations too intense for my four-year-old self. Sunlight streamed through the high windows of our grand old house, casting long, dancing shadows that transformed familiar furniture into lurking giants. Every room hummed with the energy of hushed conversations, the clinking of teacups, and the rustle of newspapers – a world of adults that felt both alluring and overwhelming.

I longed to run, to explore the hidden corners of our sprawling home, but delicate antiques and fragile knick-knacks lined every surface, creating a maze of restrictions. My small body, a whirlwind of energy, craved a refuge, a place to escape the constant reminders to be still, to be quiet, to be small.

And so, I found my sanctuary. In a shadowed corner of the hall, a large, black vase stood like a silent sentinel. Its smooth, cool surface beckoned, promising a haven from the overwhelming vastness and the endless rules. With a surge of determination, I hoisted myself onto its rim, peering into its depths.

The world within the vase was a wonderland of distorted perspectives. Sunlight filtered through the narrow opening, casting an emerald glow that transformed the familiar into something magical. The scent of dust mingled with the aroma of damp earth, whispering of hidden depths and forgotten secrets.

With a mix of excitement and trepidation, I carefully lifted our tiny, 100-year-old turtle, her wrinkled face peering back at me. Our resident turtle, seeking refuge as I was, must have been left there for safety. I gently placed her in the vase and climbed inside with my tiny four-year-old body. The smooth porcelain curves enveloped us like a comforting cocoon, shutting out the noise and demands of the adult world. Inside, the world was deliciously contained, a sanctuary of quietude where I could finally be myself.

This childhood memory, etched in the depths of my being, is a perfect reflection of the Primal Mud, the fertile darkness from which all creation arises. Just as I found solace and potential within the vase's enclosed space, the Primal Mud represents the boundless possibilities that lie dormant within each of us, waiting to be awakened.

In the ancient Egyptian creation myth, before the universe unfolded, there existed only Nun, the infinite, dark waters of chaos. From these depths arose the first mound of earth, the foundation upon which the creator god shaped the cosmos. Like the seed of the lotus, hidden within the mud, we too hold within us the potential for extraordinary growth and transformation.

The Primal Mud is a metaphor for those times when we feel overwhelmed, lost, or stuck. It's a time of gestation, of hidden growth, where the blueprint for our future self is being formed. It's in these moments of darkness and uncertainty that we have the opportunity to connect with our deepest selves, to uncover our hidden strengths, and to plant the seeds for a more authentic and fulfilling life.

As we explore the Primal Mud together, we'll uncover the wisdom that lies within the darkness, learn to value our "mud moments," and harness their transformative power to birth our most authentic selves. We'll discover that the mud is not a place of stagnation, but a fertile ground for growth, a necessary stage in the journey towards the light. Just as the lotus emerges from the mud to blossom in the sun, we too can rise from the depths of our challenges, transformed and radiant.

Journaling Prompts : Seeking Sanctuary

Reflect on a time when you sought refuge in a place that felt safe and comforting. Perhaps it was a physical space, like a favorite childhood hiding spot, a quiet corner in nature, or a cozy room in your home. Or maybe it was an internal sanctuary, a state of mind where you felt at peace and connected to yourself.

Close your eyes for a moment and allow yourself to be transported back to that sanctuary. Recall the sights, sounds, smells, and sensations that surrounded you. How did it feel to be in that space? What qualities did it embody for you?

Now, open your journal and begin to explore this memory in more detail. Describe the sanctuary, capturing its essence through words. What emotions and thoughts arise as you revisit this place of refuge?

Consider the ways in which you seek sanctuary in your life today. Where do you go, or what do you do, to find peace, solace, and a sense of connection to yourself? What practices or rituals help you create a sense of sanctuary within?

Reflect on the following questions as you write:

- What qualities do you seek in a sanctuary?
- How does your current sanctuary nourish and support you?

- How can you create more opportunities for a sanctuary in your daily life?
- How can you connect with the energy of the Primal Mud as a source of a sanctuary and renewal?

Allow your writing to flow freely, without judgment or expectation. This is a sacred dialogue between you and your inner self, a conversation with the part of you that seeks refuge and renewal.

The Oracle Silenced

The air crackled with a tension I couldn't comprehend, the clinking of glasses and murmurs of adult conversation a discordant symphony to my five-year-old ears. My aunt, usually a beacon of warmth and laughter, sat across the table, her smile strained, her eyes clouded with a longing that tugged at my heart. The adults were discussing the delicate topic of childbirth, a subject shrouded in both anticipation and apprehension in our culture. Suddenly, a knowingness surged within me, an undeniable truth that burst forth from my lips, "Aunty, you will never have children."

The room fell silent. Conversations halted mid-sentence, forks clattered onto plates, and all eyes turned towards me, wide with shock and disbelief. My aunt's forced smile crumbled, revealing a kaleidoscope of emotions – pain, resignation, and a desperate flicker of hope. My innocent pronouncement, spoken with the unwavering certainty of a child, landed like a stone in the stillness, its ripples echoing through the tense atmosphere.

That night, my father's touch was heavy, his voice thick with disappointment and fear. He saw my gift as a dangerous secret, a threat to our family's reputation in a society where childlessness was a mark of shame. His words, sharp and admonishing, cut through me: "You must never speak of such things again. It is not your place to know, to see."

His punishment, a misguided attempt to protect me from the world's judgment, felt like a betrayal. The spark of knowingness within me, once bright and clear, dimmed under the weight of his disapproval.

This early experience planted the seeds of a deep-rooted challenge – the suppression of my intuitive voice. The message was clear: my sensitivity, my ability to perceive beyond the surface, was not to be trusted, not to be shared. And so, I learned to silence the whispers of the unseen, to suppress the intuitive flashes that threatened to disrupt my carefully constructed world. I retreated into the safety of conformity, burying my true self beneath layers of self-doubt and fear of judgment.

Years blurred into decades, the memory of that fateful dinner party fading into the background, yet its impact lingered. I navigated the world with a sense of caution, afraid to fully embrace my intuitive gifts, afraid to stand out, to be different. The Primal Mud of those early years was a place of both comfort and confinement, a fertile ground where the seeds of my potential lay dormant, awaiting the awakening that would come years later.

But life, in its infinite wisdom, often has a way of revealing the hidden threads that connect our experiences. Years later, reflecting on that childhood prophecy, I realized that while my words may have seemed harsh at the time, they held a deeper truth. My aunt, though she never bore children of her own, became a mother figure to many. Her nieces, nephews, and countless others experienced her boundless love, generosity, and unwavering support. She created a family through her kindness and dedication to serving others, proving that motherhood can manifest in many forms, defying societal expectations and biological limitations. This realization deepened my understanding of the Primal Mud, a place where seemingly fixed destinies can dissolve and transform, giving rise to unexpected paths and fulfilling outcomes.

As you reflect on this story, consider the following questions:

- What parts of yourself have you buried or hidden away due to fear of judgment or societal expectations?
- How might these hidden aspects be sources of strength or growth if you allowed them to emerge?
- Can you recall a time when you expressed your true self despite feeling fear or uncertainty? What was the outcome?
- How can you embrace the fertile darkness of the Primal Mud and allow your authentic self to blossom?

Take some time to journal your responses, allowing your pen to flow freely as you connect with the whispers of your soul.

Nun's Embrace: The Waters of Infinite Potential

In the vast expanse of the cosmos, before the first glimmer of light, before the birth of stars and galaxies, there existed only Nun – the primordial waters of chaos. Imagine an endless ocean, stretching beyond the limits of perception, its depths teeming with infinite potential. This was the canvas upon which the drama of creation would unfold, the fertile ground from which all life would emerge.

Nun was a boundless, undifferentiated energy, a cosmic soup of possibilities, a womb of creation. Within its depths resided the seeds of all that would come to be – the gods and goddesses, the heavens and the earth, the very fabric of existence.

From this primordial ocean, a single mound of earth arose – the Benben stone, a symbol of creation and stability. Upon this primordial island, Atum, the self-created god, emerged, bringing with him the spark of consciousness and the power of creation.

Atum, through his divine will, began to shape the universe, giving birth to Shu, the god of air, and Tefnut, the goddess of moisture. From these two primordial forces, the rest of the cosmos unfolded – Geb, the earth god, and Nut, the sky goddess, followed by Osiris, Isis, Set, and Nephthys. The world as we know it began to take shape, emerging from the fertile darkness of Nun.

But Nun did not disappear. It remained as the underlying foundation of the cosmos, the ever-present source from which all life springs and to which all life returns. It is the embodiment of potentiality, the fertile void that holds the seeds of infinite possibilities.

Just as the lotus seed lies dormant in the mud, awaiting the right conditions to sprout and blossom, so too does our potential lie within the depths of our being, waiting to be awakened. The Primal Mud, this state of undifferentiated consciousness, is not a place of stagnation, but a fertile ground for transformation. It is in the darkness, in the stillness, that we connect with our deepest selves, uncover our hidden strengths, and plant the seeds for a more authentic and fulfilling life.

As you journey through this chapter, remember the wisdom of Nun, the primordial waters of chaos. Embrace the fertile darkness, for within it lies the potential for infinite creation and transformation. Allow yourself to be submerged in the depths of your being, to connect with the boundless possibilities that await you. Just as the lotus emerges from the mud to blossom in the light, you too can rise from the depths of your challenges, transformed and radiant.

Take a moment to reflect on the concept of Nun, the primordial waters of chaos. How does this resonate with your own understanding of creation and potentiality? Can you recall a time in your life when you felt submerged in the unknown, a time of darkness and uncertainty that ultimately led to growth and transformation? Write about your experience, exploring the ways in which the Primal Mud has shaped your journey.

Immersion: The Primordial Pool

The world softens, edges blurring as you descend into a realm of ancient whispers and forgotten magic. The air stills, heavy with the scent of damp earth and the faint echo of chanting voices. Within a vast, circular chamber, hieroglyphs shimmer and dance like fireflies in the twilight.

From the shadows emerges a figure both ancient and timeless – Nun, the embodiment of the primordial waters. Their form shifts and swirls like the cosmic ocean they represent, a being of pure potentiality, eyes holding the wisdom of eternity.

A pool of dark water materializes, its surface a mirror reflecting the star-studded ceiling above. An invitation hangs in the air, a silent beckoning to step into the waters of creation, to be embraced by the infinite potential that lies within.

The water envelops you in a warmth that feels both ancient and familiar, like a return to the source. It rises, inviting complete submersion, a surrender to the fertile darkness.

Beneath the surface, a world of profound silence unfolds. This darkness is not empty or void; it pulses with life, with the whispers of countless possibilities waiting to be born. Gentle currents caress your skin, carrying with them the secrets of creation, the echoes of the first dawn.

Gradually, pinpoints of light emerge from the darkness, like stars igniting in the vast expanse of the cosmos. Each one represents a potential, a seed of creation waiting to unfold. As you touch one, a vision floods your consciousness – a glimpse of your future self, a creative project taking shape, a transformation unfolding.

From the depths of your being, a voice whispers: From this fertile darkness, all things emerge. Embrace the unknown, for it holds the seeds of your unfolding.

An unseen force draws you upward. Breaking through the surface, the freshness of new beginnings fills your lungs. Within every challenge, every moment of uncertainty, lies the potential for transformation and growth.

[Sacred Pause]

Let the waters of creation settle within you. What visions emerged from the depths? What seeds of potential have awakened? The primordial waters continue to pulse through your being, each ripple a reminder of the infinite possibilities that await.

Integration Practice: In your journal, allow the experience to flow through you:

- What sensations linger in your body?
- What messages or visions are still echoing?
- How does this connect to your own journey through the unknown?

The Fertile Darkness: Embracing the Paradox

While Nun represents the boundless potentiality of the Primal Mud, it is essential to recognize the paradoxical nature of this fertile darkness. It is a time of both constraint and possibility, a place where we may feel stuck, overwhelmed, even lost, yet it is precisely within this darkness that the seeds of our transformation are sown.

Imagine the lotus seed buried in the mud. It is surrounded by darkness, seemingly trapped in the dense, murky depths. Yet, within this constraint, a powerful process of gestation is taking place. The seed is drawing nourishment from the mud, gathering the energy it needs to sprout and reach for the light.

Similarly, our own challenges and struggles can be seen as fertile ground for growth. When we feel stuck or overwhelmed, it is often a sign that we are in a period of deep transformation. Like the lotus seed, we are drawing upon the resources around us, gathering the strength and wisdom we need to emerge stronger and more resilient.

The Primal Mud is a paradox, a place of both darkness and fertility. It is in the depths of our challenges that we discover our hidden strengths, our resilience, our capacity for growth. It is in the darkness that we truly come to know ourselves, to understand our deepest desires, and to plant the seeds for a more authentic and fulfilling life.

Even Ra, the mighty sun god, emerged from the depths of Nun, the primordial waters. His radiant light, a symbol of life and illumination, was born from the fertile darkness, a testament to the transformative power of the Primal Mud. This reminds us that even the most brilliant manifestations have their roots in the unseen, in the fertile ground of potentiality.

Just as Ra emerged from Nun, we too can emerge from the depths of our challenges, transformed and renewed. The Primal Mud is not a place of stagnation, but a crucible of creation, a space where hidden potential is nurtured and awakened. It is in the darkness that we gather the strength and wisdom we need to step into the light.

Immersion: Cradled in the Cosmic Womb

The weight of the world melts away, replaced by boundless space and infinite possibility. Warm, silken waters envelop you, the cosmic ocean cradling you in its mother's embrace. This is Nun, the primordial waters of creation, the source of all that is, was, and ever will be.

A gentle current sways your being, a cosmic dance guided by unseen forces, carrying you deeper into the heart of existence. The primordial energy pulses within this watery abyss - raw potential that birthed the gods and goddesses, the stars and the earth themselves.

The water's caress whispers ancient myths against your skin - the first mound of earth rising from the depths, the birthplace of Ra. Golden warmth touches your face, echoing Ra's rays emerging from primordial darkness.

Vibrant energy courses through your veins as you float, the chaotic yet creative force of Nun awakening dormant potential within. Each breath draws in this primordial power, nourishing your soul, igniting your inner spark.

Thoughts and emotions rise and fall like gentle waves, ebbing and flowing with Nun's eternal tides. No need to grasp or resist - simply witness their dance against eternity's backdrop. In this boundless expanse, all possibilities reside. Your challenges, dreams, fears - all held in this nurturing embrace, seeds waiting to sprout in Nun's fertile depths.

The infinite nature of your own being unfolds - a microcosm of the vastness surrounding you. More than circumstances, more than past or imagined future. Like Nun, you hold within you seeds of endless creation, the divine spark waiting to unfold.

A gentle current beckons, pulling softly toward a distant shore - the shore of your next evolution. Within this cosmic ocean of potential, you are eternally held, eternally loved, eternally guided by the forces that birthed the cosmos itself.

The sense of boundless possibility ripples through you, Nun's embrace echoing in every cell. This knowing remains - that within you resides infinite potential for transformation, the legacy of the primordial source of all creation.

[Sacred Pause]

Integration Practice:

- Let the cosmic waters settle within you. What sensations still ripple through your being?
- What whispers emerged from the depths? What seeds of potential have awakened?
- Allow your pen to move like water across the page, flowing freely without direction or judgment
- Perhaps a symbol or vision arose - explore its contours, its messages, its gifts
- Your words may come as poetry, story, or simply fragments of feeling and knowing
- Trust what emerges, like precious artifacts washing up from Nun's infinite depths

The key is surrendering to the flow, letting your experience move through you onto the page like water finding its own path to the sea. There is no right or wrong way. You are simply witnessing what the cosmic womb has birthed within you.

Let your writing be a reflection of your journey through these primordial waters, a testament to the transformative power held in the depths of your own being.

Sekhmet's Sanctuary: A Transformation Beyond Time

The incense enveloped me in its ethereal embrace, tendrils of myrrh and frankincense dancing like spirits of the ancient past. Within Sekhmet's sacred sanctuary at Karnak, my heart pounded with a mixture of awe and anticipation. The raw power of this place hit me with the force of a tidal wave, reconnecting me to the fiery young woman I once was - defiant, passionate, unafraid to challenge societal norms.

The chapel's profound darkness seemed to swallow all light, the very essence of mystery itself. Gradually, shapes emerged from the gloom. Midday sun filtered through ancient stones, casting long shadows that danced across walls and floor, the air alive with whispers of ancient secrets.

There she stood - Sekhmet's statue, her powerful form gathering the sparse light, glowing with inner radiance. In her left hand, she clutched a papyrus scepter of unwavering strength. In her right, she cradled the ankh, promising rebirth even in destruction's wake. Her stone eyes, though inanimate, held the fury of a storm within their golden depths.

The world slowed to a crawl. The ground vibrated with otherworldly energy while profound calm anchored me, roots extending deep into the temple's sacred earth. Then, defying all logic, the impossible manifested - Sekhmet's stone form began to move with liquid grace. The cold, unyielding granite transformed into warm, living flesh before my eyes. The goddess stepped from her pedestal, each movement radiating an intensity that both awed and humbled. Her presence was a force of nature contained in physical form. The chamber crackled with power that raised the hair on my arms.

A sleek, otherworldly instrument materialized in her hand, its surface shimmering with hieroglyphs of light. Each pass over my body sent waves of golden energy coursing through me, ancient magic and divine technology working in harmony. The device's hum deepened to a resonant purr, matching the frequency of Sekhmet's own lioness heart. Layer by layer, lifetimes of fear dissolved into nothingness, replaced by a warrior's unwavering certainty.

Sekhmet's fierce countenance softened as she completed her examination. She transformed from awe-inspiring deity to wise teacher, a warrior queen acknowledging a fellow warrior. With a gesture that belied her fearsome reputation, she beckoned me forward - an invitation to step from doubt's shadows into self-realization's light.

Emerging into the blazing Egyptian sun, the heat felt invigorating rather than oppressive. Just outside the sanctuary stood an ancient sycamore tree, its gnarled branches reaching skyward, born from Sekhmet's own sweat. When my palm touched its rough bark, her untamed essence surged through me - a primal grounding of the power she had awakened. The tree stood as a living link between mortal and divine realms, connecting me more deeply to the cosmic forces than ever before.

At the tree's base lay a smooth river stone, unremarkable except for its perfectly formed center hole. Divine recognition swept through me - this was her gift, a talisman of transformation. With reverent hands, I threaded a leather cord through the hole and placed it around my neck. The stone settled against my heart, its sun-warmed surface mingling Sekhmet's energy with the patient wisdom of water-worn stone.

As I held the stone, I felt the warmth of the sun that had soaked into it merging with the residual energy from my encounter with Sekhmet. Its smooth surface, worn by countless years in the river, testified to the enduring nature of transformation. Like the stone, I too had been shaped by time and experience, emerging smoother, stronger, more defined.

This talisman would serve as a constant source of strength, a tangible link to this moment of transformation. With each touch, each glance, I would return here, drawing upon the courage discovered in the lioness goddess's presence. Even now, years later, this stone remains my faithful companion, bridging mortal and divine.

I stepped forward into the world, forever changed, carrying Sekhmet's fierce compassion and indomitable strength within me. The pilgrimage had become rebirth, and I was ready to face whatever challenges lay ahead with a lioness heart.

Immersion: Sekhmet's Crucible of Courage

The air thickens, pressing against skin with electric warmth. A heartbeat quickens, syncing with a deeper, more primal rhythm. Sun-baked earth fills the lungs, its ancient power coursing through the blood. The everyday world dissolves.

Black sand stretches endlessly, alive and pulsing with potential. Each breath stirs the obsidian grains, creating patterns of destiny. Above, the sky blazes - deep purples bleeding into fierce oranges and golds. Ancient stars pierce the twilight, witnessing what unfolds below.

A low rumble begins in the earth itself. The vibration grows, resonating through bone and sinew, filling the chest with its primal song. The black sand writhes, coalescing into a massive form.

Sekhmet rises, a lioness of living flame. Twin suns burn in her eyes, her mane a cascade of molten gold. Heat radiates in waves, stripping away all pretense. Nothing remains but raw essence before her penetrating gaze.

The ground shifts. Fire erupts in a perfect circle, surrounding everything. Within the flames, shadows twist into form - the specter of failure, the ghost of loneliness, the shade of inadequacy. Each fear manifests, more terrifying than the last.

Sweat beads despite the dry heat. Every instinct screams for escape. But Sekhmet's presence holds firm - there is only through, never away.

The heat intensifies. Defenses burn to ash. The fiery apparitions press closer, their touch paradoxically cold. Their collective weight threatens to overwhelm.

Then - transformation. Sekhmet steps into the circle, her inferno dwarfing all other flames. Her paw presses against the heart, igniting an answering fire within. Power surges outward from that point of contact, filling every cell with liquid courage.

Strength builds. The body grows tall, radiating light that pierces shadow. A roar shakes the foundations of the earth. Fear after fear dissolves, unable to withstand this newfound power. The circle of fire collapses inward, its flames absorbed rather than burning.

Power hums through every fiber. Sekhmet's approval settles like a warm mantle across the shoulders. Her gift of courage burns eternal, an inner flame to illuminate the darkest night.

[Sacred Pause]

Integration Practice:

- Let Sekhmet's fire settle in your being. Where does her courage burn brightest within you?
- What fears dissolved in her flames? What strength emerged from their ashes?
- Feel the weight of her paw still pressed against your heart. What has she awakened?
- Allow your hand to move across the page like flowing fire, capturing the essence of this transformation
- Perhaps a roar builds in your throat, or your body wishes to move with leonine grace
- Trust what emerges from this crucible of courage

Celestial Encounter at Dendera Temple

The majestic silhouette of Dendera Temple loomed before me, its ancient stones bathed in golden Egyptian sunlight. I stood there, a self-proclaimed skeptic, my mind teetering on the precipice between disbelief and wonder. The weight of decades of rational thinking pressed heavily upon my shoulders, yet something stirred within me, a whisper of anticipation impossible to silence.

As I approached the temple, the bustle of tourists faded into the background. My feet, guided by an unseen force, led me away from the crowds toward the temple's empty lake. The still waters mirrored the sky above, creating perfect symmetry between heaven and earth. I settled myself on the lake's edge, the cool stone contrasting with the warmth of the air. Inside the ancient walls of the Mimasi quiet chapel, where women sought to give birth, I found refuge as the celestial encounter began to unfold.

Reality shimmered and shifted like a veil drawing back to reveal a hidden world. The celestial realm opened before me, transforming the sky into a grand amphitheater of divine presence. The boundaries between physical and spiritual worlds dissolved, leaving me suspended in a space between realms.

The Egyptian Neteru materialized before me - vibrant, living presences radiating palpable energy that made my skin tingle. Each deity emanated a unique aura, their power and wisdom tangible even from a distance. A profound sense of familiarity washed over me, as though recognizing old friends and mentors through layers of forgotten memory.

The Neteru revealed themselves one by one: Isis with her protective wings spread wide, Osiris with his green skin symbolizing rebirth, Tehuti with his ibis head and wisdom scroll, Hathor with her sun-crowned horns. Each presence resonated deep within my being.

Years of skepticism melted away before this divine assembly. Questions poured forth about life, death, the nature of the universe and my place within it. The Neteru answered with infinite patience, their wisdom bypassing my ears to resonate directly with my soul. Each answer awakened dormant knowledge within me, ancient truths rising from the depths of memory.

The encounter shifted as they spoke of coming upheaval - a global pandemic poised to shake the foundations of our world. Despite the Egyptian warmth, chills ran down my spine at their prophetic words. Yet with this dire prediction came a sacred calling: to guide others toward their highest potential, to help unlock the dormant power within each soul. The task felt simultaneously daunting and familiar, as though my entire life had unconsciously prepared me for this role.

This celestial conference transcended mere conversation - it marked an initiation, a homecoming. The Neteru's presence and active participation in my life became undeniable, overwhelming any lingering rational resistance.

As the vision faded, I found myself again by Dendera's empty lake. The physical world had transformed, imbued with new significance. Temple stones whispered with hidden knowledge, the air charged with potential.

The following day brought a serendipitous encounter with an Akashic Records reader, another piece falling perfectly into the cosmic puzzle. This session confirmed the channeled messages and revealed eager guides ready to assist my journey. The concept of the Holographic Being emerged, reshaping my understanding of reality and my place within it.

The Akashic Records opened like an infinite ocean of knowledge, flooding me with memories, insights and forgotten wisdom. Long-suppressed psychic abilities roared back to life - no longer faint whispers or dismissible hunches, they emerged as vibrant, undeniable aspects of my being. Energy sensitivity, cosmic awareness and perception beyond the physical realm became my new normal.

This unexpected initiation reverberated through my entire being. Dendera Temple transformed from archaeological site to sacred anchor, every stone and carving holding deeper meaning. As days passed and news of a spreading virus dominated headlines, I watched in mingled awe and trepidation as the prophecy manifested. Taking the last flight from Egypt to Germany before the pandemic's grip tightened, I began opening the Akashic Records for others.

My understanding of reality expanded dramatically. Time revealed itself as fluid and malleable rather than linear. We existed as interwoven threads in existence's grand tapestry, our lives and experiences interconnected across perceived past, present and future.

This oracle's awakening stands as testament to the soul's enduring whispers across lifelines, guiding us back to our true selves. The journey that began at Dendera Temple continues unfolding, each day bringing new insights into our vast interconnected reality. The skeptic transformed into a bridge between worlds, keeper of ancient wisdom, guide for others unlocking their divine potential. The sacred mission entrusted by the Neteru resonates still, illuminating the incredible journey ahead.

Khonsu's Embrace: A Journey into the Primordial Mud

The midday sun beat down on the temple complex, casting sharp shadows that danced across the sprawling courtyard. As I approached Karnak, its massive pylons loomed overhead, their sandstone surfaces radiating the heat of a thousand suns. The familiar scent of incense and ancient stone mingled with the dry desert air, creating an atmosphere of timeless reverence.

Stepping through the towering gateway, I felt a palpable shift, a hush that descended upon me like a cool embrace. The sounds of the modern world – the chatter of tourists, the distant hum of traffic – faded away, replaced by a profound silence that seemed to echo with the whispers of centuries past.

My footsteps echoed softly as I navigated the labyrinthine complex, each step carrying me deeper into the heart of this sacred space. The hypostyle hall, with its forest of towering columns and intricate hieroglyphs, filled me with a sense of awe and wonder. Sunlight streamed through the gaps in the roof, illuminating the ancient carvings, each one a story waiting to be deciphered.

I found myself drawn to a small, secluded chapel, its entrance shrouded in shadow. As I stepped across the threshold, the air grew still and heavy, charged with an energy that prickled my skin. This was the sanctuary of Khonsu, the moon god, his presence palpable in the hushed stillness.

The walls, adorned with intricate carvings, seemed to whisper secrets in the dim light. I ran my fingers over the cool stone, tracing the outlines of ancient symbols, feeling their stories vibrating through my fingertips. The scent of antiquity filled my nostrils – dust, incense, and the faintest hint of something earthy and primal.

In the center of the chapel, bathed in a soft glow of filtered sunlight, stood the enigmatic statue of Khonsu. He was depicted not in his usual youthful form, but with the head of a baboon, the statue carved from pale limestone. The baboon sits in a compact, natural pose, its form simplified yet powerful. The statue's surface, weathered by millennia, still retained a quiet dignity. The baboon's face, though eroded by time, conveyed an expression of ancient wisdom, its gaze seeming to penetrate the depths of eternity, beckoning me to explore the primordial depths of my own being.

Settling onto the cool stone floor, I closed my eyes and breathed deeply, surrendering to the stillness and the palpable energy of Khonsu's presence. As my breath slowed, I felt myself sinking into a state of profound receptivity, drawn into the embrace of the moon god and the secrets he held within his ancient gaze.

In this liminal space between waking and dreaming, a vision unfolded:

I stood at the edge of a vast, primordial swamp, the air thick and humid, filled with the croaking of unseen creatures and the rustle of unseen wings. Before me, the muddy water stretched as far as the eye could see, its surface broken only by the occasional bubble rising from the depths.

An ancient presence made itself known, its essence neither male nor female, its energy rippling through the air like distant thunder. The message resonated within my very being - to truly know the Mud, one must become the Mud. The knowledge settled deep in my bones, compelling me forward into the waiting waters.

Taking a deep breath, I waded into the swamp. The mud squelched between my toes, cool and vicious, a sensation both foreign and strangely familiar. With each step, I sank deeper, the mud rising past my ankles, then my knees. Fear flickered in my chest – what if I sank too deep? – but something deeper than fear propelled me forward, a yearning to understand the essence of this primordial state.

As the mud reached my waist, I felt a shift. The boundaries between my body and the swamp began to blur. I was no longer moving through the mud, but becoming one with it. My consciousness expanded, spreading throughout the primordial ooze, merging with the countless lifeforms that teemed within its depths.

In this state of union, I experienced the Mud as a living entity. I felt the stirring of microorganisms, the germination of seeds, the first tentative steps of aquatic creatures venturing onto land. Each was a spark of potential, waiting for the right moment to emerge and evolve. It was a visceral reminder of a time when my own body felt like that primordial swamp – heavy, stagnant, resistant to movement.

Sacred Pause: Your Journey into the Primordial Depths

Find a quiet moment with your journal, away from the bustle of daily life. Take a few deep breaths and allow yourself to connect with your own relationship to the primal forces of creation, transformation, and renewal.

- Think of a time when you encountered an ancient or sacred space - whether a temple, a forest grove, or simply a moment of profound stillness. What shifted within you as you crossed that threshold? What whispers of wisdom arose in the silence?
- Envision yourself at the edge of your own primordial waters. What does your mud look like, feel like, smell like? What hesitations or yearnings arise as you contemplate immersing yourself in these depths?
- Consider the places in your life where transformation feels messy, uncertain, or uncomfortable. How might viewing these challenges through the lens of the primordial mud - as fertile ground for new life and possibility - shift your perspective?
- What seeds of potential do you sense stirring within your own depths? What parts of yourself are germinating in the darkness, waiting for the right moment to emerge?

Allow your reflections to flow naturally, without seeking to mirror any particular experience. Your journey with these primal energies is uniquely your own. Trust the wisdom that emerges from your personal exploration of these depths.

Immersion: The Sarcophagus of Rebirth

The air grows heavy, thick with the scent of myrrh and the faint echo of ancient chants. A sense of stillness descends, inviting you to surrender to the embrace of the unknown. You find yourself within a dimly lit chamber, its walls adorned with hieroglyphs that seem to whisper secrets of the afterlife. In the center of the chamber rests a sarcophagus, its lid slightly ajar, beckoning you to step inside.

With a mixture of trepidation and curiosity, you approach the sarcophagus. Its cool, smooth surface invites your touch, and as you run your fingers along its intricate carvings, you feel a sense of connection to the ancient ones, to those who have walked this path before you.

Taking a deep breath, you step inside the sarcophagus, the lid closing gently above you, enveloping you in darkness. The air is still and heavy, filled with the scent of earth and time. You feel the weight of the stone above you, a comforting pressure that reminds you of the earth's embrace.

As your eyes adjust to the darkness, you become aware of the subtle sounds that surround you – the gentle beating of your own heart, the soft rhythm of your breath, the distant drip of water echoing through the chamber. The world outside fades away, leaving you alone with the silence, the darkness, and the whispers of your own soul.

In this enclosed space, a sense of surrender washes over you. You release the burdens of the past, the anxieties of the future, the expectations that have weighed you down. You allow yourself to be fully present in this moment, to embrace the stillness, the darkness, the fertile ground of transformation.

Within this symbolic coffin, you are not dying, but rather undergoing a process of rebirth. In ancient Egyptian wisdom, Osiris was revered as the divine being who mastered the cycle of death and renewal - transforming the darkness of the tomb into a sacred womb of rebirth. Like this ancient archetype, you are shedding your old self, releasing the patterns and beliefs that no longer serve you. You are entering a period of gestation, a time of deep introspection and renewal, where what appears to be an ending becomes a powerful beginning.

Feel the darkness nourishing you, supporting you, holding you in its embrace. It is not an empty void, but a fertile ground teeming with potential. Within this darkness, the seeds of your future self are being sown, waiting for the right moment to sprout and blossom.

As you lie in the stillness, allow your mind to wander freely. Explore the depths of your being, the hidden corners of your soul. What fears and insecurities are you ready to release? What dreams and aspirations are waiting to be awakened? What new patterns and beliefs are you ready to embrace?

When you feel ready to emerge, gently push open the lid of the sarcophagus and step back into the light. Take a deep breath, filling your lungs with the fresh air of new beginnings. You have journeyed into the depths of your own being, confronted your shadows, and emerged transformed. Carry with you the wisdom of the darkness, the resilience of the seed, and the promise of rebirth.

Integration Practice: Embracing the Primal Mud

Find a quiet moment with your journal, perhaps near a source of water or earth to connect with the primordial energies of transformation. Allow yourself to sink into the fertile darkness of beginnings. Or perhaps you wish to light a candle to honor your journey through darkness and transformation. Take several deep breaths, allowing the echoes of your sarcophagus experience to ripple through your awareness.

Reflection Questions:

- What sensations arose in your body as you entered the darkness of the sarcophagus? Notice any areas of tension, release, or unexpected comfort.
- What feelings arose as you encountered the darkness of the sarcophagus? Like the lotus seed in the mud, how does it feel to be held in this place of profound beginning?

- The Primal Mud phase invites us to trust the fertile darkness of creation. What aspects of your life currently feel like they're in this murky, gestational phase? What might be forming beneath the surface?
- Just as the richest soil contains decomposed matter, what old patterns or beliefs are you ready to let dissolve into nourishment for new growth?

Embodied Practice: Take a moment to wrap yourself in a blanket or shawl, creating a cocoon of sacred darkness. Close your eyes and place one hand on your heart, the other on your belly. Feel the warmth building between your palms.

If possible, touch actual mud or soil as you reflect. Feel its coolness, its density, its potential for nurturing life. Let this physical connection remind you that all transformation begins in darkness, in the rich depths of the Primal Mud.

Remember that this is just the beginning of your journey. Like the lotus seed nestled in the mud, you are exactly where you need to be. Trust the wisdom of this first phase, knowing that the light will come in its own time.

Ritual: Embracing the Fertile Darkness

Venture out into the embrace of nature, seeking a sanctuary where the earth's energy whispers its secrets and the sky stretches endlessly above. Perhaps a hidden grove beneath ancient trees, their roots intertwined with the wisdom of centuries, or a secluded spot beside a gently flowing stream, its waters carrying the echoes of creation.

Gather your sacred tools: a bowl of rich, fertile mud, reminiscent of the primordial waters of Nun; a white candle, its flame symbolizing the spark of consciousness that ignited the cosmos; a small mirror, to reflect your evolving self; and a seed or small plant, a tangible representation of your dreams and aspirations.

Light the candle, its flame dancing in the stillness, and feel a sense of reverence wash over you as you connect with the energies of creation.

Settle yourself comfortably on the ground, feeling the earth's solidity beneath you, its energy rising to meet your own. Place your hands on the earth, palms open, and breathe deeply. Imagine roots growing from the base of your spine, reaching deep into the earth's embrace, anchoring you to its strength and wisdom.

With reverence, take a small amount of mud and spread it on your forehead, a symbolic anointing that connects you to the essence of creation. As you do so, feel the weight of limitations dissolving, the boundaries of your perceived self melting away.

Next, spread the mud on your heart center, feeling its coolness against your skin. Sense a wave of warmth spreading through your being, melting away any fear or resistance. Open yourself to the transformative power of the Primal Mud, allowing your heart to become fertile ground for love, compassion, and courage to blossom.

Finally, spread the mud on your palms, feeling its texture, its life-giving essence. Feel the energy of creation pulsating through your fingertips, empowering you to shape your own becoming, to emerge renewed, to craft a life that reflects your authentic self.

Close your eyes and envision yourself cocooned in the warm, nurturing embrace of the Primal Mud. Feel its weight grounding you, its darkness enveloping you, its silence quieting the chatter of your mind. Allow all thoughts and sensations to settle, like silt sinking to the bottom of a still pond. Remain in this stillness for several minutes, breathing slowly and deeply, surrendering to the transformative power of the Mud.

Now, take the seed or plant in your mud-covered hands. Feel its energy, its potential, its inherent drive towards life. Reflect on what you wish to grow or manifest in your life. What dreams do you hold within your heart? What qualities do you yearn to cultivate?

Plant the seed in the remaining mud, whispering your intentions for its growth. Visualize its roots reaching deep into the earth, drawing nourishment and strength from the Primal Mud. See its stem rising towards the light, blossoming into its full potential, mirroring your own journey of unfolding.

Slowly open your eyes and gaze into the mirror. See yourself adorned with the mud, a symbol of your willingness to embrace transformation, to dive deep into the fertile darkness and emerge renewed.

With gratitude, wash the mud from your skin with clean water. As you do so, feel the energy of the Primal Mud integrating into your being, carrying its wisdom and potential within you. Sense yourself reborn, renewed, and ready to create a life of purpose and authenticity.

Extinguish the candle, leaving its lingering fragrance as a reminder of your journey. Carry the planted seed with you or place it in a special spot as a reminder of this ritual and the boundless potential you carry within.

Whispers from the Primordial Waters

Close your eyes and sit in stillness for a moment, allowing the echoes of your journey through the Primal Mud to settle in your being. Feel the weight of your body, the rhythm of your breath, the quiet stirring of life within.

Now, open your journal to a fresh page. Let your pen become a divining rod, seeking the deep waters of your unconscious. Begin writing and keep your pen moving continuously across the page. Don't pause to think, edit, or judge. Write through any discomfort or resistance. Write past what you think you should say into what needs to be expressed.

The wisdom of the Primal Mud speaks in images, sensations, fragments, and feelings - trust them all. Keep writing until you feel complete, even if what appears seems strange or disconnected. You are not here to understand, but to allow the mud of transformation to move through you.

Let your writing flow until it naturally comes to rest, like sediment settling in still water.

Mud Immersion Meditation

Step out of your dwelling and into the embrace of the dark earth. Find a place where the soil is rich and damp - perhaps beneath ancient trees where leaves have decomposed for centuries, or near a stream bank thick with primordial mud. Settle yourself here, allowing your body to sink into the ground.

With reverence, scoop the cool mud or soil into your palms. Don't try to shape it or give it form yet. Instead, feel its raw potential - the decay that creates fertility, the chaos that precedes creation. Let its primal scent fill your nostrils, connecting you to the ancient wisdom of dissolution and becoming.

Close your eyes and breathe deeply, inhaling the musty perfume of decomposition and possibility. Feel the mud between your fingers, how it defies containment, how it holds the memories of all that has returned to the earth to be transformed.

Let yourself become mud. Release the need to grow, to manifest, to become anything yet. Simply be with the fertile darkness, the sacred matrix from which all life emerges. Feel yourself softening, dissolving, returning to your most primal essence.

Sit with this feeling of formlessness, of pure potential. There is no need to plant seeds yet - that will come later. For now, simply surrender to the mud, to the dark waters of creation, to the blessed nothing-and-everything of the primal source.

When the meditation feels complete, gently wipe the mud from your hands, knowing it has left its mark on your soul. Carry this connection to the fertile darkness within you, trusting that all transformation begins in the depths.

Primal Mud Communion

Find a quiet space and gather natural clay or mud. Let its cool, damp presence remind you of the primordial waters from which all life emerged. Close your eyes and breathe deeply, allowing your consciousness to sink into the ancient memory held within this substance.

Place your hands in the mud. Rather than shaping it, let it shape you. Feel how it moves between your fingers, resisting definition, maintaining its essential formlessness. Notice any urge to create or control, and gently let these impulses dissolve back into the mud.

Allow your hands to play in the substance without purpose or goal. Experience its pure potential - too raw yet for form, too wild for containment. Feel its coolness against your skin, its primal invitation to return to the state before shape, before structure, before becoming.

Let the mud teach you about surrender. About the wisdom of remaining undefined. About the power of chaos and possibility. Notice how it claims your hands, marking you with its darkness, initiating you into the mysteries of the depths.

When you feel complete, simply let the mud be mud. No need to shape it into anything. No need to find meaning or extract lessons. Simply honor its essential nature - formless, fertile, full of unmanifest potential.

Let your hands remain dirty for a while, carrying the memory of this communion with the primal source. When you do wash them, watch the mud return to water, completing the cycle of dissolution that is so sacred to this phase.

Reflections from the Depths: A Primal Mud Integration

Take time to sit with your journal, allowing the wisdom gathered from your journey through the Primal Mud to settle into your bones. Let the rich silence embrace you as you prepare to write.

Consider:

- The moments when you surrendered to the fertile darkness. How did your body feel? What emerged in these times of deep receptivity?
- The ancient memories that stirred within you as you connected with primordial waters. What ancestral wisdom surfaced? Which whispers from the depths still echo in your being?
- The places where you experienced dissolution and transformation. How did the mud reshape your understanding of creation? What emerged from these formless spaces?
- Your relationship with the fertile chaos of unfolding. How has your perception of uncertainty and possibility evolved? What depths have you discovered within yourself?
- The sacred wisdom of stillness and gestation. Which seeds lie dormant in your depths? How has your trust in the dark waters deepened?

Remember, this writing practice serves as a vessel for raw truth. Let your words flow directly from the mud of your being. Write until you feel complete, until the depths have spoken through you.

As you close your journal, honor this phase of your journey. Touch the earth beneath you, feeling its ancient presence. You carry the primal waters within you now, their creative power flowing through your veins. The mud remains your teacher, your womb of transformation, your eternal source.

Your exploration of these depths continues to unfold, each moment pregnant with infinite possibility. The wisdom of the Primal Mud lives in you, awakening new channels of creation with every breath.

II. SEEKING LIGHT

Isis, Mistress of Mysteries, unlock our slumbering sight,
To see within the ordinary, a symphony of light.
Stardust sings within us, a joyful, wondrous song,
May childlike innocence guide us where we belong.
Isis, Keeper of Earth's Wisdom, tune our ears to nature's call,
The wind's whispered secrets, where ancient echoes fall.
Bird and wave and beating heart, a universal rhyme,
May their tides awaken us, reshaping space and time.
Isis, Weaver of Life's Tapestry, teach us to behold,
The silent script of leaf and stone, stories you unfold.
Resilient like the seed, may we reach for radiant skies,
Part of the grand design, where love eternal lies.

Dawn's Call

Pre-dawn mist swirls around my bare feet at the Nile's edge. The air trembles with possibility, heavy with the river's breath. First light paints ripples in amber and gold, each ray igniting memories etched deep within my bones.

One morning here changed everything. The rising sun awakened a primal yearning - a hunger for understanding that burned bright as desert flame. That same fire now guides me as whispers rise from the flowing waters, each ripple sparking questions.

Morning light streams across the river's surface, weaving pathways of radiance. I follow their golden trails, drawn by an insatiable curiosity. The wind carries echoes of seekers: scribes pouring over papyrus by lamplight, priestesses studying stellar maps, sages contemplating birds' patterns against dawn sky. Their quest pulses in my blood.

The seeking phase unfolds in nature's mirror - sunrises painting wisdom across the sky, ideas flaring like shooting stars, understanding flowing steady as the river itself. Each heartbeat brings new questions, each breath carries mystery.

By the river's edge, curiosity burns as sacred flame. Wonder illuminates hidden pathways. The Nile flows on, its waters reflecting infinite possibilities, calling us ever deeper into exploration's embrace.

Dawn Light: First Stirrings of the Seeker

Find a quiet moment as the sun rises. Let these questions guide your pen across fresh pages:

- What awakens your curiosity? Write about a moment when wonder caught your breath - perhaps a shaft of light through clouds, a passage in a book, a strain of music that opened your heart to mystery.
- Which questions live in your heart right now? Pour them onto the page without seeking immediate answers. Let them breathe and expand.
- Recall the first time you felt yourself becoming a seeker. What sparked that initial flame of curiosity? How did it feel in your body, your heart, your spirit?
- Where do you find wisdom speaking to you? Through nature, through art, through silence, through movement? Describe these encounters in rich detail.
- Draw a map of your current seeking path. What beacons guide you? What mysteries call to you? What terrains of knowledge or understanding do you yearn to explore?

Allow your writing to flow freely, following wherever curiosity leads. Trust that each question opens a door, each wondering lights a path forward. Your journal becomes sacred ground where seeking takes root and understanding begins to flourish.

The Ibis and the Scroll

The air in Khan el-Khalili market shimmered with heat as Ra's sun blazed overhead. I stood at the entrance, my heart pounding with the rhythm of creation itself. The narrow, winding alleyways stretched before me like pathways through the Egyptian otherworld, each turn promising wisdom as deep as the sacred texts themselves.

A breeze caressed my face, carrying whispers of Ma'at - the divine force of truth, balance, and cosmic harmony. The scents of cardamom, cumin, and saffron mingled with the earthy aroma of papyrus and sacred incense, weaving together earthly and celestial realms in an intoxicating perfume. Each fragrance, each sound found its perfect place in Ma'at's eternal dance of order.

My fingers traced the worn edges of a crumbling papyrus, its surface alive with hieroglyphs pulsing with hidden meaning. Here lay fragments of universal memory, holding the wisdom of Tehuti - divine scribe, keeper of sacred knowledge, who stands with Ma'at to weigh the truth in every heart.

A flash of white caught my eye. An ibis, magnificent and pure as those painted in temple walls, swept down and lifted the papyrus in its beak. My breath caught - here stood Tehuti himself in his bird aspect, master of wisdom, measurer of time, who works in harmony with Ma'at to maintain the balance of creation.

I followed, drawn by an irresistible pull. Each step carried me deeper through the market's maze. The usual clamor of voices transformed into whispers of ancient spells and rustling scrolls. In the seeming chaos, Ma'at's ordering principle revealed itself - every vendor, every transaction, every movement part of a greater cosmic dance.

The ibis led me to a hidden courtyard where time itself seemed to pause. The air grew thick with the sweet scent of blue lotus, carrying memories of creation's first morning when Ma'at emerged from the waters of possibility. A fountain stood at its heart, carved with sacred writings - mysteries of balance and truth meant for those ready to receive them.

The ibis perched there, dark eyes gleaming with the light of ages. Its wings spread wide like the sky goddess Nut embracing the earth. A single white feather spiraled down, landing beside the now-opened papyrus. The hieroglyphs danced, shifting into messages of Ma'at's eternal truths, singing in my blood.

As I reached for the writings, cosmic knowledge flowed through me. The market's patterns revealed themselves - each sound, scent, and movement in perfect relationship with all others. Here Ma'at's work was made visible: harmony within complexity, divine order expressed through everyday life.

I emerged from that courtyard carrying more than papyrus and feathers. A golden thread now connected me to streams of ancient wisdom, to Ma'at's cosmic law that keeps the stars in motion and truth alive in human hearts. The market had become my teacher, every moment an initiation into the dance between seeking and divine order.

After walking the winding paths of Khan el-Khalili with Tehuti and Ma'at, let us pause to explore your own journey of seeking:

- Recall a moment when wisdom appeared unexpectedly - through an animal, a stranger, a sign that caught your attention. How did your body respond to this encounter? What sensations awakened in your cells?
- Which smells, sounds, or sights open doors to deeper understanding in your life? Like the market's spices and incense, what sensory experiences awaken your inner knowing?
- Where do you glimpse Ma'at's divine order in your daily life? Describe a time when apparent chaos revealed an underlying

pattern, when seemingly random events aligned to show you truth.

- What spaces feel charged with mystery to you? Like the hidden courtyard in the market, where do you find sanctuary for seeking? What makes these places sacred?

Let these reflections guide you as we prepare to enter Tehuti's realm of divine wisdom...

Immersion: The Seeker's Market

Find a quiet space where questions can arise freely. Rest your feet firmly on the ground, awakening your seeker's curiosity.

Feel the warmth of Ra's sun on your skin. The threshold of Khan el-Khalili beckons. Breathe in deeply as the market's essence surrounds you.

Scents weave stories: cumin speaks of desert caravans, frankincense carries temple secrets, papyrus holds wisdom's earthen breath. Each aroma awakens a question in your heart. Let these questions rise without grasping for answers.

Listen as the market's symphony unfolds. Merchant calls blend with prayer songs. Footsteps write rhythms on stone pathways. Every sound invites deeper wondering. What mysteries echo in this ancient dance?

Feel textures beneath your fingers - smooth alabaster, rough papyrus, cool metal, warm silk. Each touch opens another door of curiosity. What knowledge lives in these sensations?

Through this awakening of senses, you begin to read the market's hidden language. Every detail holds a clue, every moment offers a thread of understanding to follow.

Integration Practice: The Seeker's Journal

After emerging from the market's embrace:

1. Create a Sensory Map

   - Draw five concentric circles on your journal page
   - In each circle, record the sensations that sparked deepest curiosity:
     - Center: What drew your strongest wondering?
     - Second ring: Which sounds raised questions?
     - Third ring: What scents opened doors?
     - Fourth ring: Which textures invited exploration?
     - Outer ring: What sights called for deeper understanding?

2. Follow the Threads

   - Choose three sensations from your map
   - For each one, write:
     - The initial question it sparked
     - Three related questions that arose
     - A possible path of exploration
     - A symbol to represent this line of seeking

3. Daily Practice

   - Carry a small notebook
   - Each day, record one moment when your senses awaken curiosity
   - Note the questions that arise
   - Draw connections between these daily wonderings

Let this practice guide you deeper into the art of seeking, training your senses to read wisdom's subtle signs.

Childhood Awakening: The Spark of Yearning

The library, a hushed sanctuary within our bustling Cairo downtown home, held a magic all its own. Sunlight, filtering through stained-glass windows, painted the room in a kaleidoscope of colors, transforming the towering bookshelves into gateways to fantastical realms. The scent of aged paper and leather-bound volumes mingled with the faintest hint of incense, creating an atmosphere of timeless wisdom and whispered secrets.

I, a child of four or five, a whirlwind of untamed curiosity, found myself drawn to this haven of knowledge, my small hands reaching for the forbidden treasures that lined the shelves. My father, a renowned artist and lover of knowledge, had always envisioned me amongst the brightly colored children's books in my own little corner. But on this day, a rebellious thrill, a yearning for the unknown, guided me towards the oversized art volumes that towered above me like ancient monoliths.

With a surge of determination, I pulled a massive tome from its perch, its weight almost exceeding my own. The book, its faded cover whispering promises of worlds unseen, became a portal to another realm. As I sank onto the cool wooden floor, the book splayed open in my lap, its pages revealing a riot of colors and forms that stole my breath away.

Klimt's "The Kiss," shimmering with gold leaf and vibrant hues, ignited a spark within me, a longing for beauty and connection that I couldn't yet name. I traced the intricate patterns with my fingertip, marveling at how something so flat could evoke such depth of emotion.

The library became my sanctuary, a place where I could lose myself in the wonders of art and knowledge. I devoured the books, their heft a testament to the worlds they contained. I stood on tiptoes, straining to glimpse the enigmatic sculptures that adorned the high shelves, their forms hinting at stories yet to be discovered.

A replica of Nefertiti's bust, perched just out of reach, became my confidante. I whispered my dreams and fears to her serene visage, imagining her as a rebel queen who defied expectations and embraced her own truth. In the soft afternoon light, I could almost swear I saw her lips curve into a knowing smile, as if acknowledging our shared secret of quiet defiance.

This moment in the library, this awakening of curiosity and yearning, was the beginning of my lifelong quest for knowledge, beauty, and understanding. The spark ignited that day would grow into a flame, guiding me through the twists and turns of my journey, always urging me to seek the light of wisdom hidden in the most unexpected places.

The Gallery Muse: Storytelling Awakens

The art books in our family library were gateways, but the fire they ignited truly blazed in galleries. My father, a pioneer of modern art, often took me to exhibitions in downtown Cairo. Here, art pulsed with life, colors and textures demanding to be felt, beyond mere sight.

At one particular exhibition, the air hummed with the quiet murmurs of art connoisseurs and the subtle scent of linseed oil. As my father engaged in deep discussions with curators and fellow artists, I felt a familiar restlessness stirring within me. Without thinking, I snatched an official pamphlet from a nearby stand – holding it upside down, of course, adding a touch of delightful chaos to my impromptu performance.

Transforming myself into a tiny, unconventional docent, I began to weave tales about each piece. My voice rose and fell dramatically, filling the hushed gallery with childish enthusiasm and wild imagination. "Look here," I'd exclaim, pointing to a swirling abstract canvas, "This is clearly a dragon's dying breath! See how the crimson paint curls like smoke? And there, that glint of gold leaf? That's the last of the dragon's treasure, scattered as it fell from the sky!"

At first, visitors and artists alike were taken aback by this pint-sized tour guide. But soon, their initial surprise gave way to amusement and genuine interest. They leaned in, faces alight with curiosity, as I regaled them with invented narratives that grew more elaborate with each artwork. A stark minimalist piece became a map to a hidden world, while a vibrant expressionist painting transformed into a musical score for alien symphonies.

In those moments, surrounded by attentive adults twice and thrice my size, I discovered the power of storytelling to transform how we perceive the world around us. Each artwork became a portal to infinite possibilities, limited only by the boundaries of imagination. This experience taught me that seeking light isn't just about finding what's already there, but about the creative act of illuminating the world with our own unique vision.

As the afternoon wore on, I noticed my father watching from a distance, a mixture of pride and wonder in his eyes. He later told me that in my fanciful interpretations, he saw a spark of the same creative fire that drove him to push the boundaries of modern art. It was a moment of connection, of mutual understanding across generations, united by the transformative power of creativity.

This day in the gallery became a cornerstone in my journey of seeking light. It showed me that the act of seeking is not passive, but a dynamic interplay between the seeker and the world around them. Just as I had breathed new life into static artworks with my stories, I realized that we all have the power to illuminate the world with our unique perspectives and creative expressions.

Awakening the Inner Child's Light

- Think back to a space from your childhood that felt magical and transformative. What made this place special?
- What sights, sounds, smells, and textures do you remember most vividly?
- How did this space nurture your emerging curiosity and sense of wonder?
- If you could write a letter to your younger self in that sacred space, what would you say?
- Recall a time when you felt drawn to something that was considered "too advanced" or "not for you." What attracted you to it?
- How did you navigate between others' expectations and your own deep yearnings?
- What inner wisdom were you following, even if you couldn't name it at the time?
- How has that early act of reaching beyond boundaries influenced your life's path?
- Remember a moment when you first dared to interpret the world in your own unique way. What gave you the courage?
- How did others react to your unconventional perspective? How did their reactions affect you?
- What "dragon's breath" do you see in the abstract patterns of your own life today?
- How can you reclaim that childlike ability to transform the ordinary into the extraordinary?
- What stories did you tell as a child - to yourself, to others, to your toys or imaginary friends?
- When did you first discover your power to captivate others with your unique way of seeing?

- What "galleries" in your life are waiting for your creative reinterpretation?
- How can you nurture and protect your inner storyteller today?
- Think of a moment when an adult truly saw and appreciated your unique gifts. How did it make you feel?
- What creative sparks have you inherited from your family, whether through genetics or inspiration?
- How do you honor both tradition and innovation in your own creative expression?
- What legacy of creative courage do you wish to pass on to future generations?
- Like the young gallery guide holding the pamphlet upside down, what "delightful chaos" do you bring to formal spaces?
- How do you balance respect for established forms with the need to subvert them?
- What expectations are you ready to defy in service of your authentic expression?
- How can you create safe spaces for others to explore their own sacred defiance?
- What forgotten aspects of your childhood creativity are asking to be reclaimed?
- How can you create or find spaces that nurture your soul's continuing expansion?
- What stories are you ready to tell that only you can tell?
- What concrete steps can you take this week to honor your inner child's wisdom?

Remember: Take your time with these prompts. Let your responses flow naturally, without judgment. Feel free to write, draw, doodle, or express yourself in whatever way feels most authentic. The goal is not perfection, but connection with your own journey of awakening and seeking light.

Seshat's Celestial Records: A Journey of Illumination

The scent of ancient papyrus and starlit incense fills your nostrils as you stand before a towering ebony door. Your fingers trace the hieroglyphs etched into its surface, each symbol warm to your touch, pulsing with hidden meanings. The stone floor beneath your feet hums with a deep, cosmic resonance that travels up through your body.

Warmth brushes your skin as Seshat's presence emerges. The air around you sparkles with stardust, and your skin tingles as if touched by countless points of light. A leopard skin cloak materializes, its surface rippling with living constellations so vivid you could reach out and pluck the stars from its fabric. The seven-pointed star above radiates waves of knowledge that wash over you like warm honey.

As the massive doors part, your breath catches at the vastness before you. The chamber stretches beyond physical possibility, its boundaries shifting like a mirage. Your ears catch whispers of ancient wisdom carried on currents of ethereal air. Scrolls and tablets hover around you, their surfaces shimmering with moving images that draw your gaze. Each breath you take tastes of stardust and possibilities.

Your feet carry you to a crystalline pedestal at the chamber's heart, where a blank papyrus scroll glows with inner light. The reed pen beside it thrums against your palm as you lift it, its starlight essence flowing into your veins like liquid moonlight. Energy courses through your arm, making your fingers tingle with creative power.

As you begin to write, the chamber comes alive around you. The scratch of pen on papyrus echoes like music. Constellations wheel overhead, their movements matching the flow of your words. Colors you've never seen before spiral through the air, painting your thoughts in cosmic light. The very air vibrates with the frequency of creation.

The completed scroll rises from beneath your hands, its surface glowing with your newly-written truth. Its essence crystallizes in your palm as a seven-pointed star amulet, cool to the touch yet pulsing with inner warmth. The metal seems to merge with your skin, becoming part of your own radiance.

The chamber's vast energy flows through you now, a river of starlight and wisdom that has forever altered your perception. Even as the grand space begins to fade from view, your body holds the resonance of this cosmic alignment. Each breath draws in the lingering scent of stardust, each heartbeat echoes with the rhythm of celestial spheres.

Integration Practice:

1. Create your own miniature celestial archive using seven small scrolls
2. On each scroll, write one insight or truth discovered during your seeking
3. Arrange the scrolls in a seven-pointed star pattern
4. Each morning, select one scroll at random
5. Spend time contemplating its wisdom while holding a starlit crystal
6. Journal how this wisdom illuminates your path that day
7. At week's end, gather all seven scrolls and synthesize their collective light into a personal codex of transformation

Through this practice, we anchor Seshat's celestial wisdom into earthly form, allowing it to guide and illuminate our continued journey of seeking.

The Seeker Emerges: A Berlin Journal for Self-Discovery

The years flowed like the Nile, carrying me from the sanctuary of my father's library to the vibrant, divided streets of Berlin. That childhood spark had grown into a blazing fire, demanding expression. In 1987, at 22, I stepped into a city still scarred by history, its infamous Wall a stark testament to division and longing.

My first home was a tiny attic room in Kreuzberg, its slanted ceiling pressing down as if urging me to break free of constraints. As I regained strength after a debilitating illness, I began to explore. The streets of Berlin became my canvas, each walk a journey through a fragmented yet vibrant universe.

The energy of Berlin crackled around me, a symphony of raw creativity and untamed expression. In the gaps and abandoned spaces left by the Wall, a new generation of artists flourished. I was drawn to the underground scene in Mitte and Prenzlauer Berg, where forgotten factories transformed into impromptu galleries.

My sketchbooks overflowed with attempts to translate the swirling visions in my mind onto paper, but soon even that felt confining. I experimented with photography, sculpting, street art – anything to bring my inner world to life.

When the Wall fell in 1989, it was as if the city itself exhaled a long-held breath. The artistic community exploded with newfound freedom. Tacheles, an artist squat in a bombed-out department store, became a symbol of this creative renaissance.

Berlin became more than just a city to me – it was a living metaphor for the process of seeking light. The fall of the Wall symbolized the breaking down of inner barriers, the abandoned spaces transformed into galleries that mirrored the potential waiting to be awakened within us all.

Seeds of Transformation: A Journey into Your Creative Awakening

- Think of a time when you arrived somewhere new - physically or metaphorically. What emotions surfaced? How did your senses absorb this unfamiliar environment?

- Describe a space in your life that feels like that tiny attic room in Kreuzberg - somewhere that both constrains and challenges you to break free. What lies beyond its slanted ceilings?
- What "illness" (physical, emotional, or spiritual) have you had to recover from? How did it transform your way of seeing the world?
- Map the evolution of your creative expression. What medium first called to you? Which ones followed? What still waits to be explored?
- Like Berlin's abandoned factories becoming galleries, what spaces in your life are waiting to be transformed? What potential lies dormant in your "forgotten" places?
- When have you felt most creatively alive? Describe that moment in vivid detail - the sounds, smells, textures, and emotions that made it electric.
- What "walls" in your life are ready to fall? List them, then explore what lies on the other side of each one.
- Like post-Wall Berlin, what parts of yourself are experiencing a creative renaissance? What has been liberated in you recently?
- What symbols of division in your life could become bridges of connection? How might you transform these barriers into gateways?
- If your life were a city, what would its map look like? What are its vibrant districts, quiet corners, and underground scenes?
- Where is your personal "Tacheles" - the raw, authentic space where your truest creativity emerges?
- What metaphor best describes your current journey of seeking light? How is it evolving?

Take time to read back through your responses. What patterns emerge? What surprises you? Write a letter to yourself about the journey ahead, incorporating the insights you've gained through these reflections.

Remember: Like Berlin itself, you are constantly in a state of unfolding. Each day offers new opportunities to break down walls, transform abandoned spaces, and let your creative light shine brighter.

Immersion: Unveiling the Hidden City

The air shimmers with the heat of a thousand untold stories as you step off the train, your senses bombarded by the symphony of a city you've never encountered before. The scent of exotic spices mingles with the diesel fumes of ancient buses, creating a fragrance that is both alluring and unsettling. The cacophony of voices, a chorus of unfamiliar languages, rises and falls like the tide, punctuated by the rhythmic calls of street vendors and the distant wail of a siren.

Your eyes, wide with curiosity, scan the bustling streets, taking in the vibrant tapestry of humanity that unfolds before you. Women draped in brightly colored fabrics glide past businessmen in crisp suits, their paths intertwining like threads in a vibrant tapestry. Children with mischievous grins dart through the crowd, their laughter echoing off the weathered walls of ancient buildings.

The ground beneath your feet is a mosaic of cobblestones and cracked pavement, each step a tactile reminder of the city's history, its resilience, its enduring spirit. The sun beats down with an intensity that mirrors the vibrant energy of the city, casting long shadows that dance and distort, creating an ever-shifting landscape of light and darkness.

As you wander deeper into the city's embrace, your senses heighten, attuned to the symphony of urban life. The taste of freshly baked bread mingles with the smoky aroma of street food, tantalizing your taste buds with unfamiliar flavors. The rhythmic beat of distant drums blends with the melodies of street musicians, creating a soundtrack that pulses with the city's heartbeat.

You find yourself drawn to a hidden alleyway, its walls adorned with vibrant murals that depict scenes of both celebration and struggle, a reflection of the city's soul. The air here is cooler, the sounds of the bustling streets muted, replaced by the gentle trickle of a fountain and the chirping of birds nesting in the eaves.

In this quiet sanctuary, you stumble upon a hidden door, its weathered wood hinting at untold stories and forgotten dreams. Curiosity piqued, you push the door open, and step into a world of creative wonder.

The space is bathed in a soft, golden light, its walls lined with bookshelves overflowing with volumes of poetry, philosophy, and art. Easels stand scattered throughout the room, their canvases blank, awaiting the touch of inspiration. Musical instruments rest in shadowy corners, their strings humming with the potential for melodies yet to be born.

This is a haven for artists and dreamers, a sanctuary where creativity flourishes, where the boundaries between imagination and reality dissolve. You feel a surge of inspiration, a yearning to express your own unique voice, to contribute to the symphony of creation that resonates within this space.

What will you create in this haven of unlimited potential? Will you pick up a brush and paint a masterpiece that captures the city's vibrant soul? Will you compose a melody that echoes the rhythm of its streets? Or will you weave words into a tapestry of stories that reflect the dreams and aspirations of its inhabitants?

Integration Practice:

As you stand in this golden-lit sanctuary of creativity, let the question of what you will create settle deeply into your being. Close your eyes and feel the resonance of each artistic possibility - the brush waiting to dance across canvas, the strings yearning to sing, the blank pages whispering for your stories.

But instead of rushing to grasp one of these tools, take a moment to simply breathe in the creative potential that surrounds you. Let each inhale draw in the layered symphony of your journey - the spice-laden air of the streets, the laughter of children, the echo of street musicians' songs. Let each exhale settle you deeper into this moment of infinite possibility.

Now, with eyes still closed, allow one artistic medium to call to you. Trust that your soul knows which form of expression needs to emerge. Perhaps it's the brush that sends a tingle through your fingers, or maybe a melody rises unbidden to your lips. The blank page might magnetize your hand, or your body might begin to sway with an unspoken choreography.

Open your eyes and approach your chosen medium with reverence. Before you begin, place one hand over your heart and whisper: "Through this art, I weave my thread into the city's tapestry." Then let yourself create without judgment or expectation. Let the sights, sounds, scents, and sensations of your journey flow through you and into your chosen form of expression.

Create for exactly thirty-three minutes - the time it takes for a stick of incense to burn, for shadows to shift across the floor, for the city outside to write another chapter in its endless story. When time flows to completion, step back from your creation and bow to it with gratitude.

Before you leave this sanctuary, choose one small element of your art - a single line from your writing, a particular color from your painting, a phrase from your song, a gesture from your dance - and vow to carry it with you into the world beyond the hidden door. This will be your key, allowing you to rediscover this sacred creative space wherever your journey leads.

Let this practice be your bridge between the extraordinary and the everyday, between the hidden and the revealed, between the city's dreams and your own creative awakening.

Immersion: Dancing with Tehuti, the Master Shapeshifter

Beloved seeker, prepare to embark on a journey of profound transformation. Find a quiet space where you won't be disturbed. Take a deep breath, feeling the air fill your lungs with the ancient power of change. As you exhale, let go of all preconceptions about who you are and what you're capable of becoming.

Before you materializes Tehuti, the ibis-headed god of wisdom and magic, master of shapeshifting. His form flickers and changes – one moment an ibis, the next a baboon, then a man with piercing eyes that hold the knowledge of ages. His presence fills the air with crackling energy, the scent of papyrus and stardust. Feel Tehuti's energy envelop you. The world around you dissolves into swirling mist, shot through with threads of golden light. These are the strings of possibility, the very fabric of creation that Tehuti manipulates with his magic.

Now, let your body begin to move. There's no right or wrong way – simply allow the energy of transformation to guide you. As you dance, feel your form start to shift. Your arms elongate into wings, feathers sprouting along your skin. You are an ibis, Tehuti's sacred bird, soaring high above the Nile. Feel the wind beneath your wings, see the world from this new, expansive perspective. What truths become clear from this vantage point?

Another turn in your dance, and you shrink, your body becoming dense and powerful. You are a baboon, wise and mischievous. Feel the strength in your limbs, the acute intelligence in your gaze. What hidden knowledge can you access in this form? What mysteries can you unravel with your clever hands?

Keep moving, letting the dance carry you through a myriad of forms. Become a lotus, rooted in the mud but reaching for the light. Transform into a scarab beetle, rolling the sun across the sky. Shape yourself into a scribe's reed pen, feeling the power of words flow through you.

With each transformation, pay attention to the sensations in your body, the shift in your perceptions. How does each form change the way you interact with the world? What new understanding does it bring?

As the dance reaches its crescendo, you find yourself face to face with Tehuti once more. His eyes meet yours, filled with approval and challenge. Slowly, your dance brings you back to your human shape. But you are not the same. You carry within you the memory of flight, the wisdom of the baboon, the resilience of the lotus, the transformative power of the scarab, the creative force of the reed pen. You are all of these and more – a being of infinite potential, constantly seeking, constantly transforming.

Carry the energy of Tehuti's shapeshifting dance within you. The world around you may look the same, but you now perceive it through the lens of infinite possibility. You are the seeker and the sought, the creator and the created, constantly dancing on the edge of transformation.

This immersion aligns deeply with the Seeking Light phase. It embodies the spirit of exploration, the willingness to see from new perspectives, and the courage to reinvent oneself in the pursuit of wisdom and enlightenment. It encourages breaking down barriers and embracing the unknown.

Reflect on your shapeshifting journey with Tehuti. Which form resonated most deeply with you? How can you incorporate the wisdom and perspective of that form into your daily life? What limitations or self-definitions are you now ready to shed as you continue your journey of seeking light?

Integration Practice: The Seeker's Shapeshifting Light

Stand before your reflection as the final echoes of your dance with Tehuti fade, but notice how your transformed body seems to glow from within. The ibis's wings have left trails of light across your shoulders, the baboon's wisdom sparkles in your eyes, the lotus's journey toward illumination still pulses in your chest.

Bring your awareness to this inner radiance - the light of seeking that burns within every seeker of truth. Let it pool in your heart center, growing brighter with each breath. As you watch your reflection, allow this light to shape-shift just as your body did during the dance. Let it become the soaring illumination of the ibis's flight, revealing truth from new heights. Transform it into the penetrating insight of the baboon's gaze, cutting through illusion. Feel it stretch like the lotus stem, reaching through darkness toward greater understanding.

Now, focus on the form that called to you most powerfully in your dance with Tehuti. What unique way of seeking light did this form reveal to you? Perhaps the ibis showed you how to rise above limitations to gain a broader perspective. Maybe the baboon taught you to seek wisdom through playful curiosity. Or the lotus demonstrated how to trust your journey through darkness toward light.

Speaking softly to your reflection, ask:

"What shadows have I been afraid to explore?"
"What light am I truly seeking?"
"How can my way of seeing guide my search?"

Let the wisdom of your chosen form answer through movement. Your body remembers its shapes - trust it to show you new ways of seeking, new paths toward illumination.

Complete this integration by drawing your inner light into your hands. Cup them before your heart, feeling the warmth of your seeking spirit. Bring to mind one truth this shapeshifting journey has revealed - one new way of seeking that you'll carry forward. Release your hands outward, offering this light of understanding to illuminate the path for other seekers.

Remember: Every new perspective, every transformation, is another way of seeking light. You are not just changing forms - you are expanding your capacity to perceive and embody truth.

Art Academy: Where Rebellion Breeds Brilliance

The energy of Berlin had awakened a hunger within me, a yearning to express the swirling visions that danced behind my eyes. With this fire burning in my soul, I entered the Art Academy Berlin in the 1990s, my heart a canvas for dreams, my mind a palette of ideas yearning to take form.

But the academy, with its echoes of tradition and whispers of "pure" art forms, presented a new kind of challenge. My professors, those guardians of the established order, couldn't see beyond the confines of their canvases and sculptures. Their voices, steeped in the language of brushstrokes and chisels, met my passion for multidisciplinary art with resistance, their skepticism a barrier I struggled to overcome.

I remember one particularly frustrating critique session. I had presented a mixed-media piece, a tapestry woven with video elements alongside a traditional painting. As I explained my vision of blending time-based media with static art, I could see the frowns deepening on my professors' faces, their brows furrowed like hieroglyphs etched in disapproval.

"This is not a painting," one of them declared, his voice heavy with the weight of tradition. "It's not a sculpture either. What is it you're trying to do here?"

I fumbled for words, trying to articulate the swirling visions in my mind, the yearning to break free from the confines of a single medium. "I'm trying to capture movement, the passage of time, the way memory works..." I trailed off, seeing only confusion in their eyes, their expressions mirroring the fragmented reflections in my artwork.

Another professor, her silver hair pulled back in a severe bun, shook her head, her disapproval as palpable as the texture of the canvas before me. "You must master the basics before you can break the rules. Focus on your brushwork, your composition. Leave the experimentation for later."

Their words felt like chains, attempting to tether my wild imaginings to the safe harbor of tradition. But even as I nodded and promised to focus on the fundamentals, I knew in my heart that I couldn't contain the stories bursting to be told, the visions yearning to break free from the confines of convention.

Driven by this hunger for multidisciplinary expression, I began to explore beyond the academy's walls. I discovered workshops led by Ernest Berk, the last living student of the renowned Mary Wigman. Despite being confined to a wheelchair, Berk's passion for movement and expression was infectious, his spirit soaring beyond the limitations of his physical form. His teachings opened my eyes to the power of dance and physical storytelling, adding new dimensions to my artistic vocabulary.

I started creating installations, pushing the boundaries of what my classical art professors considered "art." These experiments, a rebellion against the established order, nearly cost me my bachelor's degree, with some professors threatening to deny my graduation. But amidst the resistance, I found an ally in my sympathetic Japanese professor, her eyes twinkling with encouragement as she witnessed the fire burning within me.

"Your art doesn't belong in the confines of a studio," she told me one day, her words like a gentle breeze fanning the flames of my creativity. "Travel. Explore. Take your creations out into the world."

Her words were a key to unlocking a door I hadn't even known was there. They resonated with a deep yearning within me, a desire to break free from traditional boundaries and explore the vast possibilities of artistic expression.

It was during this time of exploration that I met the director of the film academy, his presence a beacon of light in the midst of my struggles. Seeing my yearning to transcend the limitations of traditional mediums, he encouraged me to consider filmmaking. "Film can be your canvas," he said, his voice filled with possibility, "a medium that encompasses all your loves – visual art, storytelling, movement, sound."

With this encouragement, I began to explore the world of cinema, my curiosity ignited like a torch in the darkness. I snuck into lectures at the film academy, soaking in every word about framing, editing, the power of the moving image to capture the essence of life itself. My sketchbooks, once filled with static images, now overflowed with storyboards, each frame a portal to a world waiting to be born. My hands, accustomed to brushes and charcoal, learned to cradle cameras with reverent care, capturing fleeting moments and weaving them into tapestries of light and shadow.

I started creating short films, experimenting with laymen artists and actresses to create hybrid, poetic pieces that defied categorization. These films became a way to explore the duality of my existence, depicting a holographic life, a fusion between the vibrant world of Cairo and the stark beauty of Berlin.

This period of struggle and evolution taught me a profound lesson about seeking light. Sometimes, the light we seek cannot be found within established boundaries. It requires us to push against constraints, to venture into uncharted territories, to embrace the fertile chaos of experimentation. The resistance I faced became a catalyst for growth, pushing me to seek new forms of expression, new ways of bringing light into the world. I learned that true creativity often lies in the spaces between disciplines, in the fusion of seemingly disparate elements. Most importantly, I discovered that seeking light is not just about finding illumination, but about having the courage to create it where none existed before.

Imagine a time when you were standing at a crossroads, unsure of which path to take. Perhaps you were considering a new career, ending a relationship, or moving to a different city. Recall the moment you decided to take a leap of faith and choose a new direction.

- What were you afraid of?
- What gave you the courage to take the leap?
- How did the outcome of your decision shape your life?

Think about a time when you stumbled upon something that ignited a spark within you. Perhaps it was a hobby, a skill, or a cause that you became deeply passionate about.

- How did you discover this passion?
- What obstacles or challenges did you face in pursuing it?
- How has your passion enriched your life?

Have you ever experienced a creative block, a period when your inspiration seemed to dry up? Recall a time when you felt stuck and unable to create.

- What was causing your creative block?
- How did you overcome it?
- What did you learn about yourself and your creative process?

The China Crucible: Visions and Rebirth

Following my professor's advice, I embarked on a journey that would reshape my understanding of reality. Beijing in 1996 was a city caught between worlds, ancient traditions colliding with the relentless march of modernity. As I navigated the narrow hutongs and stood in awe before Tiananmen Square, I felt the pulsing energy of a nation in flux coursing through my veins.

The ancient Silk Road beckoned, a ribbon of dust and dreams stretching into China's heart. Dunhuang rose from the desert like a mirage, its market, a sensory explosion that left me reeling. That first day, I stood paralyzed, my senses overwhelmed by the kaleidoscope of life swirling around me.

The air, thick with spices and incense, carried whispers of a world both foreign and achingly familiar. Voices rose and fell in a language I couldn't understand, yet their cadence echoed the markets of my childhood in Cairo. My mind reeled, struggling to reconcile this sensory assault with the comfortable predictability I'd left behind in Berlin.

Days passed in a haze of sensory overload. Slowly, like a photograph developing, the chaos began to coalesce into recognizable patterns. The shouted greetings of vendors, the vibrant swirl of silk scarves, the steam rising from bubbling pots of mysterious broths – each element sharpened into focus, revealing a world as rich and complex as the one I'd known in my home Egypt.

In quiet teahouses, I fumbled through conversations with weathered locals, their faces maps of lives lived fully. Each interaction was a bridge, not just between languages, but between worlds. The Chinese characters I practiced felt like hieroglyphs come to life, each stroke a key to unlocking ancient wisdom.

As I ventured beyond the cities, the landscape unfolded like a scroll painting come to life. Mist-shrouded mountains gave way to emerald rice terraces, each vista more breathtaking than the last. In remote villages, I found echoes of rituals that resonated deep within my bones, as if some part of me recognized a truth older than memory.

It was in Guangzhou that the fever struck, a fire that consumed me from within. The world dissolved into a swirling vortex of visions, reality bleeding into dream. In the depths of my delirium, I felt a presence – ancient, powerful, yet achingly familiar.

The fever raged for days, each moment a battle between light and shadow. I descended into the depths of my own psyche, confronting fears and desires long buried. The Neteru were my guides, illuminating the darkest corners of my soul with their divine presence.

When the fever finally broke, I emerged transformed. The woman who had arrived in China – eager, yet still clinging to the safety of the known – was gone. In her place stood someone new, someone who had glimpsed the vast, interconnected web of existence and could never again see the world through the same eyes.

As strength returned to my limbs, I found myself drawn to the bustling markets once more. This time, the sensory onslaught was a symphony, each element a note in the grand composition of life. I moved through the crowd with newfound grace, the language now flowing from my lips as if I'd always known it.

In a small, incense-filled temple, I sat in meditation, feeling the pulse of chi flowing through me. The energy was at once foreign and intimately familiar – the ka of my Egyptian heritage given new form. The boundaries between cultures, between the physical and spiritual realms, had blurred. I was a bridge, a living embodiment of the connection between worlds.

This crucible of fever and vision in China became a pivotal moment in my journey of seeking light. It taught me that sometimes, we must be broken open to let the light in. The illness stripped away layers of conditioning, allowing me to see the world – and myself – with new eyes. I learned that seeking light isn't always a gentle process; sometimes it requires us to face our deepest fears, to lose ourselves in order to find a greater truth. The experience reinforced the interconnectedness of all things, showing me that the light we seek is not confined to one culture or tradition, but pulses through the very fabric of existence. Most importantly, it revealed that true transformation often comes when we are at our most vulnerable, when we surrender to the process of unfolding.

Reflection: The Seeker's Crucible

Beloved seeker, find a quiet moment and a blank page. Light a candle if you wish, its flame a reminder of the transformative fire that burns within each of us. Let your pen become a bridge between worlds as you explore these gates of understanding:

Recall a time when life stripped away your familiar comforts, when illness, challenge, or radical change forced you into unknown territory. How did this experience break you open to new light? What veils of perception dissolved in that crucible of transformation?

Imagine yourself in a foreign land where nothing is familiar - the language, the smells, the rhythms of daily life. What fears arise? What excitement stirs? Write about a moment when strangeness transformed into recognition, when the foreign became intimately known.

Describe a fever dream, real or metaphorical, that changed how you see reality. What visions emerged from your depths? What ancient wisdom surfaced? What truths were you finally ready to face?

Paint with words the moment you emerged from your own crucible of transformation. How had your inner landscape shifted? What new light illuminated your path? What could you never unsee?

Finally, trace the golden threads that connect your most challenging experiences to your deepest awakenings. How has surrender - to fever, to foreignness, to the unknown - opened doorways to light? What mysteries still beckon from beyond the veil of the familiar?

Let your writing flow without judgment, knowing that each insight is another step on the endless journey of seeking light. Trust that even in recording these reflections, new layers of understanding may emerge.

Immersion: The Dragon's Breath: A Healing Journey

The air crackles with a vibrant energy as you stand at the base of a majestic mountain, its peak shrouded in swirling mists, a symbol of the unknown depths within your own being. Sunlight filters through the leaves, casting dappled patterns on the forest floor, where a carpet of moss and wildflowers invites you to begin your ascent.

Feel the earth beneath your feet, solid and supportive, grounding you in the present moment. The air grows cooler with each step, carrying the scent of pine needles and damp earth, a reminder of the healing power of nature. Your breath deepens, your heart rate quickens, as you embark on this journey of inner exploration.

Halfway up the mountain, you encounter a cave bathed in a warm, inviting light. This is the lair of the Dragon, a mythical creature of immense power and wisdom, its breath a source of healing and transformation. The entrance to the cave beckons you, promising a sanctuary of renewal and rejuvenation.

Step into the cave, and feel the warmth enveloping you, not as a scorching flame, but as a gentle, soothing embrace. The air here vibrates with a subtle energy, a healing balm that soothes your weary soul. The sounds of the outside world fade away, replaced by the gentle dripping of water and the echo of your own heartbeat.

In the center of the cavern, coiled in majestic repose, lies the Dragon. Its scales shimmer with iridescent hues, reflecting the spectrum of emotions and experiences that have shaped your journey. Its eyes, ancient and wise, meet yours, and you feel a sense of deep recognition, a knowing that this creature holds the key to your healing.

The Dragon's breath washes over you, a gentle breeze that carries the scent of healing herbs and the whispers of ancient wisdom. It penetrates your being, seeking out the places where you hold pain, fear, or unresolved trauma. Feel the tension melting away, the knots of emotional blockage dissolving, the wounds of the past gently healing. The fire within you is not destructive, but transformative, burning away what no longer serves you, making space for renewal and growth.

Visions arise, shimmering glimpses of your own resilience and strength. You see yourself navigating challenges with courage and grace, emerging from the darkness stronger and more empowered. The Neteru appear beside you, offering their support and guidance. Isis, the healer, gently tends to your wounds. Tehuti, the wise scribe, offers words of encouragement and understanding. Anubis, the guardian of the underworld, reminds you that even in the darkest depths, transformation is possible.

The Dragon's breath intensifies, its warmth penetrating every cell of your being, activating your innate healing abilities. You feel a surge of energy, a revitalization of your spirit, a deep sense of connection to the life force that flows through all creation.

As you emerge from the cave, the world around you shimmers with newfound vibrancy. The sunlight filtering through the leaves seems brighter, the air crisper, the scent of pine needles more invigorating. You feel lighter, stronger, more alive. The Dragon's healing breath has ignited a spark within you, a flame of resilience and self-love that will illuminate your path forward.

The mountain path, once a daunting challenge, now beckons you with a gentle invitation. Your steps are lighter, your breath deeper, your spirit soaring with the newfound clarity and strength that flow through your being. You continue your ascent, guided by the whispers of the wind and the warmth of the sun on your skin, eager to explore the hidden wonders that await you on the summit.

Integration Practice: The Healing Flame Within

As you descend the mountain path, the Dragon's healing warmth still pulsing through your being, pause in a quiet grove. Here, where sunlight dapples the earth and the wind whispers through pine needles, you'll integrate this transformative experience through the practice of the Healing Flame.

Find a comfortable seat on the soft earth. Place one hand over your heart, where the Dragon's breath still resonates, and the other on your belly, connecting to your own inner fire. Feel how the ground supports you, just as it supports the mountain that houses your mystical healer.

Begin to breathe deeply, imagining that with each inhale, you draw in the Dragon's healing essence - that perfect balance of warmth and power that transformed you in the cave. With each exhale, direct this healing breath to any part of your being that still calls for attention.

Now, begin to hum softly, allowing your voice to carry the vibration of healing throughout your body. Let the sound emerge naturally, shifting and changing like the Dragon's iridescent scales. Your voice becomes a bridge between the mystical experience and your physical form, helping to anchor the transformation.

As you continue humming, slowly begin to sway, letting your body move in response to the healing energies flowing through you. Perhaps your movements echo the Dragon's sinuous grace, or maybe they express the unfurling of your own renewed spirit. Trust whatever emerges.

When your movement naturally stills, sit quietly and speak aloud three truths that the Dragon's healing has revealed to you. Let these words carry the power of declaration, of claiming your restored wholeness. The trees stand witness to your words, the earth receives them, the wind carries them into the world.

Complete your practice by drawing the infinity symbol (∞) on your heart center with your finger, sealing the connection between the Dragon's transformative power and your own innate ability to heal and renew. This symbol becomes your touchstone - a simple gesture you can repeat whenever you need to reconnect with the healing flame that now burns within you.

Rise slowly, bow in gratitude to the mountain and its mystical guardian, and continue your journey carrying the Dragon's gift of healing within your heart. Remember: you are now a keeper of the sacred flame, capable of igniting healing warmth wherever your path may lead.

Inner Journeys and Philosophical Explorations

The fever that had gripped me in China subsided, but its effects lingered, reshaping my perception of reality like a potter's hands molding clay. As

I returned to the familiar streets of Berlin, I found myself a stranger in my own life. The cobblestones beneath my feet felt alien, the rhythms of the city out of sync with my newly awakened consciousness. The art that had once consumed me now felt hollow, a pale reflection of the vast, interconnected reality I had glimpsed in my transformative experience.

It was in this state of inner turmoil, walking through the bustling Alexanderplatz with its mix of socialist architecture and burgeoning consumerism, that I first encountered the teachings of Krishnamurti. The title, "Freedom from the Known," leaped out at me from a small, tucked-away bookshop, its words resonating with a deep yearning within my soul.

His words fell upon my consciousness like rain on parched earth, awakening a thirst I hadn't known I possessed. "The ability to observe without evaluating is the highest form of intelligence," he wrote, and I felt a profound resonance, as if Krishnamurti had given voice to the ineffable experiences I had undergone in China.

Driven by an insatiable hunger for understanding, I immersed myself in his writings. The parks of Berlin became my open-air study halls. The Tiergarten, with its sprawling greenery and winding paths, became my sanctuary. Its labyrinthine walkways mirrored the journey of self-discovery I was undertaking, each turn revealing new vistas of understanding.

I would spend hours beneath the ancient oaks, their gnarled branches a canopy above me, Krishnamurti's books spread before me like sacred texts. His words were a chisel, chipping away at the calcified beliefs and assumptions I had accumulated over years.

"Belief is poison," he declared, and something within me cracked, like a fault line suddenly giving way. It revealed a space where I'd thought certainty lay, a void that was both terrifying and exhilarating. The collapse of my belief systems was disorienting, leaving me feeling untethered. Yet in the rubble lay a startling question that would become my compass: "If not belief, then what is the foundation of my life?"

This question became a koan, a riddle I turned over and over in my mind as I wandered the streets of Berlin. From the graffitied remnants of the Wall to the sleek modernity of Potsdamer Platz, every corner of the city became a backdrop for my philosophical musings. I began to see how my identity as an artist, as a seeker, even as a human being, was constructed of beliefs – some inherited, some chosen, but all ultimately limiting.

As my exploration of Krishnamurti's teachings deepened, I found myself increasingly at odds with the academic world I had been part of. The University of the Arts, once my haven, now felt constricting. The rigid structures of university life, the emphasis on categorization and specialization, felt increasingly at odds with the holistic understanding I was developing. Lectures that once inspired now felt like cages, each theory and methodology a bar limiting the free flow of creativity and understanding.

Friends and colleagues looked on, baffled and concerned, as I abandoned what they saw as a promising academic career for the unpredictable realm of independent art. At 30, an age when many were settling into established paths, I was uprooting myself from the known. Leaving behind the security of academia seemed like madness to them, but I felt a deep inner certainty that thrummed through my being like a tuning fork struck against the edge of the universe.

Each new discipline I explored became a threshold to cross, an expansion of myself. I dove into filmmaking, capturing the interplay of light and shadow that mirrored my inner journey. International affairs drew me in, revealing the complex web of global interconnections that echoed the unity I had glimpsed in my visions. Healing modalities became a way to integrate body, mind, and spirit, while my growing ability to channel the Egyptian Neteru opened doors to wisdom beyond the rational mind.

Krishnamurti's words lingered, a constant refrain: the outer journey is the inner journey. I began to see how true freedom lay not in external circumstances, but in facing the unknown within, in confronting the shadowy corners of my psyche that I had long avoided. Yet this understanding brought its own challenges. His promise of boundless joy through freedom clashed jarringly with society's relentless regulations, a dissonance I felt not just in the world around me but mirrored in my own mind, conditioned by years of societal norms.

This period of philosophical exploration and inner journeying was a series of spirals, each cycle bringing me back to familiar ground yet with new insights. It taught me that seeking light is about learning to live with questions. The discomfort of uncertainty, which I had once fled from, became a trusted companion, a sign that I was pushing against the boundaries of my understanding.

I discovered that true wisdom often lies in the spaces between certainties, in the fertile void of not-knowing. This wasn't an easy lesson - there were nights of existential angst, days when the lack of solid ground left me feeling adrift. But gradually, I learned to trust the process, to find exhilaration in the freefall of uncertainty.

Perhaps the most profound lesson of this period was that seeking light sometimes means dismantling the very structures we've built our lives upon. It requires courage - the courage to question everything, to let go of the identities and beliefs we've clung to for safety. It's a process of breaking down in order to break through, of clearing away the accumulated debris of a lifetime to uncover the bedrock of our true nature.

As I navigated this landscape of philosophical inquiry and personal transformation, I came to a startling realization: the light we seek is a constant unfolding, a dance between questioning and understanding, between the known and the unknown. It is the very process of seeking that illuminates our path, each step forward casting light on the next.

The journey that wove through the parks and studios of Berlin, guided by the words of Krishnamurti and the presence of the Neteru, had brought me to a new threshold. I stood poised between worlds - the academic and the artistic, the rational and the mystical, the personal and the universal. The path ahead was unclear, but one thing was certain: the journey of seeking light, of unfolding into my fullest potential, had just begun.

Reflection

- Krishnamurti often spoke of the limitations of belief systems. Describe a belief that you once held with unwavering certainty, but have since questioned or released. How did this shift in perspective impact your understanding of yourself and the world around you?
- Krishnamurti emphasized the importance of looking inward for truth and wisdom. Close your eyes and visualize yourself standing before a wise being, a guide who embodies the qualities you most admire. Who is this being? What wisdom do they impart? How can you cultivate these qualities within yourself?
- The path of Seeking Light is often filled with uncertainty and ambiguity. Imagine yourself embarking on a journey through a dense forest, its paths winding and obscured by mist. How do you navigate this unknown terrain? What tools or instincts do you rely on to guide your steps? What discoveries await you in the heart of the forest?

- Krishnamurti's teachings often highlighted the interconnectedness of opposites. Reflect on a time when you experienced the merging of seemingly contradictory forces within yourself or the world around you. How did this experience challenge your understanding of duality? What new perspectives emerged?

- The Seeking Light phase is about embracing the journey itself as a source of wisdom and transformation. Imagine yourself dancing through life with a sense of curiosity and wonder. What does this dance look and feel like? How can you cultivate a playful spirit of exploration in your daily life, approaching each experience as an opportunity for growth and discovery?

Immersion: A Journey Through the Seven Rays

You stand at the foot of a towering pillar, its surface etched with ancient hieroglyphs that pulse with living light. The symbols seem to breathe, each one singing a tone that resonates with your very cells. As you reach out, your fingertips tingle with recognition - this is no mere stone, but a key to awakening the spectrum of divine wisdom within you.

The pillar's glow builds like a rising sun, each heartbeat intensifying its radiance until light explodes in a prismatic cascade. Time slows as the first ray emerges...

Red light pools at your feet like molten earth, spiraling up through your legs. The scent of rain-soaked soil fills your lungs as Geb's presence grounds you into unshakeable stability. Your bones hum with the deep resonance of mountain roots while a warm breeze carries the whisper: I am grounded and secure, as ancient as stone, as steady as earth itself.

The red light transforms, blooming into a vibrant orange that dances around your sacred center. Isis's creative fire ignites within you as orange blossoms perfume the air. Your cells remember their power to shapeshift and transform. Your body sways with serpentine grace as you hear: I am infinitely creative, eternally adaptable, forever flowing with life's dance.

Yellow light bursts from your solar plexus in a radiant sun-star. Ra's presence fills you with liquid gold confidence. The beat of distant drums matches your strengthening heartbeat. Heat builds in your core as power flows through you unobstructed. Your spine straightens as truth reverberates: I am a sovereign creator, shining with divine purpose and strength.

A soft green glow emanates from your heart like aurora borealis. Hathor's love pours through you in waves of compassion that dissolve all barriers. Bird song weaves through the air as your heart expands beyond its boundaries. Tears of joy fall as you hear: I am love itself, infinite in compassion, one with all beings.

Crystal blue light springs from your throat like a mountain stream. Tehuti's wisdom flows through you in a clear cascade of expression. The sound of gentle waves carries your voice to new depths of authenticity. Words of power form on your tongue as you declare: I am truth spoken clearly, wisdom expressed purely, divine voice ringing true.

Deep indigo blooms between your brows like a midnight flower. Horus awakens your inner vision until you see with the eyes of eternity. A bell's pure tone opens doorways of perception. Stars wheel in your mind as insight dawns: I am seer of mysteries, knower of truth, visionary of divine light.

Finally, violet-white light crowns you in cosmic radiance. Nut's infinite presence dissolves all boundaries until you are vast as space itself. The sacred hum of creation vibrates through your being. You expand beyond form as revelation sounds: I am one with the divine, infinite awareness, eternal light.

The rays continue their dance around and through you, no longer separate but flowing together like a living rainbow. You have become a prism of divine light, able to refract universal wisdom into every color needed. With each breath, the rays pulse in perfect harmony. You are earth and sky united, a bridge between realms, carrier of the eternal flame.

Feel the seven affirmations merge into a single truth in your heart: I am a living temple of light, awakened to my full spectrum of being. As it is above, so it is within me. So it is, so it shall be.

Integration

As the seven rays continue their dance around you, place one hand over your heart center. Feel how each ray has left its unique signature within you - red's groundedness, orange's creativity, yellow's power, green's love, blue's expression, indigo's vision, and violet-white's connection to the divine.

Take seven conscious breaths, each one honoring one of the rays. With each exhale, speak its affirmation with your entire being. Let each truth settle into your cells, becoming part of your essential nature.

On your final breath, imagine all seven rays merging into a single point of rainbow light in your heart. This is your inner prism, always ready to refract divine light into whatever color, whatever quality you need at any moment.

Draw a small circle over your heart with your finger, sealing this rainbow light within you. From this day forward, whenever you need to access any of these divine qualities, simply touch this spot and remember: you are a living bridge between earth and sky, carrying all the colors of divine wisdom within you.

Remember - you don't need to search outside yourself for these qualities. They are your inheritance, your birthright, your true nature. You are the prism through which divine light shines.

Awakening the Divine Within

The Nile River flows gently past Philae Island, its waters reflecting the golden hues of the setting sun. As you approach the island by boat, a sense of anticipation builds within you, a yearning to connect with the sacred feminine energy that permeates this ancient land.

The island emerges from the mist like a jewel, its lush palm trees swaying in the gentle breeze, their fronds whispering secrets of the goddesses. The temple of Isis stands tall and proud, its sandstone walls bathed in the warm glow of the Egyptian sun, its intricate carvings hinting at the mysteries that lie within.

Stepping onto the island, you feel a profound sense of peace wash over you. The air is alive with the sweet scent of jasmine and the rhythmic chirping of birds, their melodies weaving a tapestry of tranquility. The temple's entrance is framed by two towering obelisks, their hieroglyphs etched with stories of the gods and goddesses, their presence a reminder of the ancient wisdom that resides within these sacred walls.

As you enter the temple, the grandeur of the interior takes your breath away. The walls are adorned with intricate carvings and paintings, depicting scenes from the myths and legends of ancient Egypt, each one a portal to a world of magic and wonder. The light filters through stained glass windows, casting a soft, ethereal glow on the temple floor, illuminating the path towards the heart of the sanctuary.

In the center of the temple, a circular pool shimmers with an otherworldly light, its surface as still as a mirror, reflecting the starry sky above. This is the Well of the Divine Feminine, a source of primordial wisdom and power, its waters infused with the essence of Isis, the goddess of magic, healing, and creation.

Approach the well, feeling the energy emanating from its depths, a gentle pull towards the source of your own feminine power. As you gaze into the waters, the goddesses begin to emerge, each one a facet of the sacred feminine power that dwells within you.

Isis steps forth first, her wings of protection spreading wide to embrace you. She who gathered the scattered pieces of Osiris, who breathed life back into death through the power of her love, who protected her son Horus in the marshes - she knows the alchemy of transformation. Through her reflection in the well, you see your own power to make whole what has been broken, to nurture seeds of possibility in the darkest places, to weave magic from the threads of everyday life.

Hathor emerges next, her cow ears framing her face of infinite compassion. She who holds the sistrum that shakes the stars into dance, who offers divine milk that nourishes souls, who embodies sacred pleasure and joy - she awakens your capacity for ecstatic celebration of life. In her reflection, you recognize your own ability to find beauty in every moment, to nurture others through music and dance, to embrace the sensual power of being alive.

Sekhmet appears in a shimmer of heat, her lioness face fierce with protective love. She who breathes fire to defend the innocent, who transforms rage into healing power, who burns away all that prevents growth - she ignites your warrior spirit. Through her eyes, you see your capacity to set and defend sacred boundaries, to speak truth to power, to transform destructive forces into creative ones.

Bastet slinks forth with feline grace, her presence a reminder of playful sovereignty. She who guards hearth and home, who sees in the dark, who balances fierce protection with tender nurturing - she awakens your sensual wisdom. In her reflection, you recognize your ability to land on your feet after any fall, to move with grace between worlds, to embody both power and pleasure.

The goddesses begin to dance around the well, their energies merging into a spiral of divine feminine power. You glimpse yourself as a fierce warrior, clad in shining armor, her sword raised in defense of truth and justice. You see yourself as a nurturing mother, her arms cradling a newborn child, her heart overflowing with unconditional love. You witness yourself as a wise crone, her eyes filled with the wisdom of ages, her voice whispering ancient secrets. And you see yourself as a playful child, her laughter echoing through the temple chambers, her spirit dancing with the joy of creation.

Embrace these reflections, acknowledging each aspect of the divine feminine within you, the warrior, the nurturer, the wise woman, and the playful child. They are all part of your sacred wholeness, the tapestry of your being.

As you reach down and touch the surface of the water, you feel a surge of energy coursing through your body, awakening every cell, every atom. This is the elixir of the divine feminine, a potent brew of intuition, creativity, nurture, and strength.

Cup your hands and bring some of this sacred water to your lips. As you drink, feel the elixir spreading through your being, flowing to all the places within you that have felt unloved, unworthy, or wounded. Feel it soothing, healing, empowering.

The elixir reaches your heart, and you feel it expanding, opening like a lotus flower, its petals unfurling to reveal the radiant light within. From this open heart, tendrils of light begin to spread throughout your body, illuminating the channels through which the divine feminine flows – through your intuition, your creativity, your capacity to nurture and heal.

As you drink, imagine your inner temple forming within you. This temple is a sacred space dedicated to the divine feminine, adorned with symbols of wisdom, creativity, and nurturing. Within the temple, visualize a vast library filled with ancient scrolls, each containing the wisdom of the ages, waiting to be explored and integrated into your being.

A scroll materializes before you, its surface inscribed with hieroglyphs that shimmer with golden light. As you unroll it, the words reveal themselves, their message resonating deep within your soul: "The Divine Feminine is the source of all creation. She is the nurturing Mother, the wise crone, the fierce warrior, and the playful child. Embrace all aspects of her within you."

As this energy flows, you might feel a warmth in your womb space (regardless of your biological sex). This is your creative center, the place from which you birth new ideas, new aspects of yourself, new ways of being in the world. Place your hands here and feel the pulsing potential, the creative fire that burns within.

Now, become aware of your feet. Feel them connecting deeply with the earth, roots growing down into the soil, anchoring you to the strength and wisdom of the planet. You are a conduit between earth and sky, a living embodiment of the divine feminine in all her forms.

As you emerge from this immersion, feel the blessings of the goddesses upon you. Isis, Hathor, Sekhmet, Bastet – their energies merge with yours, bestowing upon you the strength, wisdom, and love of the divine feminine. Carry this elixir within you, beloved. Let it guide you on your journey, illuminating your path and empowering you to transform both yourself and the world around you.

Integration: The Goddess Seal

As the divine feminine power continues to pulse through you, place both hands over your womb space - your creative center. Feel the warmth building between your palms, a sacred fire of manifestation.

Begin to tone softly, allowing your voice to emerge from this center. Let it carry all the aspects you've awakened - Isis's power of transformation, Hathor's joy, Sekhmet's strength, Bastet's grace. Your sound becomes a bridge between the realm of the goddesses and your everyday life.

Draw a circle clockwise around your womb space seven times, sealing in these awakened powers. With each circle, speak one quality you are claiming:

"I claim my power to transform..." "I claim my power to nurture..." "I claim my power to protect..." "I claim my power to create..." "I claim my power to heal..." "I claim my power to dance..." "I claim my power to love..."

Complete this sacred activation by placing one hand on your heart and one on the earth, becoming a living pillar connecting heaven and earth. Speak your dedication:

"I am a vessel of the divine feminine, awake to all her powers. May I use these gifts with wisdom, grace, and love, for the benefit of all beings. As it was in ancient days, so it is now, so it shall ever be."

Carry this seal of the goddesses within you. Return to it whenever you need to awaken these sacred powers, knowing that the goddesses dance eternally within your own heart.

Sinai Sojourns: A Tapestry of the Soul

The Sinai sun, a relentless companion, beat down on me as I stood at the foot of Mount Moses, its heat a fiery embrace against my youthful skin.

Yet, an inner defiance surged within me, pulling me away from the well-trodden path towards the stark, shadowed face of Mount St. Catherine. It was a yearning for a challenge that mirrored the wildness within my own heart, a desire to climb higher, to explore the uncharted territories of my being.

A chance encounter with a weathered Swiss climber became an unexpected turning point. I was sixteen, a bud on the verge of blossoming, my senses alive with a newfound curiosity and a yearning for connection. His calloused hands, rough yet gentle, guided mine onto the jagged rocks, his quiet strength a testament to the mountain's power. With each upward struggle, each stinging scrape, a dormant strength within me awakened. It wasn't just the thrill of the climb, but the audacity of claiming this ancient, unforgiving land as my own, a place where my will and determination could shape my destiny.

Years blurred, each return to Sinai a pilgrimage into the depths of my being. The monastery's hushed beauty held a comforting constancy, a sanctuary for the battles raging within. The cool, stone walls offered respite from the desert heat, the scent of incense and ancient prayers lingering in the air, a balm for my restless spirit. Yet, it was in the tenacious desert blooms – the resilient almond blossoms, the fragrant rosemary, the ethereal desert roses – that I found a true reflection of my own enduring spirit, a testament to the beauty that can flourish even in the harshest of environments.

Sinai's true gift unfolded during a solitary three-day retreat I imposed upon myself as a young woman, nestled amidst the rugged peaks and sun-baked valleys near St. Catherine's Monastery. I sought out a secluded spot, a rocky outcrop where a Greek monk had retreated into silence and solitude. I mirrored his isolation, seeking the stark confrontation with my own inner landscape.

For three days, I existed in this desolate yet awe-inspiring realm, exposed and vulnerable, with only the relentless buzz of flies and the silent offerings of a young Bedouin boy, who brought us meager provisions once a day, for company. The vastness of the desert mirrored the expanse of my own soul, its silence amplifying the whispers of my doubts and fears, the echoes of past hurts and unfulfilled desires.

The sun beat down with relentless intensity, a fiery crucible that tested the limits of my endurance. The wind, a restless spirit, whipped through the canyons, carrying with it the whispers of forgotten travelers and the echoes of ancient prayers. The nights were a symphony of stars, their brilliance a stark contrast to the darkness that shrouded my soul.

During those three days, I wrestled with the demons that lurked within me, the shadows that had followed me from the bustling streets of Cairo to the quiet solitude of the desert. I confronted the fears that held me back, the doubts that whispered insidious lies, the insecurities that threatened to consume me.

It was a raw, unfiltered encounter with my own shadow self, a descent into the depths of my being where I unearthed the hidden wounds and unresolved traumas that had shaped my life. Tears flowed freely, mingling with the sweat that stung my eyes, a cathartic release of pent-up emotions that had long been buried beneath the surface.

I emerged from that solitary retreat transformed, my spirit weathered yet strengthened, my heart filled with a newfound clarity and resolve. The desert had become my crucible, forging me anew, preparing me for the journey ahead.

Nights under Sinai's vast, star-studded canvas held a different kind of awe. The universe's indifference was liberating, shrinking my worries and desires against the backdrop of eternity. The stars, like diamonds scattered across a velvet cloth, whispered tales of cosmic creation and the infinite possibilities that lay before me. Yet, even in this solitude, the land asserted its power. A night lost in the canyon, found by Bedouin trackers who navigated by starlight and an ancient language of the stones, was a stark reminder of my dependence on this land and its people, a humbling lesson in interconnectedness and the wisdom of those who walked a different path.

I remember the terror of realizing I was lost, the encroaching darkness seeming to mirror my inner disorientation. As panic threatened to overwhelm me, I reached into my pocket and felt the reassuring coolness of a smooth, polished crystal. In that moment, it became a lifeline, a tangible reminder of all the journeys that had brought me to this point, all the challenges I had overcome.

When the Bedouin trackers found me, their eyes shining with a mixture of concern and amusement, I was struck by their deep connection to the land, their ability to read the stars and stones as easily as I might read a book. Their knowledge, passed down through generations, was a living testament to the wisdom that can be found in the embrace of nature, in the whispers of the wind and the secrets held within the earth.

It was during one of these visits that the seed of "Nomad's Home" was planted. I met Selema, a Bedouin woman whose eyes sparkled with a fierce determination, her weathered face a map of resilience and strength. Over cups of sweet tea, fragrant steam rising between us, she spoke of her dream – a handicraft business that would empower the women of her tribe, giving voice to their creativity and sharing their artistry with the world.

This conversation ignited a fire within me, a passion to tell their stories, to weave their voices into a tapestry of film that would celebrate their strength and resilience. But the path ahead was far from smooth. The cultural barriers were high, the traditions deeply ingrained. The very idea of women appearing on camera was taboo, a threat to centuries of custom.

Yet, with patience and persistence, the doors began to open. One by one, the women emerged from the shadows, their hands skilled in the art of weaving, their voices carrying the wisdom of generations. We filmed in the soft light of dawn and the hushed stillness of dusk, capturing their stories, their laughter, their dreams for a future where tradition and progress could dance hand in hand.

Seven years passed, each frame of film a testament to the trust and collaboration that had blossomed between us. "Nomad's Home" became more than just a documentary; it was a bridge between worlds, a celebration of the feminine spirit, and a testament to the power of storytelling to illuminate the hidden corners of human experience.

When the film premiered, traveling to festivals around the world, it carried with it the spirit of those Bedouin women. Each award, each accolade, felt like a victory not just for me, but for Selema and every woman who had dared to share her story, their voices echoing through the grand halls of international recognition.

In my late fifties, Sinai beckoned me once more. This time, the journey led to the hidden Hathor temple, its weathered carvings whispering of ancient floods and forgotten histories, a testament to the enduring power of the feminine. Within those crumbling walls, I underwent an initiation, a reawakening of the potent force that resided within.

As I stood before the faded image of Hathor, her cow-eared face still radiating serenity after millennia, I felt a profound shift within myself. All the experiences, all the seeking, all the transformations – they coalesced in that moment into a deep understanding. I was not just an observer or a documentarian; I was a living embodiment of the very energies I had been exploring.

As I left the temple that day, I felt a profound sense of coming full circle. The seeker who had first set foot in Sinai years ago had been transformed, like the desert itself – weathered, stripped to essentials, yet vibrant with life and possibility. I knew that this was not an end, but a new beginning.

Sinai became more than just a place on my journey of seeking light – it became a living metaphor for the process itself. The harsh desert sun illuminated the hidden corners of my own being. The mountains taught me that seeking light often requires us to climb, to push beyond our perceived limits. The Bedouin women showed me that light can be found in the most unexpected places, in stories long silenced, in traditions reimagined. Through "Nomad's Home," I learned that seeking light is a journey that has the power to illuminate the paths of others. Most profoundly, Sinai taught me that the light we seek is not always a gentle glow, but sometimes a fierce fire that burns away what no longer serves us, leaving us raw, renewed, and ready to begin again.

Journaling Prompts

- Close your eyes and imagine yourself standing atop Mount Sinai, the wind whipping through your hair, the vast desert landscape stretching out before you. Feel the ancient wisdom of the land pulsating beneath your feet, the whispers of the ancestors echoing in the canyons. What secrets does the desert hold for you? What truths are revealed in the silence and solitude?
- The desert blooms of Sinai – the resilient almond blossoms, the fragrant rosemary, the ethereal desert roses – are a testament to the beauty that can flourish even in the harshest environments. What seemingly barren landscapes have you encountered in your own life? How have these experiences shaped your

understanding of resilience and the potential for growth in unexpected places?

- The Bedouin women of "Nomad's Home" shared their stories with courage and vulnerability, their voices weaving a tapestry of strength and resilience. Whose voices have inspired you on your journey? How have their stories illuminated your path and empowered you to embrace your own truth?

- Recall a time when you felt lost and disoriented, your inner compass spinning like the desert sands. How did you find your way back to yourself? What guides or inner resources did you rely on to navigate the unknown?

- The Sinai desert is a place of constant change, where the landscape shifts with the rhythm of the wind and the cycles of the sun and moon. Reflect on the transformations you have experienced in your own life. How have these experiences shaped your understanding of impermanence and the cyclical nature of existence?

Quantum Light Play: A Living Ritual

Find your spark point - that place where light dances differently, where silence holds music, where possibilities whirl like dust motes in sunbeams.

Place your crystals where they want to play. Watch them catch light, throw rainbows, whisper to each other across space and time. Let them guide your hands - some demand center stage, others prefer the edges where dimensions blur.

Three flames arise. Feel how they pulse together, creating patterns of shadow and radiance that mirror the dance of particles through the cosmos. Each flame holds a story - past, present, future merging in a single point of light.

Let vibrations move you. Start small - a fingertip conducting quantum symphonies, a toe tapping out the rhythm of reality itself. The energy builds, ripples outward, transforms you into a living wave of light and sound.

Make music with the universe. Tap crystalline rhythms on your altar. Hum frequencies that awaken ancient memories in your cells. Ring bells that send ripples through the quantum field. Let your body become an instrument of cosmic play.

Stand in your power point. Feel light coursing through you, photons dancing between neurons, consciousness expanding outward in concentric rings of radiance. You are observing and observed, creator and creation, a living paradox of light expressing through form.

Move as stars dance. Let your body discover new geometries, new ways of being in space and time. Float. Spiral. Pulse with the heartbeat of the cosmos. Find those exquisite points of balance where all possibilities converge.

Right here, right now - this moment holds everything. Feel joy bubbling up from the quantum realm, pure delight in being alive, in being light, in being. Let it overflow, ripple outward, transform everything it touches.

Beam gratitude through every cell. Let it shine from your eyes, pulse through your palms, radiate from your heart. You are a lighthouse of appreciation, broadcasting on frequencies that reshape reality.

Carry this light forward. Let it infuse each breath, each step, each interaction with sparkles of quantum possibility. You are light walking, light loving, light creating, light playing in human form.

The ritual lives in you now, a continuous dance of light and wonder unfolding in every moment.

A Playful Twist

Now, let's infuse this ritual with a touch of playful curiosity and unexpected delight. As you light the candle, imagine it is a tiny portal to a realm of pure light. Peek through this portal and see what wonders await you - perhaps a field of luminous flowers, a sky filled with dancing stars, or a city built entirely of shimmering crystals.

As you cleanse your space, create a symphony of sound! Gather pots, pans, and any other objects that can make noise. Bang them together, creating a joyful cacophony that banishes stagnant energy and invites in the playful spirits of light.

Instead of simply visualizing a path of light, imagine yourself hopping along it like a child playing hopscotch. With each hop, land on a different color, experiencing the unique vibration and energy of each hue.

As you chant or play singing bowls, let your body move spontaneously. Wiggle, jiggle, and shake your way into alignment with the frequency of light. Laughter is encouraged!

Instead of just standing tall, try embodying different creatures of light. Spread your arms like a majestic eagle soaring through the sunlit sky, or curl into a ball and roll around like a playful firefly illuminating the night.

And as you express gratitude, shout your intentions from the rooftops! Let your voice ring out with the joy and confidence of a child discovering their own radiant power.

This playful twist on the Illumination Path ritual reminds us that seeking light can be a joyful and spontaneous adventure. Embrace the unexpected, let your inner child guide you, and discover the transformative power of playfulness on your journey towards illumination.

Seeking Light Ritual: The Whispering Path

Gather your tools: a blindfold, a mismatched pair of socks, a small drum or rattle, and a handful of flower petals. Find a place in nature where you can move freely and feel the earth beneath your feet. It could be a forest path, a garden, or even a rooftop overlooking the city.

As the sun begins its descent, casting long shadows across the land, slip on your mismatched socks, their contrasting colors and textures a playful reminder of the duality within you. Feel the soft earth beneath your bare feet, grounding you in the present moment.

Now, place the blindfold over your eyes, surrendering to the darkness, trusting your intuition to guide your steps. Take a deep breath and begin to walk, allowing your feet to find their own path, your body to move in harmony with the whispers of the wind and the rustling leaves.

As you walk, shake the rattle or drum softly, creating a rhythmic beat that echoes the pulse of your heart, the rhythm of the earth, the symphony of the universe. Feel the vibrations resonating through your body, awakening your senses, opening you to the subtle energies that surround you.

With each step, imagine yourself stepping into a different realm of possibility, a hidden dimension where magic and wonder intertwine with the mundane. Feel the presence of the Neteru guiding your journey, their whispers carried on the breeze, their light illuminating your path.

Reach out with your hands, feeling the textures of the world around you – the rough bark of a tree, the delicate petals of a flower, the smooth surface of a stone. Each touch is a message, a symbol, a story waiting to be deciphered.

As you wander through this unseen landscape, allow your imagination to soar. Envision yourself dancing with the stars, conversing with the spirits of the trees, weaving your dreams into the fabric of reality.

Suddenly, you stumble upon a clearing bathed in a soft, golden light. Remove your blindfold, and gasp in amazement. Before you lies a field of luminous flowers, their petals shimmering with iridescent hues, their fragrance intoxicating your senses.

This is your inner garden, a sanctuary of light and beauty, a reflection of your own radiant potential. Step into this garden, and feel the warmth of the sun on your skin, the gentle caress of the breeze, the soft earth beneath your feet.

Gather a handful of flower petals, their vibrant colors a reminder of the diverse facets of your being. As you hold them in your hands, whisper your intentions for your Seeking Light journey, your dreams for the future, your yearning for truth and understanding.

Now, scatter the petals to the wind, allowing them to carry your intentions to the far reaches of the universe. Watch as they dance and twirl, their vibrant colors painting the sky with a tapestry of your dreams.

As the last petal falls to the ground, feel a sense of peace and gratitude wash over you. You have planted the seeds of your intentions, and the universe has heard your call. Trust in the unfolding of your journey, and embrace the light that guides your way.

Seeking Light: The Symphony of Sacred Questions

Light falls differently now. Each ray carries messages your Inner Being has learned to read. The ordinary world shimmers with extraordinary meaning - market vegetables hold cosmic wisdom, children's laughter contains creation stories, even dust motes dance with divine intention.

Remember how this seeking began? That first quickening in your chest, that subtle shift when shadows started speaking and questions bloomed like desert flowers after rain. Now pause. Feel how your inner architecture has transformed. Where walls once stood, doorways open to infinity. Where certainty lived, mystery now dances. Your very cells pulse with newfound frequencies of wonder.

The Egyptian sun paints different colors across your consciousness now. You've learned to see beyond its fierce gold into spectrums that exist between light and shadow. Markets that once felt chaotic now reveal their sacred geometries. Temple walls that seemed solid now breathe with ancient rhythm. Even your own reflection surprises you - there's a depth in your eyes that speaks of worlds explored between heartbeats.

You've become fluent in the language of light - how it bends around questions, pools in spaces of not-knowing, sparks in moments of holy curiosity. Your hands have learned to read the braille of starlight written across reality's skin. Your feet remember how to dance between dimensions while staying rooted in earth's sacred soil.

The Neteru's whispers weave through your daily breath. Tehuti's ibis wings fan the flames of your questioning. Aset unveils mysteries in your morning coffee's steam. Hathor's laughter echoes in unexpected moments of illumination. Even Sekhmet's fierce light has become a familiar companion, teaching you that seeking requires courage as much as curiosity.

You've discovered teachers everywhere - in the flight patterns of birds, in the wisdom of mismatched socks, in the geometry of broken shells on temple steps. Each question asked has created ripples through the cosmic web. Each moment of wonder has planted seeds of future illumination. Each step into uncertainty has added new notes to your soul's expanding symphony.

The light you sought was never separate from your seeking. Every question marked a doorway. Every doubt outlined a window. Every uncertainty pointed toward truth. You've learned to trust the spiral path, to find stability in spinning, to see how seeking itself shapes both seeker and sought.

Now stand at this threshold between seeking and ascending. Feel the momentum gathering in your bones, stardust crystallizing into new constellations within your being. The next phase beckons - Luminous Ascent calls with the voice of dawn breaking over temple walls.

Before you step forward, let the treasures of your seeking flow through you like golden honey, sweet with accumulated light. Each breath becomes a teaching, wisdom moving through your body like wind through desert valleys. Holy uncertainty dances in your cells, a sacred partnership with mystery that makes your spirit soar. Light sparkles in life's smallest corners - a dewdrop holding universes, a child's laugh containing creation stories, a fallen leaf inscribed with cosmic scripture.

Mystery calls and your soul answers, curiosity flowing like Nile waters through the landscape of your consciousness. Freedom blooms in the spaces between your questions, petals of possibility unfurling in the fertile void. Your seeking moves with the grace of ibis wings through morning mist, touching truth without grasping, discovering without demanding. Love flows through every sincere question like sunlight through stained glass, painting cathedral colors across reality's canvas.

Your seeking has altered reality's fabric, rewoven the threads of existence with patterns of wonder. Each question birthed new constellations in consciousness, stars of understanding blazing trails across your inner sky. Every moment of wonder opened another door in the universe's heart, revealing chambers of light previously unseen.

You stand ready now for the next movement in this cosmic symphony - prepared to rise with all you've gathered, to shine with all you've learned. The light falls differently now through the prism of your transformed perception, breaking into spectrums only awakened hearts can see.

And this - this is just the first note of an eternal song, the initial brush stroke on infinity's canvas, the opening breath of creation's endless dance.

Sacred Questions for Integration:

Allow these inquiries to spiral through your consciousness like light through crystal:

- What questions have become your most beloved companions?
- Which mysteries now feel like home?
- How has your relationship with uncertainty transformed?
- What new frequencies of light can you perceive?
- Where do you find teaching in each moment?
- How has seeking shaped your soul's unique signature?
- What doorways of perception have opened within you?
- Which sacred questions will you carry forward?

Let your responses flow like light across water. Draw them, dance them, dream them into being. This is your unique light signature, your soul's symphony of seeking.

III. LUMINOUS ASCENT

Isis, Skyward Guide, on your wings my spirit takes flight,
Cosmos mirrored in dewdrops, a dazzling, wondrous sight.
Through starlit realms and landscapes unknown,
May my own wings find strength, as seeds of courage are sown.
Isis, Painter of Worlds, your vibrant hues I boldly wield,
Rainbow and ocean, where secrets are revealed.
Cast off the shackles, let our inner light ignite,
Radiant reflections of your love's eternal might.

The Lotus Awakens: A Dawn by the Nile

The journey of the Luminous Ascent is akin to the lotus bud rising through the murky depths, gathering strength and resilience before it bursts forth into its full glory. It's a phase of overcoming challenges, of shedding limitations, of preparing to embrace the radiant light within.

I remember a dawn by the Nile, years ago, when I witnessed this process unfold before my very eyes. The pre-dawn air hung heavy with moisture, the world shrouded in a soft, ethereal glow. As the first rays of sunlight began to paint the sky in hues of rose and gold, I settled onto a weathered stone at the water's edge, my gaze drawn to a lotus bud emerging from the depths.

The river flowed gently before me, its surface a mirror reflecting the awakening sky. The lotus bud, its green stem stretching upwards from the murky depths, swayed gently with the current, yet maintained its unwavering trajectory towards the light. Time seemed to slow as I watched its journey, each subtle movement a testament to its inherent drive to reach the surface.

The water around the bud shimmered, changing from deep indigo to turquoise as the sun climbed higher in the sky. Slowly, ever so slowly, the bud neared the surface, its tightly furled petals holding the promise of the blossom to come.

My breath caught as the lotus finally breached the water's plane. Droplets clung to its petals, catching the light like tiny prisms, scattering rainbows across the surface. As the sun's warmth touched it, the bud began to unfurl, revealing layers of pristine pink petals, each one a masterpiece of delicate beauty.

In that moment, a profound understanding washed over me. The lotus's ascent mirrored our own journey – from the nurturing darkness of self-discovery, through the challenges of growth, to the moment of emerging towards the light. I saw how this phase of the Lotus-Born Heart process bridged the gap between seeking and the future blossoming, a time of preparation and strengthening before the full radiance of our being could be revealed.

As I continued to observe the lotus, another realization dawned. This flower, emerging from the mud to blossom in the light, carried everything it needed within itself. Its beauty, its strength, its potential for growth – all were inherent in its being from the very beginning.

In that moment, I understood that I too carried an innate abundance within me. Like the lotus, I had journeyed through dark and murky periods, faced challenges that threatened to hold me back. Yet here I sat, witnessing the dawn, alive and full of potential.

Tears welled up in my eyes as I recognized the wealth of experiences, knowledge, and love that I had accumulated over the years. Each challenge I had faced, each joy I had experienced, each connection I had made – all of these contributed to an inner richness that I had often overlooked.

Filled with inspiration, I reached for my journal, my fingers leaving damp marks on the pages as I captured this revelation. The concept of Luminous Ascent flowed through me, each word rising from a deep well of knowing. As I wrote, I felt my own spirit lifting, resonating with the promise of continuous growth and transformation.

The sun now hung high in the sky, its heat burning away the last wisps of mist. The lotus stood in partial bloom, a testament to the beauty of becoming. I gathered my things, sand clinging to my clothes, my heart full of purpose. The next phase of the Lotus-Born Heart journey had revealed itself, and I knew this insight would shape my path for years to come.

As I finally rose to leave, I gave silent thanks to the lotus, my unexpected teacher. Its simple act of emerging and beginning to bloom had opened my eyes to the vast reservoir of potential within me, waiting to be recognized and expressed. I understood that this Luminous Ascent was not the end, but a crucial step towards full blossoming and, eventually, the sacred seeding that would follow.

Sacred Reflection: The Journey of Your Inner Lotus

Find a quiet moment and a comfortable space. Light a candle if you wish, its flame representing the light you're moving toward. Let these prompts guide you into deeper understanding of your own luminous ascent:

- Recall a time when you felt submerged in life's "murky waters." What strengths or insights did you discover in that darkness?
- Like the lotus drawing nourishment from the mud, how have your challenges contributed to your growth?
- What "nutrients" in your current situation - even if challenging - might be feeding your future blossoming?

- What is calling you to rise right now in your life? What light are you naturally reaching toward?
- Like the lotus maintaining its course despite the current, what helps you stay true to your path when forces pull you off course?
- Describe a moment when you felt yourself "breaching the surface" of an old limitation. What changed in that breakthrough?
- The lotus carries everything it needs within itself. What inner resources have you discovered in yourself that surprised you?
- What qualities or strengths do you possess that you might be overlooking?
- What experiences have revealed your resilience? How has each challenge contributed to your inner richness?
- Like the lotus's petals catching the light, what aspects of yourself are beginning to shine?
- What parts of your being are still tightly furled, waiting for the right moment to unfold?
- How might you honor both your current state of partial bloom and your continued unfolding?
- What "droplets of wisdom" from your journey would you like to share with others?
- How has your understanding of transformation evolved through your own process of emergence?
- What gratitude would you express to your own inner lotus - that part of you that knows how to grow through darkness toward light?
- What new phase of growth do you sense emerging within you?
- How might you support your continued ascent while honoring the timing of your natural unfolding?
- What would it mean to trust that, like the lotus, you carry everything you need for your next phase of growth?

Daily Practice

Choose one of these practices to maintain connection with your inner lotus:

1. Morning Reflection: Each dawn, acknowledge one way you're rising toward the light
2. Evening Gratitude: Thank the "mud" that's nourishing your growth
3. Breakthrough Journal: Document moments when you feel yourself breaking through old limitations
4. Growth Snapshots: Like photographing a lotus's emergence, record the subtle signs of your own unfolding
5. Wisdom Collection: Gather the insights that arise as you navigate your ascent

Sacred Waters: The Lotus Journey

Cool, silky mud embraces you like a lover's caress, your consciousness settling into the form of a lotus seed nestled in the sacred depths. The waters of creation pulse around you, their ancient rhythms humming through your being. Secrets whisper through the darkness - tales of transformation, promises of light, memories of countless souls who have made this journey before you.

A stirring awakens deep within your essence - the first flutter of becoming. Your spirit responds to a call as old as time itself, compelling you toward transformation. Your form begins to shift, tender green life extending through your seed-self, reaching through layers of nurturing mud. Though darkness surrounds you, an inner knowing guides you upward. This is your luminous ascent beginning, the sacred journey of your unfolding.

The waters press against your emerging form, currents tugging at your tender stem. Each push threatens to bend you, to turn you from your path. Yet with every challenge, your being responds - roots reaching deeper into the fertile mud, stem growing stronger and more flexible. You learn to dance with the waters, to find strength in yielding, power in persistence.

Inky blackness gradually shifts to midnight blue. Tiny motes of light drift past like fallen stars, casting brief illumination through the depths. A flash of movement - a fish glides by, its scales shimmering like polished lapis lazuli in the dim light. Its presence reminds you that even in this solitary journey, you are held within the web of life. Sacred waters teem with unseen companions.

The pool trembles, stone walls vibrating with unexpected energy. From a hidden alcove emerges Bes, the dwarf god of protection and joy, his lion's mane floating like a golden cloud around his grinning face. He tumbles through the water with divine playfulness, sending swirls of bubbles dancing around your stem. His laughter ripples through the depths, a reminder that even profound transformation can be filled with delight.

As Bes's presence fades, his joy lingers in the waters around you. The heavy depths lighten to luminous turquoise. Your stem has grown tall and strong, able to bend without breaking, anchored in deep wisdom while reaching toward promise.

A change ripples through the waters above - dawn's first rays piercing the surface, calling you upward. Yet the final stretch brings its own trials. The water thickens, as if the depths themselves resist your leaving. In this moment of challenge, warmth surrounds you like a loving embrace. Nefertem, the lotus god himself, infuses your being with solar power and divine strength.

Anticipation builds with each subtle movement upward. The boundary between water and air shimmers just above, so close now. Every cell of your being yearns toward that threshold, while wisdom reminds you to savor each moment of emergence.

With one final surge of divine effort, you pierce the surface. Cool morning air caresses your first unfurling leaves. Droplets cling to your nascent bud, each one a prism transforming dawn light into tiny rainbows. You have done it - ascended from sacred depths into a world of infinite light and possibility.

Your petals slowly open to greet the sun, each one a testimony to the journey that has shaped you. The being that began as a seed has transformed through darkness and challenge into an expression of divine beauty. Yet this too is just a beginning. Like the lotus, you contain endless cycles of death and rebirth, of diving deep and rising again, each journey revealing new facets of your limitless nature.

The world shimmers with heightened awareness as you settle back into human form. Colors appear more vivid, sounds carry deeper meaning, scents tell stories of distant realms. Your consciousness has expanded through embodying the lotus journey. The challenges that once felt like obstacles now reveal themselves as strengthening forces, currents of grace sculpting you into your highest potential.

You are changed, transformed by moving through the sacred waters as the lotus. Divine light fills you, awaiting its moment to blossom forth in ever greater radiance. The journey continues, but you carry within you now the eternal wisdom of emergence.

Integration: Anchoring the Lotus Journey

Take a few moments to integrate this experience:

1. Remain seated comfortably, keeping your eyes soft and gently focused.

2. Place one hand on your heart and one on your belly, connecting to both your emotional center and your root energy.

3. Take three deep breaths, each one remembering a different phase of your journey:

   - First breath: Feel the nurturing darkness of the mud
   - Second breath: Sense the strength you gained pushing through water
   - Third breath: Experience again that moment of breakthrough into light

4. In your journal, capture your experience with these simple prompts:

   - What challenged you most in your ascent?
   - Where did you find unexpected joy?
   - What strength did you discover?
   - What is beginning to unfurl in your life?

5. Choose one simple anchor for today:

   - Touch water mindfully when washing your hands
   - Pause to feel sunlight on your face
   - Notice where support appears in unexpected ways
   - Celebrate small moments of breakthrough

Close by touching your heart center and whispering: "Like the lotus, I rise."

Carry this essence with you as you move through your day.

Laughter on the Nile:

The summer heat of Cairo enveloped our makeshift theater like a thick, shimmering veil. Backstage, the air buzzed with a frenetic energy, heavy with the scent of kohl, spirit gum, and youthful anticipation. I stood before a cracked mirror, watching in wonder as layers of greasepaint transformed my sixteen-year-old face into the visage of Zahra, a wizened crone.

The weight of my costume - black velvet adorned with a thousand tiny, captured stars - settled on my shoulders, whispering tales of faraway deserts. Each fold seemed to contain a story, a secret waiting to be revealed. Sweat beaded on my brow, threatening to mar the intricate lines that aged me decades in mere minutes. Yet beneath the padding that altered my lanky frame, a thrill of excitement crackled like static electricity.

"Five minutes!" The director's voice, a frantic whisper through the worn stage curtain, barely registered above the excited chatter of our young troupe. I cupped a hand around my ear, straining to hear, while my other hand gripped an ornate cane. Its carved serpent head tapped a playful rhythm against the wooden floorboards, echoing the quickening beat of my heart.

As I shuffled onstage, inhabiting Zahra's arthritic gait, the world beyond the footlights disappeared. The creaky boards beneath my feet became a sun-baked village square, the painted backdrop a mud-brick wall weathered by countless desert winds. In that moment of transformation, I felt the weight of Zahra's years settle upon me - the mischievous glint in her rheumy eyes, the lifetime of stories etched into her wrinkles.

Then came the miscue that would ignite a storm of laughter. My on-stage granddaughter, barely a year my senior, delivered her line with perfect solemnity: "Grandmother, fetch the water jug."

But in my ears, powered by some impish spirit of theater, her words transformed. With exaggerated glee, I cackled, "Sail the Nile on a hippopotamus? What a splendid idea, my girl!"

The look of utter bewilderment on her face was priceless. For a heartbeat, silence reigned. Then, like a dam bursting, laughter erupted - from the audience, from backstage, from deep within my belly. It bubbled up, unstoppable, shaking my frail character's frame with very un-grandmotherly mirth.

The laughter was contagious, rippling through the audience like waves on the Nile. It lifted us all, transforming our modest production into something magical. The rickety stage trembled beneath our feet, creaking in gleeful protest. Through a gap in the scenery, I caught a glimpse of our youngest members in the wings, their eyes wide with a delightful mix of awe and mischief.

As Zahra's cackles subsided into chuckles, I felt a profound shift. Age, character, and reality blurred. In that moment, we were simply souls united in joy, co-creators of a world spun from imagination and mirth. The laughter had bridged a gap, connecting us all in a shared moment of pure delight.

That summer, as we traveled through Egypt's provinces, each performance became a new opportunity for transformation. Under open skies and before audiences in dusty town squares, we spun tales and wove laughter. The heat, the long bus rides, the shared meals under canopies of stars - all of it blended into a tapestry of joy and discovery.

We were more than a theater troupe; we were alchemists, turning the base metal of words and gestures into pure gold. With each laugh, each moment of wonder we created, I felt myself ascending, reaching for something greater than I had known before.

The laughter that echoed through that Cairo theater still resonates within me, a reminder of the transformative power of joy and playfulness. It calls to mind the energy of Bes, that impish dwarf god we encountered in our lotus journey. As we continue our exploration of luminous ascent, let's embrace the spirit of the trickster, allowing ourselves to see the world – and ourselves – through new, playful eyes.

Journaling Prompts: The Alchemy of Laughter

- Recall a moment when something "went wrong" but transformed into unexpected delight
- What shifted in that moment? How did the energy change?
- How did shared laughter create connection with others?
- Think of a time when you stepped into a different role or version of yourself
- What freedoms or insights did this new perspective bring?
- How did playfulness help you access deeper truths about yourself?
- Where in your life could you invite more lightness and spontaneity?
- What "serious" situations might benefit from a touch of divine mischief?
- How can you honor both wisdom and playfulness, like the character of Zahra?
- What "base metals" in your life are waiting to be transformed into gold?
- How might approaching challenges with a playful spirit change their nature?
- Where do you feel called to be an alchemist of joy in your community?

- How does your body feel when you laugh deeply? Where do you hold tension? Where do you feel release?
- What gestures or movements help you access your playful spirit?
- How can you use your physical presence to uplift others?

Draw, doodle, or write freely. Let your inner trickster guide your pen. Remember - like the stage, this page is a safe space for exploration and transformation.

End your writing with a moment of gratitude for laughter's healing power and joy's ability to transcend all boundaries.

Immersion: The Trickster's Touch: Dancing with Bes

The air shimmers with ancient mystery, heavy with the scent of kohl and sacred incense. Here in this Egyptian temple-theater, where the gods once danced to ward off evil and bring protection to households, time bends and flows like the Nile itself. Elaborate costumes hang from wooden beams, their beadwork catching the light like captured stars, each pattern an echo of Bes's sacred symbols - the ostrich feathers, the lion's mane, the tambourine that drives away darkness.

For Bes is unlike any other Egyptian deity - a dwarf god of immense power, fierce yet playful, grotesque yet beloved. The protector of households, women in childbirth, and children, he dances and laughs to drive away evil spirits. His lion's face and protruding tongue may seem fearsome, but they mask a heart full of joy and protective love. The ancient Egyptians welcomed his image into their homes, carved his likeness on their headrests to guard their dreams, and celebrated his power to transform fear into laughter.

A golden thread of curiosity pulls at the heart, drawing attention to what appears to be an ordinary stage curtain. But nothing is ordinary in Bes's sacred space, where boundaries blur between protection and play, wisdom and foolery. The fabric ripples like water, transforming into a portal of liquid light. The body moves forward of its own accord, drawn by the magnetic pull of divine mischief.

The world dissolves and reforms into a labyrinth of mirrors, each surface alive with reflection and possibility. Like the walls of ancient birth houses where Bes's image watched over new life coming into being, these mirrors reflect infinite potential. Here stands a child-self, eyes sparkling with untamed wonder. There leans an ancient one, face etched with the wisdom of countless moons. Every reflection reveals another facet of being - the dancer, the dreamer, the sacred fool.

A giggle echoes through the maze, ricocheting off mirrored walls like drops of mercury. This is Bes's signature sound - the laugh that banishes demons, the joy that transforms fear into power. His presence fills the space with electric joy, his lion's mane wild and untamed, his dwarfed figure radiating the strength that comes from embracing one's unique nature. His eyes hold the glint of stars and ancient mysteries, reflecting the same mischievous protection that guarded Horus as a child.

The mirrors pulse with invitation. Movement begins, slow at first, then building like a desert wind. Each reflection dances to its own rhythm - the child-self flowing with elder's grace, the ancient one leaping with youthful abandon. This is Bes's sacred dance, the same movements that have protected households and birthing chambers for millennia. The body responds instinctively, moving between order and chaos, finding wisdom in the spaces between.

The dance deepens. Feet stumble purposefully, arms wave in delightful disorder. Each "mistake" births a new possibility, each awkward movement reveals hidden grace. This is Bes's greatest teaching - that imperfection holds power, that what seems misshapen may carry the strongest magic. Laughter bubbles up from some ancient spring, transforming the maze into a kaleidoscope of joy and revelation.

The mirrors begin to spin, reality blurring at the edges. Faces flash past - ancestors, descendants, possible selves yet unborn. Just as Bes bridges the divine and human worlds, this spinning transcends time itself. The laugh that emerges comes from everywhere and nowhere, expanding the heart beyond its usual horizons. This is the same laughter that has echoed through Egyptian homes for thousands of years, bringing protection through joy.

As the spinning slows, Bes's presence grows stronger, his divine mischief wrapping around like a warm cloak. The wisdom gained through play settles into bones and blood, lightening the spirit while deepening the roots of being. Like the ancient Egyptians who wore his amulets and placed his image above their doors, we carry his protection in our awakened joy.

Integration Practice:

1. Let the body settle into this new lightness, feeling Bes's protective presence
2. Touch three surfaces nearby with playful curiosity, remembering how Bes guards the household
3. Make a small, deliberate "mistake" - perhaps holding a pen awkwardly or sitting slightly off-balance - and find the power in imperfection
4. Feel how the space around you has shifted, protected by sacred laughter
5. Record in your journal one truth that revealed itself through play today
6. Create or carry a small token (perhaps drawing Bes's image or choosing an object that makes you smile) as a reminder of his protective, playful presence.

Baba Yaga's Wisdom. A Journey into Crone Magic

The mist parts to reveal a primordial forest where worlds and times interweave. Pine needles crunch underfoot, giving way to the smooth roots of ancient baobabs. Here the veil between worlds grows thin, and wisdom whispers through rustling oak leaves. The sharp scent of juniper purifies the air, preparing body and spirit for deep revelation.

In a moonlit clearing stands the infamous hut, its chicken legs shifting restlessly against moss-covered earth. The structure creaks and turns, ancient magic stirring the fallen leaves into spiraling patterns. The doorway yawns open, darkness beckoning with the promise of transformation.

The interior unfolds into a vast crystalline cave, its walls glittering with countless mirrors catching the light of bubbling cauldrons. Shelves stretch endlessly upward, laden with the mysteries of existence - bottled starlight, preserved dreams, herbs that flower in darkness. The air itself feels alive, thick with the potential of unbounded knowledge.

From the depths emerges the ancient one, her presence both wild and wise. Her silver hair moves like living smoke, her eyes holding the sharp glint of stars and secrets. The scent of earth and herbs clings to her form, marking her as a keeper of nature's deepest mysteries.

The cave shifts, revealing a massive bronze mirror whose surface ripples like disturbed water. Within its depths, time flows strange and fluid. Reflections age and transform, revealing the face of future wisdom. Silver threads appear in hair, laugh lines deepen around eyes that have seen countless moons rise and set. This elder self gazes back with eyes that hold both shadow and light, having walked through the fires of transformation and emerged stronger.

At the cave's heart bubbles the great cauldron of knowing. Its surface swirls with visions of wise women through the ages - Cerridwen brewing inspiration's brew, triple-faced Hecate guarding life's crossroads, dancing Kali spinning worlds into being. Their combined wisdom creates currents of possibility in the sacred liquid.

The moment of deepest magic approaches. The surface of the cauldron beckons, its waters warm and alive with potential. As hands break the surface, something solid takes form - a personal talisman of power, unique to each seeker's journey. This object holds the essence of inner knowing, a bridge between present self and future wisdom.

But the talisman is only the beginning. The cave itself seems to lean in, shadows dancing with anticipation as deeper truths emerge. The very air grows thick with questions that must be answered:

What untamed wisdom lies dormant in the bones, waiting to be claimed? Which fears, once guardians, have become prison walls to be dismantled? What truth needs to be spoken, what power reclaimed, what aspects of self finally embraced or released?

The answers rise from some deep well of knowing, surprising in their clarity and strength. This is the gift of the crone's cave - the mirror that reflects not just what is, but what could be. Each revelation builds upon the last, weaving a tapestry of understanding that transforms the very air.

As the vision begins to fade, a profound knowing remains. The wisdom of ages pulses in the blood now, a living force that can never be lost. The talisman's weight in hand serves as anchor and reminder - the crone's power was never something to be reached for, but a force that dwelled within all along, waiting to be recognized and claimed.

Integration Practice:

Settle into a quiet space, allowing the cave's energy to linger. Let your talisman - whether physical object or visualized symbol - rest in your hands or your mind's eye. Feel its connection to your own deep knowing.

Allow your awareness to spiral inward through these layers:

- First, acknowledge the wisdom already earned through lived experience
- Then, sense the ancestral knowing that flows through your lineage
- Finally, touch the timeless wisdom that resides in your very cells

Let your journal capture what emerges:

- What taste does your wisdom have? What color? What texture against your skin?
- Where in your body do you feel its strongest resonance?
- How does it wish to be expressed in your daily life?
- What gift does it ask you to share with the world?

Close by touching three points on your body - forehead, heart, and belly - sealing in the integration of mind, spirit, and instinct. The crone's cave journey continues to unfold within, its mysteries illuminating the path ahead one revelation at a time.

Carry this knowing forward: You are not seeking wisdom, but remembering it. You are not becoming the crone, but unveiling her presence within. The wild wisdom of the ages dances in your blood, ready to guide your luminous ascent.

The Storyteller's Journey: Tales on Marsa Matrouh Beach

The sun dips towards the horizon, painting Marsa Matrouh's vast, expanse beach in hues of fiery orange and soft pink. I dig my toes into the cooling sand, feeling the day's accumulated warmth radiating through my feet. The air carries the tang of salt, mingling with the smoky aroma of distant campfires being lit for the evening. The gentle lapping of waves provides a soothing backdrop to the growing excitement around me.

As twilight descends, a sense of anticipation builds. Children begin to gather, their laughter echoing across the beach, a joyous counterpoint to the rhythmic sea. Their eyes are wide with excitement, reflecting the last glimmers of daylight. I smile, realizing that word has spread – the storyteller has arrived.

A young boy, perhaps eight or nine, plops down directly in front of me. His face is lit with a spark of mischief that mirrors the glint in my own eyes. He leans forward conspiratorially, the scent of sea and sun clinging to his skin, and whispers, "Tell us about the djinn in the old fisherman's lamp!"

That single request ignites something within me. Stories begin to flow, as natural and unstoppable as the tides. I weave tales of magical creatures emerging from the sea foam, their scales glistening with otherworldly light. I speak of hidden oases in the desert where trees bear golden fruit that chimes like bells in the wind. My voice rises and falls as I describe stars that descend to earth, walking among us in human form, leaving trails of stardust in their wake.

As I speak, I feel a profound connection forming. The children lean in, their silence a testament to the captivating power of a story. I see wonder reflected in their eyes, feel the collective gasp as I unveil a plot twist. With each word, each flourish of imagination, the boundary between storyteller and audience blurs. We are co-creators in this moment, spinning worlds into existence through our shared imagination.

The stories flow from my lips; they ignite within me. I feel the heat rising in my face, mirroring the last rays of the setting sun. My hands move of their own accord, painting pictures in the air – the graceful arc of a flying carpet, the sinuous coils of a sea serpent, the delicate unfurling of a magical lotus.

Between tales, I become aware of my surroundings with heightened sensitivity. The grains of sand clinging to my skin feel like a galaxy of tiny stars. The cool evening breeze caresses my face, carrying whispers of distant lands. I taste salt on my lips – from the sea spray or my own exertion, I'm not sure.

As night deepens, the stories take on a life of their own. They intertwine with the rhythm of the waves, the twinkling of the first stars, the murmur of women preparing the evening meal in nearby tents. A tale of a brave sailor navigating storm-tossed seas coincides with a particularly large wave crashing on the shore. The children squeal in delight at the timing, and I feel a thrill of connection to something larger than myself.

In this moment, I understand the true power of storytelling. It's more than entertainment; it's a bridge between hearts, a thread connecting us to our shared humanity. I've found my voice, but more than that, I've discovered the joy of awakening imagination in others.

As the last tale comes to a close, a hush falls over the group. The night air has grown cool, but I feel warm from within. Exhaustion mingles with exhilaration. The children disperse slowly, their whispers carrying fragments of stories into the night.

I remain seated on the sand for a while longer, watching the moon cast a silvery path across the water. My six-years old heart is full, not just with the stories told, but with the ones yet to be born. This beach, this moment, has become a turning point. I know now that my journey as a storyteller – as a weaver of dreams and awakener of imagination – has truly begun.

As I finally rise to leave, I feel the weight of unseen worlds within me. My feet leave imprints in the sand, and I smile at the thought that even these small marks are the beginning of new stories, waiting to be told.

The power of storytelling lies in its ability to transport us, to help us imagine new possibilities. In my own life, there came a moment when I had to step beyond the realm of imagination and into a very real journey into the unknown. This experience of crossing both physical and cultural thresholds became a pivotal part of my luminous ascent.

Seeds of Story: Journaling Journey

Imagine yourself on Marsa Matrouh beach as the sun sets, toes buried in cooling sand, the rhythm of waves carrying ancient whispers. Let these prompts guide you into your own storytelling depths:

Remember a story that changed you - perhaps told by a grandparent, read in childhood, or whispered around a campfire. What made it magical? How did it shift something within you? What sensations arise as you recall this moment? Let your pen trace the pathways of memory, capturing the sights, sounds, and feelings that made this story come alive.

When did you first discover your voice? Perhaps it emerged in sharing a dream, recounting an adventure, or making a child laugh. Explore a moment when words flowed naturally, when you felt the power of weaving reality with imagination. What awakened in you then? What stories are sleeping in your bones, waiting to be told?

Recall an instance when the universe seemed to collaborate with your tale - like the wave crashing at the perfect moment in the story. Write about times when life itself became part of your narrative, when synchronicity danced with your words. How did these moments change your understanding of story's power?

What connections have you forged through sharing stories? Write about a time when a story created invisible threads between you and others, when boundaries dissolved in the magic of shared imagination. How did it feel to co-create these moments of wonder?

What stories do you carry that need to be shared? What wisdom, wonder, or wild dreams are asking to be voiced? Write about the tales that wake you in the night, the ones that pulse in your blood like distant drums. How might your stories illuminate paths for others?

Let your writing flow like waves on the shore, each word carrying seeds of story to new shores of understanding. End by capturing one story you'll share today - perhaps with a child, a friend, or even whispered to the wind.

Crossing Thresholds: From Cairo To Germany

The familiar cacophony of Cairo downtown faded behind me as I stepped into the cool, sterile environment of Frankfurt Airport. The contrast struck me immediately – gone were the warm sandstone buildings, the melodic calls to prayer, the ever-present aroma of spices and shisha. In their place stood sleek glass and polished metal, a sea of unfamiliar faces moving with purposeful efficiency.

My heart raced, a mix of excitement and apprehension coursing through my veins. This was it – the dream I'd nurtured in the quiet corners of the Goethe Institute library downtown Cairo had become a tangible reality. As I clutched my suitcase, its weight seemed to anchor me to the world I was leaving behind.

The familiar words of German swirled around me, yet Frankfurt Airport unfolded like an alien labyrinth. Corridors branched endlessly, each turn revealing a new sensory assault. The rapid-fire announcements, though perfectly understandable, carried an urgency that set my heart racing. I grasped my suitcase tighter, a lifeline in this maze of steel and glass.

Approaching the train schedule, I faltered. The flickering board, its letters and numbers dancing with maddening speed, mocked my years of German schooling. Understanding each word didn't translate to comprehending this dizzying whole. I was adrift in a sea of authentic German, the gulf between classroom fluency and real-world navigation yawning wide before me. In this moment, Frankfurt Airport became a crucible, reshaping my confident student self into something new – a traveler, uncertain yet exhilarated, standing on the threshold of a world both familiar and thrillingly unknown.

Arriving at my host family's home in rural Germany felt like stepping into another dimension. The landscape spread before me as a patchwork of neatly ordered fields and forests, so different from the urban sprawl of Cairo or the vast expanses of Egyptian deserts. The air carried the scent of pine and recent rain – a world away from the dry heat and exotic spices I knew so well.

Inside the house, I encountered my first true culture shock. As we sat down for breakfast, my eyes were drawn to a strange sight hanging above the table – a strip of flypaper, dotted with its unfortunate victims. To my hosts, this was a mundane, practical solution. To me, it served as a stark reminder of just how far I'd traveled, in miles and in cultural norms.

Yet, amidst this foreignness, I found an unexpected connection. The daughter of my host family, a young woman close to my age, shared with me her dreams of visiting Egypt. As she spoke of pyramids and ancient mysteries, her eyes shone with the same wanderlust that had brought me to her country. In that moment, I saw our journeys mirrored – each of us yearning for a world the other knew intimately.

The days that followed became a whirlwind of new experiences. Each challenge – deciphering train schedules, navigating unfamiliar city streets, grappling with a language that tied my tongue in knots – became a step on my path of transformation. I felt myself stretching, growing, adapting in ways I never imagined possible.

There were moments of frustration, of course. Times when the weight of cultural differences and the language barrier seemed overwhelming. But with each small victory – successfully ordering a meal in German, finding my way through a new town without getting lost – I felt a surge of confidence. I had become more than just a girl from Cairo; I was becoming a citizen of the world.

As weeks turned into months, I found myself viewing both my new surroundings and my homeland through a different lens. Germany, with its orderly efficiency and lush landscapes, became familiar. Yet, I also gained a new appreciation for the vibrancy and warmth of my Egyptian heritage. I learned to hold both worlds within me, to find balance in the space between cultures.

This journey across thresholds – from Cairo to Frankfurt, from the familiar to the unknown – became more than a physical relocation. It marked an ascent into a broader understanding of myself and the world. Like a lotus rising through murky waters towards the light, I grew, reaching towards a higher perspective that encompassed both where I came from and where I was going.

As I look back on that young woman stepping off the plane in Frankfurt, I see now that she embarked on more than a trip. She began an alchemical process, one that would transform her very essence. In crossing that threshold, I had initiated my own hero's journey, one that continues to unfold with each new experience and every boundary crossed.

Thresholds of Transformation: A Journey Within

Find a quiet moment to settle with your journal, perhaps near a window where two worlds meet - the inside and outside, the known and unknown. Let these pathways guide your exploration:

Return to a moment when you stood at the edge of profound change - perhaps arriving in a new country, starting a life-changing job, or stepping into an unfamiliar role. What sensations filled your body? What scents, sounds, and sights marked this threshold? Write with all your senses, capturing the texture of transformation.

Recall an encounter with the utterly foreign - a custom that startled you, a tradition that puzzled you, a way of being that challenged your assumptions. Like the flypaper above the breakfast table, what seemingly simple things revealed the vast distances between worlds? How did this experience reshape your understanding?

Think of a time when you recognized yourself in someone from a different world, like the host family's daughter dreaming of Egypt. What bridges formed in that moment of connection? How did sharing dreams across cultural divides illuminate your own journey?

Remember instances when you had to communicate beyond the boundaries of shared language. What gestures, expressions, or moments of wordless understanding created connection? How did these experiences change your perception of what it means to truly communicate?

Consider how crossing thresholds has transformed you. What parts of yourself emerged only after leaving the familiar behind? Like carrying both Cairo and Germany within, how do you hold seemingly contradictory aspects of your identity? What wisdom has emerged from straddling different worlds?

Explore a time when feeling lost led to unexpected discovery. Like navigating Frankfurt Airport's labyrinth, how has disorientation shaped your growth? What gifts have you received from embracing uncertainty?

Close your writing by contemplating the threshold before you now. What new crossing awaits? What parts of yourself might be born in the space between here and there?

Baptism by Waves: A Greenhorn's Unexpected Helm

In my fifties, life threw me an unexpected curveball – one that would challenge every comfort I'd known. My partner, a man with saltwater in his veins, introduced me to Nefertiti, our weathered sailboat. Named for the enigmatic Egyptian queen, she became the vessel of my transformation, though I didn't know it then.

I remember that first day vividly. The sky hung heavy with clouds, a detail I barely registered as we approached Nefertiti. She swayed gently in what I assumed was a calm harbor. The scent of salt and seaweed filled the air, mingling with the metallic tang of the marina. My partner's eyes gleamed with excitement as he helped me aboard, the deck creaking softly beneath our feet.

"Ready for an adventure?" he asked, his grin infectious.

Before I could form a response, he guided me straight to the helm. No preliminaries, no gentle introduction to life aboard. His hands placed mine on the rudder, the rough wood beneath my fingers telling stories of countless voyages.

"Here," he said, "you're going to steer us out."

My eyes widened. "Now? Just like that?"

He nodded, pointing to a buoy in the distance. "Aim for that. Feel the boat respond to your touch."

And with that, he was off, adjusting ropes and sails, leaving me alone with the wheel and my racing thoughts.

As we moved away from the dock, the true nature of the day revealed itself. What had seemed like gentle swells from shore transformed into rolling waves. The "calm" harbor waters churned with unexpected ferocity, the weather shifting rapidly. The wind whipped my hair, carrying spray that stung my eyes and left a salty film on my skin.

Each wave sent Nefertiti lurching. The wheel pulled in my hands, alive and willful. My arms strained to keep us on course, muscles I'd never known I had screaming in protest. The boat creaked and groaned, the sails snapping taut in the wind.

"How are you doing?" my partner called over the growing wind.

"Fine!" I shouted back, my white-knuckled grip betraying me.

The buoy that had seemed so close now danced on the horizon, mocking my efforts to reach it. Rain began to fall, fat drops obscuring my vision. I blinked rapidly, trying to clear my eyes without letting go of the rudder. The taste of salt was strong in my mouth, a mixture of sea spray and my own nervous sweat.

In that moment, the enormity of the situation crashed over me like the waves battering Nefertiti's hull. Here I was, a complete novice, steering a boat through increasingly rough waters. No manual, no practice run, just the raw experience washing over me.

Fear mingled with a strange exhilaration. Each time I managed to correct our course, a small thrill ran through me. I was doing this. Somehow, against all odds, I was sailing. The rhythmic slap of waves against the hull became a drumbeat, urging me on.

Hours seemed to pass, though it might have been minutes. Time lost meaning in the rhythm of the waves and the singular focus of keeping Nefertiti on course. My world narrowed to the feel of the rudder, the tilt of the deck, the distant buoy that was our goal.

Finally, my partner returned to the helm. "Well done," he said, taking the wheel. "You've got a natural touch."

As I relinquished control, I realized my hands were shaking. Every muscle ached. I was soaked to the bone, chilled, and utterly exhilarated. The taste of accomplishment was sweeter than any I'd known before.

That baptism by wave became the foundation of my sailing journey. No gentle introduction, no calm waters to ease me in. Instead, I was thrust into the heart of the experience, forced to sink or swim – or in this case, sail.

In the days that followed, I learned the basics - knots, terminology, the rhythm of life aboard. But nothing quite matched that first, intense lesson at the helm. It set the tone for everything that followed, teaching me that the sea waits for no one, and that sometimes, the only way to learn is to dive in headfirst.

Looking back, I'm grateful for that tumultuous start. It stripped away any illusions I might have had about sailing being a gentle, easy pursuit. Instead, it showed me the raw beauty and challenge of life on the water, igniting a passion I never knew I had.

That day, steering Nefertiti through unexpectedly rough waters, I discovered a strength within myself I'd never known existed. It was the beginning of a journey that would reshape my understanding of myself and the world around me, one wave at a time.

Deep Waters: A Journey into the Unknown

Settle into a quiet space where you can hear your own inner tides. Let the rhythm of your breath become like waves lapping against a shore as you explore these waters:

Think of a time when life thrust you into deep waters without warning. Like being placed suddenly at Nefertiti's helm, what moments have demanded you take control before feeling ready? Write about the sensations in your body, the thoughts racing through your mind, the taste of salt and fear and possibility on your tongue.

Remember an experience that revealed capabilities you didn't know you possessed. What storms have you weathered that showed you your own power? Like discovering unknown muscles at the wheel, what parts of yourself emerged in the face of challenge? Trace the map of your newfound territories.

Explore a moment when fear transformed into exhilaration. When has terror given way to triumph? Like those first lurching waves that became a rhythm, how have you learned to dance with the unknown? What did your body know before your mind caught up?

Recall an experience that dropped you into timeless space - when the world narrowed to just you and the challenge before you. Like focusing solely on the distant buoy, what moments have demanded your complete presence? What gifts waited in that suspended time?

Write about a triumph that soaked you to the bone with its intensity. What accomplishments have left you trembling and transformed? Like the sweetness of that first sail, what victories still sing in your blood? How did they change the way you face new challenges?

Consider the initiations that have shaped you. What experiences have stripped away illusions and shown you raw truth? Like that first day at sea, how have life's baptisms prepared you for deeper waters? What wisdom emerged from being thrown in deep?

Close by contemplating the horizons that call to you now. What distant buoys beckon? What new waters await your exploration? Let your pen chart these unknown seas.

Celestial Encounters. Nut's Celestial Embrace

The sky above the Dahkla Oasis stretched endlessly, a canvas of deepest indigo studded with countless stars. I lay on my back, the cool desert sand a stark contrast to the lingering heat of the day. The Milky Way arched overhead, a river of light that seemed close enough to touch. As I gazed upward, the very act of looking seemed to call more stars into existence, filling the sky with an impossible multitude of twinkling lights.

Slowly, imperceptibly at first, the stars began to shift. They coalesced into a form both familiar and awe-inspiring - the great arching body of Nut, the sky goddess. Her star-studded form stretched across the heavens, fingertips and toes touching the distant horizon. Within her cosmic embrace, galaxies and planets danced in eternal, celestial rhythms.

A gentle tugging sensation pulled at my consciousness. Nut's star-filled eyes seemed to focus on me, extending an invitation to join her celestial realm. I closed my eyes, surrendering to the experience, and felt myself floating upward, drawn into the vast expanse of the night sky.

When I opened my eyes again, I found myself suspended among the stars, cradled within Nut's cosmic form. The Earth hung below, a beautiful blue marble against the velvet darkness of space. From this vantage point, I could see the intricate web of connections linking every particle of existence.

Nut's voice resonated through me, not as sound but as pure vibration: "Beloved child, you are more vast than you know. Within you lies the power of creation itself."

As these words washed over me, I began to see myself differently. My body became translucent, revealing an inner cosmos as vast and complex as the one surrounding me. Every cell, every atom, mirrored the dance of the stars and planets. I was at once infinitesimally small and unimaginably vast.

Gradually, I felt myself descending back to Earth. As my feet touched the cool desert sand, I opened my eyes to find the night sky as it was before – yet everything had changed. The stars still glittered overhead, but now I saw them as old friends, co-dancers in this cosmic ballet.

Immersion: Nut's Embrace - The Sky Goddess Beckons

The ancient temple air shimmers with sacred presence, heavy with the scent of time and mystery. Massive stone columns rise like silent guardians, their shadows dancing in the flickering light of oil lamps. Above, stretching across the vast ceiling, a breathtaking mural captures the eye and stirs the soul.

There she is - Nut, the great sky goddess, her body an infinite arch over the earth. Her skin glows with the deep blue of endless night, galaxies spiraling across her form like cosmic jewels. Her fingers and toes touch the distant horizons, grounding celestial power in earthly form. Along the curve of her body, the sun makes its eternal journey - born each dawn from her mouth, traversing her star-studded form, only to be swallowed again at dusk.

The air grows thick with possibility. The mural begins to pulse with life. Nut's star-filled eyes blink open, focusing with ancient knowing. Her smile holds the mystery of creation itself. The temple floor seems to dissolve, gravity releasing its hold. The boundary between art and reality blurs as her painted form becomes a gateway to the cosmos.

Rising weightless into her embrace, the mortal world falls away. Here, floating in the living body of the sky goddess, planets and constellations perform their eternal dance. Stars whirl in patterns of impossible beauty, their light singing ancient songs of creation. This is the cosmic womb, where celestial bodies are born and cosmic order maintained.

The very essence of space vibrates with Nut's presence. Her energy flows through every atom, awakening a profound transformation. Skin begins to shimmer with stellar light, constellations mapping themselves across flesh. The boundary between self and cosmos dissolves - each cell a galaxy, each breath a solar wind.

Perspective expands exponentially. From one angle, you are but a mote of stardust in Nut's vast form. Yet focus shifting reveals universes contained within your own being, equally vast, equally infinite. The truth becomes clear - there is no separation between above and below, between cosmic and corporeal. All is one in Nut's eternal dance.

Her joy ripples through space like waves of starlight, awakening new understanding. The limitations of earthly existence fall away, revealing infinite potential. In her embrace, you are both child of earth and cosmic dancer, both singular being and universal force.

Descending gently back to the temple floor, the world appears transformed. The mural above is now recognized as a gateway rather than mere paint and plaster. Earth itself is revealed as a sacred participant in the cosmic dance, and every being upon it a bridge between realms.

Integration Practice:

Rest your awareness in your body as the cosmic energies settle. Notice:

- The weight of your form, anchoring stellar light into earth

- The rhythm of your breath, moving like cosmic winds
- The pulse of your blood, flowing like rivers of stars
- The space within your cells, vast as galaxies

Let your hands explore this transformed vessel:

- Trace the constellations that now map your skin
- Feel the places where earth and sky meet in your form
- Notice where cosmic energy gathers and flows

Connect with your surroundings through new eyes:

- Observe how ordinary objects hold cosmic light
- Feel the dance between gravity and celestial pull
- Sense the starlight hiding in every shadow

Ground this experience through mindful action:

- Take three steps, feeling yourself as a bridge between realms
- Touch something nearby, experiencing it as both matter and stardust
- Speak your name, hearing how it echoes through cosmic spaces

In your journal, map this journey through:

- Colors that capture your cosmic transformation
- Sensations that linger in your earth-star body
- Wisdom that whispers from the space between realms
- Ways you'll carry Nut's infinite embrace into everyday life

Encountering Hathor's Vibration

On another trip, I found myself in a different kind of sacred space - the temple of Hathor at Hatshepsut's mortuary temple. The first rays of dawn painted the sky in hues of pink and gold as I made my way up the ramp to the second terrace. Though I had visited countless temples before, something about this pilgrimage felt different, charged with an energy I couldn't quite name.

As I stepped into Hathor's chapel, the air seemed to shift. The stone beneath my feet hummed with an ancient power, each step connecting me more deeply to the sacred ground. The mammoth columns, adorned with Hathor's serene face, loomed above me, their presence both intimidating and comforting.

I found a quiet corner and settled onto the cool stone floor. My intention was simple: to meditate, to connect with the energy of this place. Closing my eyes, I began to focus on my breath, allowing the sounds of early morning birds and distant voices to fade away.

At first, everything seemed ordinary. But as I sank deeper into my meditation, a subtle vibration began to build. It started as a gentle hum in my fingertips, barely noticeable. Gradually, it intensified, spreading up my arms, through my chest, until my entire body seemed to resonate with this mysterious frequency.

The sensation was unlike anything I'd experienced before. It was as if every cell in my body was awakening, singing in harmony with an ancient, cosmic song. In my mind's eye, I saw swirling patterns of light, reminiscent of the intricate carvings on the temple walls.

Suddenly, a wave of pure joy washed over me. It wasn't the fleeting happiness of everyday life, but a profound, all-encompassing sense of bliss. Tears streamed down my face, but I was laughing too, my body unable to contain the sheer magnitude of this feeling.

In that moment, I understood. This was Hathor's energy, the vibration of divine joy and love that she embodied. The goddess of music, dance, and healing was making her presence known, not through visions or words, but through this incredible resonance within my very being.

Time lost all meaning as I sat there, bathed in this vibrational embrace. When I finally opened my eyes, the temple was filled with golden light. My body felt lighter, as if a great weight had been lifted. But more than that, I felt profoundly changed on an energetic level.

As I rose to my feet, a bit unsteady from the intensity of the experience, I noticed something extraordinary. The pain in my lower back, a constant companion for years, had vanished. The persistent knot of tension between my shoulder blades had melted away. I felt renewed, reborn.

In the days and weeks that followed, I found myself spontaneously humming or swaying to unheard rhythms. Joy bubbled up within me at unexpected moments. It was as if Hathor had attuned me to a higher frequency, one that resonated with the very pulse of life itself.

Immersion: Hathor's Resonance: A Vibrational Journey

Press your fingertips to the mirror's surface. Let them dance across the glass, creating rhythms that pulse through your arms, awakening ancient memories. The mirror shimmers, quicksilver rippling outward from your touch, inviting you deeper, deeper...

Through the portal, floating on golden light thick as honey. The air itself sparkles with bell-tones, each one awakening cellular memory. Skin tingles with celestial frequencies, remembering creation's first song.

A priestess emerges from radiant mist, her form flowing like water caught in sunlight. The sacred sistrum in her grasp seems alive - Hathor's face adorning its handle while suspended discs capture and release light like imprisoned stars yearning to sing.

A gentle nod, an offering. The sistrum passes from her hands to yours. Divine electricity dances through flesh and spirit the moment skin meets metal.

One shake transforms everything. A single bright tone cracks the universe wide open. Space expands infinitely while awareness spirals inward, consciousness becoming smaller than stardust. Here, inside the sistrum's cosmic architecture, simple metal discs reveal themselves as celestial dancers, planetary beings swaying through void.

Sound manifests in waves of living color: sapphire frequencies resonate through bone marrow, emerald vibrations unfold the heart like dawn's first lotus, rose-gold harmonies transmute ancient grief into pure light. Swimming through oceans of vibration, each note revealing more of the soul's radiant essence.

Divine presence surrounds, vast and tender as universal love. Hathor's energy, pure frequency beyond form, ripples through awareness like waves of starlight. Understanding floods every atom - joy flows as creation's fundamental tone, the primordial song birthing universes.

The body becomes living music. Every cell vibrates as a note in cosmic symphony. Movement conducts orchestras of stars, composing with colors transcending earthly language. Dancing with waves of sound-light, flesh and spirit become instruments of divine play.

Boundaries dissolve. Dancer and dance unite. Singer and song merge into one. Pure creation bursts forth, new harmonies spiraling from movement, intention, essential nature.

Return brings transformation. The temple shimmers with elevated frequencies, joy radiating as a fundamental tone. A sacred rhythm pulses through the heart center, the sistrum's song now dwelling in the soul's deepest chambers.

Integration Practice: Sacred Sound Alchemy. Embodied Harmonics

Create sacred space with sensory anchors - flowers releasing their perfume, crystals catching light, objects that spark wonder. Candlelight optional but welcoming.

Choose your sound vessel - rattle, bell, bowl, or voice. Plant feet firmly yet softly upon earth.

Begin with one pure tone. Let vibration ripple through flesh and bone. Feel sound moving through the body like light through water.

Explore the inner symphony:

- Send vibrations through each energy center, awakening their songs
- Let bones hum their ancient rhythms
- Release the wild soul's ecstatic dance
- Sound the frequencies of highest destiny

Weave these voices together. Allow them to play, merge, transform. Let the body move as music moves.

Create a personal sound signature - perhaps three beats, silence, then two beats. A unique pattern that instantly reconnects to these frequencies.

Complete by resting both hands over the heart, feeling its pulse align with divine rhythm. The body radiates as an instrument of cosmic joy, attuned to creation's song.

Carry these vibrations into each moment. Let them inform voice, movement, creative expression. The being shines as joy incarnate, playing its singular note in the universal symphony.

Each heartbeat echoes cosmic drums. Words ring as sacred sound. The entire being flows as music in human form. Pure symphony resounding through all creation.

Play on, beloved light. Play on.

Marriage of Death and Rebirth: My Dance with Osiris and Aset

Moonlight spilled across the temple floor at Abydos, turning ancient stone to liquid silver. My bare feet traced paths worn smooth by millennia of pilgrims, each step resonating with memories older than time. Here, in this sacred space where Aset restored her beloved Osiris, the veil between myth and reality shimmered gossamer-thin.

The scent of blue lotus and myrrh hung thick in the air, carrying me deeper into trance. My fingertips brushed cool stone walls, feeling the pulse of stories carved in hieroglyphs. Each touch connected me more profoundly to the eternal dance of death and rebirth, loss and restoration, separation and sacred reunion.

The chamber seemed to expand, stone walls dissolving into infinite space. Stars wheeled overhead, countless as grains of sand. Through half-closed eyes, I watched Aset's story unfold in the constellations - her tireless search for the fragments of her beloved, her wings spreading dark against the star-strewn sky as she hovered above Osiris's broken body, breathing life back into his form through the power of her love.

My own breath deepened, synchronizing with this ancient rhythm. Each inhale drew in Aset's fierce devotion, each exhale released into Osiris's surrender to transformation. The polarities began to dance within my being - the divine feminine and masculine, death and regeneration, endings and beginnings spiraling together in perfect harmony.

Heat built at the base of my spine, rising like golden serpents of light through my body. When it reached my heart, something cracked open - grief and love pouring forth in equal measure. I felt Aset's anguish as my own, her determination burning through my blood. My arms became her wings, spreading wide to embrace both death and life, darkness and light.

The rising energy crescendoed at my third eye. Colors exploded behind closed lids - deepest indigo, royal purple, electric blue-white. My consciousness expanded beyond body, beyond temple, beyond time itself. In this vast space, Osiris and Aset moved as pure energy - no longer separate beings but complementary forces weaving the tapestry of existence.

Understanding flooded every cell: this myth lived within me, within all of us. Each fragment of Osiris represented aspects of self waiting to be gathered, healed, reintegrated. Aset's journey mapped the soul's eternal quest for wholeness. Their sacred marriage demonstrated the power of love to transform even death into new life.

Dawn found me still sitting in the temple, tears drying on my cheeks. The first rays of sun painted the walls gold, illuminating Osiris's djed pillar - symbol of stability rising from chaos. My body hummed with residual energy, cells vibrating at a new frequency. The third eye awakening revealed itself as part of this larger mythic pattern: death and rebirth, fracturing and reintegration, the eternal dance of cosmic forces within human form.

This lived experience became my initiation into deeper mysteries, preparing me for direct communion with these divine energies. The myth had transformed from ancient story into embodied wisdom, awakening new ways of seeing, being, and unfolding.

Immersion: Vision Awakening: Dancing with Osiris and Horus

Ancient stone radiates coolness against your palms as you enter the temple depths. Lotus and myrrh weave through the air, mingling with an otherworldly essence that speaks of mysteries beyond time. Oil lamps cast living shadows across walls alive with hieroglyphs, each symbol pulsing with hidden meaning.

The Eye of Horus beckons from a far wall, its sacred geometry seeming to ripple and dance in the flickering light. Energy builds in your forehead's center, a warmth spreading like honey between your brows. Your pineal gland awakens, responding to the ancient call.

A point of radiance emerges in your inner vision, expanding into a sphere of pure white brilliance. Colors dance and spiral - royal indigo depths giving way to electric purple lightning, cosmic blue flames painting stories across the canvas of consciousness.

The colors weave themselves into a vast celestial tapestry. Stars pulse with living light while constellations dance, telling tales in the language of pure knowing. Through this cosmic expanse moves a figure of ineffable power - Osiris in his aspect of eternal renewal, skin shimmering green with the promise of endless rebirth.

His sacred dance begins, body fragmenting into countless points of starlight that scatter across space like seeds of creation. These fragments of divine light swirl and coalesce, reforming into an even more radiant being. Here lies the mystery at existence's heart - through dissolution comes rebirth, through surrender comes transformation.

Your own awareness expands into this cosmic dance. Boundaries dissolve as you merge with the endless cycles of death and renewal. Each star becomes a node in the vast web of being, each atom a universe unto itself, all connected in the grand choreography of creation.

The light and wisdom gather, condensing into a pulsing star between your brows. Your third eye thrums with celestial frequencies, a living bridge between worlds. Colors deepen, sounds clarify, reality reveals its subtle layers and hidden harmonies.

Through awakened senses, you perceive the world anew - each moment fresh with possibility, each breath an opportunity for transformation. Like Osiris eternally renewed, you emerge reborn, carrying the seed of divine vision within.

Integration Practice: The Alchemist's Spiral

Create a sacred space with elements representing the four directions - incense for air, a candle for fire, water in a bowl, and crystals or stones for earth.

Begin a spiral walk, moving inward while focusing on dissolution. With each step, release an old pattern, belief, or limitation. At the spiral's heart, pause in perfect stillness.

Now spiral outward, gathering wisdom from the Neteru encountered on your journey:

- Invoke Nut's cosmic embrace, expanding into infinite possibility
- Dance with Hathor's joyful frequencies
- Rise with Osiris's power of renewal
- Soar with Horus's divine vision

At each cardinal point, create a gesture or movement expressing the unique gifts received:

- East: Third eye awakening with Horus
- South: Creative fire with Sekhmet
- West: Deep wisdom with Osiris
- North: Grounding with Geb

Complete the integration by sitting at the spiral's outer edge. Place your hands over your heart, feeling the pulse of ancient wisdom beating within. Let the energies of all encountered deities weave together into a symphony of transformation.

Sacred Verses for the Journey:

Through Nut's star-strewn body we expand
Beyond all bounds of space and time
In Hathor's dance we find our joy
Each movement sacred and sublime

With Osiris we die and rise again
Through darkness into dawning light
While Horus grants the vision clear
To see beyond the veil of night

In cosmic cycles ever turning
We spiral up the sacred way
Each ending holds a new beginning
As night gives birth unto the day

Carry these frequencies forward, letting them inform your way of being. You walk now as a living bridge between worlds, your awakened vision illuminating paths of possibility. The Neteru dance within you, their wisdom flowing through your words and works, their power expressing through your unique creative force.

The eternal spiral continues, beloved initiate. The eternal spiral continues.

The Sacred Dance of the Mismatched Socks

Dawn light spills through bedroom windows, painting ordinary space with extraordinary potential. The sock drawer quivers with unmistakable energy, ancient rhythms pulsing behind wooden panels. One gentle pull unleashes pure magic - an explosion of color, pattern, texture bursting forth into morning air.

Polka dots whirl in ecstatic spiral dances, their spots trailing stardust as they spin. Stripes tango with fierce passion, their linear patterns dissolving into pure light. Fuzzy companions flow in tai chi movements smooth as silk, their softness leaving trails of comfort in the air.

Then... oh then! The mismatched ones emerge in their full glory. Electric green nylon embraces formal black cotton, their unlikely union creating sparks of pure possibility. They breakdance across floorboards, defying gravity, weaving stories of cosmic rebellion. A thick hiking sock, still singing mountain songs, sweeps a delicate lace anklet into an ethereal waltz. Their dance speaks of forest meets fairytale, wilderness touching grace.

Joy bubbles up from earth's core, through feet and belly and heart, erupting in waves of laughter that shake the foundations of reality itself. Each giggle releases another layer of gravity's hold. Bare feet begin to float, skin tingling with stardust static.

Two extraordinary companions claim this moment of ascension - one sock swirled with spiral galaxies, the other sequined with countless stars. They weave themselves around earthbound ankles with loving mischief, becoming living launching pads into infinite space. Up and up, trailing comet-tail laughter, soaring through the ceiling turned to stardust, into the waiting sky.

Earth transforms below into an artist's palette - greens and blues bleeding into abstract beauty. Higher still, until our blue marble home hangs suspended in velvet void, precious and perfect. Here, in the space between stars, the true celebration unfolds.

Dancing souls float in zero gravity's embrace, each adorned with magical mismatched messengers. A CEO's power suit cannot contain the joy of rubber ducks paddling across one foot while quantum equations spiral around the other. A grandmother's floral dress perfectly complements one sock alive with prowling tigers, the other decorated with cosmic cupcakes. Children spin past like living kaleidoscopes, their socks defying any earthly logic of color or pattern, their delight painting new constellations across space.

In this realm beyond gravity, beyond matching, beyond rules, pure connection ignites between souls. Age dissolves. Culture melts. Beliefs transform into stardust. Only joy remains, expressed through the sacred art of cosmic sock-wearing. Here floats the ultimate truth - life blossoms most beautifully in glorious mismatched chaos, in unexpected combinations that sing their own perfect harmony.

Descent comes gently, bedroom reforming like a dream taking solid shape. Yet the magic lingers. That sock drawer will never appear ordinary again. And there, in the shadowed corner, one sock offers the faintest starlit wink - keeper of cosmic secrets, guardian of joy's mysteries.

From this day forward, matching becomes sacrilege. Each consciously mismatched pair forms a prayer of remembrance, an invocation of cosmic dance. Sometimes, in moments of deep silence, these fabric mystics still hum their celestial tune - the universe's heartbeat, translated into thread and wool and infinite possibility.

The socks have spoken. The cosmic dance continues. And somewhere in space, a CEO's rubber ducks paddle eternal through quantum equations, leaving trails of starlit joy in their wake.

The Sacred Ritual of Cosmic Socks: A Playful Path to Enlightenment

Begin in the hour before dawn, when stars still whisper and the veil between worlds shimmers thin. Gather your sacred tools:

- A collection of unpaired socks, the more varied and vibrant the better
- One pair of pure white socks, unworn, to receive cosmic impressions
- Crystal points or stones to anchor the sock circle's four directions
- Starlight (or moonlight) captured in a mirror or bowl of water
- Sacred oils of joy (orange, bergamot, rose)

Create your cosmic sock mandala. Arrange socks in a spiral, starting from the center with the white pair crossed in infinity symbol. Let each sock find its own placement - trust that apparent chaos holds divine order. The mandala grows organically, socks flowing outward like a galaxy spiraling through space.

Anoint your feet with sacred oils. Each toe receives its own blessing:

- Big toe: grounding and earth connection
- Second toe: joy and playfulness
- Middle toe: courage to be uniquely you
- Fourth toe: cosmic connection
- Little toe: divine mischief and transformation

Step into the center of your sock spiral. Raise your bare feet to the stars (or ceiling - the cosmos exists everywhere). Wiggle your toes, activating their newly blessed powers. Feel energy spiraling up from Earth's core, through your feet, igniting each chakra with sparks of cosmic laughter.

Now comes the Sacred Sock Selection. Eyes closed, hands open, allow the socks to choose you. First right foot, then left. Trust whatever combination manifests - the more mismatched, the more powerful the magic.

Don your cosmic companions with reverence and playful ceremony. As each sock embraces your foot, speak its unique qualities:

"Striped one, your lines connect earth and sky!"
"Polka dot messenger, your spots mirror the stars!"
"Fuzzy guardian, your warmth ignites my soul!"

Begin the Dance of Ascending Joy. Start small - perhaps just toe wiggles. Let movement grow organically. Your socks will guide you. They remember the cosmic dances. Trust their ancient wisdom.

As energy builds, feel yourself getting lighter. Your feet may leave the ground - this is natural. The socks remember their celestial origin. Dance with zero gravity. Let your sock-clad feet lead you through constellations.

Invite fellow cosmic dancers to join your ritual:

- Place socks on your hands - new dance partners!
- Create sock puppets that speak star language
- Build sock constellations on walls or floor
- Trade one sock with another dancer, mixing cosmic codes

End by returning to your sock spiral. Place your danced-in socks at the mandala's edge - they're now charged with cosmic frequencies. The white pair at center will have absorbed the dance's energy, becoming your new sacred tools.

Keep one sock from your ritual night unpaired. Let it be your cosmic messenger, appearing mysteriously in unexpected places, reminding you of the night you danced with stars.

Integration Practice:

- Wear consciously mismatched socks to important meetings
- Create sock altars in hidden corners
- Listen for the hymn of the lost dryer socks - they've simply ascended
- Notice which socks "want" to come together - they're sharing cosmic messages
- Let one sock guide your day's adventure

Remember: Every lost sock creates potential for sacred mismatch. Every hole is a portal to new dimensions. Every laundry day becomes a ceremony of cosmic reunion.

The Great Sock Mystery is solved at last - they've been leading us to enlightenment all along, one mismatched pair at a time.

Advanced Practice:

Host monthly sock ceremonies at full moon. Create sock mandalas large enough for cosmic sock communities to gather and dance. Document mysterious sock manifestations. Begin sock-based divination systems.

The socks know. Trust their wisdom. Dance their mystery.

Let the great cosmic sock revolution begin.

The Infinite Spiral: Where Worlds Merge

Cairo's usual veil of dust and modernity suddenly dissolves, swept away by an otherworldly breath. The megalopolis shimmers, its concrete and chaos transmuting through waves of golden light. From my balcony, I witness the city's magical metamorphosis: smog transforms to sacred incense, traffic sounds become temple bells, tower blocks shift to crystalline minarets piercing twilight's veil.

The eternal Nile burns molten gold, its waters remembering their first flow from celestial realms. Above, impossibly bright stars pierce through the urban haze, defying all mundane physics. This is Cairo as it exists in dreams, in visions, in moments when the veils between worlds grow gossamer-thin.

Something calls from beyond the city's edge - a frequency that vibrates in my bones. The desert beckons, its ancient voice carried on winds that sweep through time itself. Without hesitation, I answer its summons, leaving the transformed city behind.

Miles of pavement give way to sacred sand. Here, under the infinite dome of desert stars, reality shifts again. Every grain of sand becomes a tiny sun, each dune a wave in the cosmic ocean. The night sky opens completely, unveiling its full grandeur - galaxies upon galaxies spiraling overhead, mirroring the spiral path of consciousness ascending.

In this liminal space between worlds, my own luminous journey unfolds like a living papyrus scroll. Each turn of the spiral blazes with accumulated light - the young priestess discovering theater's ancient magic, the seeker stepping into unknown lands, the sailor learning wisdom from wind and wave aboard Nefertiti.

Sacred temples pulse with remembrance, their stone walls dissolving to reveal the Neteru dancing through my awakening consciousness. Sekhmet's fierce flame, Hathor's golden resonance, Tehuti's mercury wisdom - all aspects of the eternal light now flowing through my veins. Every cell sings their story, tiny suns in the constellation of becoming.

The desert sun that once seemed adversary now reveals itself as beloved teacher, its fierce rays calling forth inner radiance. Past initiations shine like jewels strung on the spiral's curve - each challenge a crucible where lead transformed to gold, where shadows became stepping stones toward greater luminescence.

Desert stars mirror the light we carry, their ancient rays reminding me of countless souls ascending this cosmic spiral throughout time. Though our paths spiral at different rhythms, we dance in exquisite harmony, our combined light illuminating the way for all.

Night-blooming jasmine releases its intoxicating perfume - nature's incense marking this moment of profound revelation. The journey spirals ever upward yet has no final destination. Each summit reached reveals new peaks emerging from light's infinite mist. Every mystery solved opens doors to deeper wonder.

Electric joy courses through my being as I contemplate the spiral's next revolution. The unknown shimmers with possibility's rainbow light. What new frequencies of consciousness await discovery? What undreamed dimensions of self will emerge in love's expanding glow?

Gratitude wells up as vast as the desert itself, deep as starlit space. For every teacher, challenge, joy and sorrow that shaped this vessel of light I've become. For the infinite potential still dormant, cosmic seeds waiting to flower. For the eternal dance of light and shadow that teaches us to shine.

The cool night breeze carries tomorrow's whispers, stories yet unlived, light yet unconceived. Each breath connects me more deeply to the living tapestry of existence, every cell vibrating in harmony with universal light.

My reflection shimmers in a pool of starlight - familiar yet startlingly new. These eyes now hold galaxies, these hands shape light itself. The being gazing back stands ready to spiral into even greater radiance, to share accumulated light with a world awakening to its own luminous nature.

This phase of ascension, magnificent as it has been, simply prepares the way for the full flowering yet to come. Like a lotus rising through ancient waters, each petal holds light gathered from the depths. What new songs will emerge as consciousness unfolds in ever-widening spirals of illumination? What nectar of wisdom will flow when the flower of light fully opens?

The journey spirals onward, each turn adding new frequencies to existence's eternal song. As constellations wheel overhead and sand shifts beneath my feet, I stand ready to dance the next movement of this cosmic symphony. The light gathered in Luminous Ascent flows naturally into Radiant Blossoming, each phase a note in creation's unfolding chord.

Here at the threshold between rising and blooming, certainty fills me - the most beautiful music, the most brilliant light, still awaits its moment to shine through our awakening hearts.

Sacred Reflection: Journaling the Spiral of Light

- Map your own spiral of illumination. What key moments ignited new frequencies of consciousness within you?
- How has your relationship with light - both inner and outer - transformed through this journey?
- Which shadowed places in your being now shine with unexpected radiance?
- How have you woven together the different lights encountered - Sekhmet's flame, Hathor's gold, Tehuti's quicksilver wisdom?
- What new harmonies emerge as these frequencies dance within you?
- How does your unique light signature contribute to the greater symphony?
- What base metals of your being have transformed into gold through this process?
- How has your understanding of "rising" evolved beyond physical or mental concepts?

- What divine frequencies now pulse through your everyday existence?
- Where do you sense the spiral leading as you transition toward full blossoming?
- What aspects of your light feel ready to be shared with the world?
- How has your relationship with the unknown transformed through gathering your inner radiance?
- How do you experience your connection to the greater field of ascending consciousness?
- What unique note does your light contribute to creation's song?
- What becomes possible when we rise together in harmony?

End your reflection by creating a light mandala - through art, movement, or pure intention - that captures the essence of your luminous ascension. Let it serve as both celebration of the journey so far and beacon lighting the way toward even greater flowering of consciousness.

The spiral continues. The light ascends. The dance goes on.

IV. Radiant Blossoming

Isis, Voice of Thunder, your love a cleansing storm,
Shake loose the chains, let our true selves be reborn.
Lightning-swift compassion, each word a vibrant flame,
Weaving hearts together, erasing doubt and shame.
Isis, Sinai's Witness, in each dawn humility we find,
Humbled by the vastness, may our souls be open and kind.
Sunrise ignites our colors, a radiant blossoming,
With each new day unfolding, your eternal love we sing.

The Lotus Unfurls: A Dance with Hapi

The Nile's waters mirror the sunrise, turning molten gold. A figure emerges from the depths - blue-green skin shimmering, body a perfect harmony of curves and angles, strength and grace intertwined. The Egyptian God Hapi dances between forms like light playing on water, each movement a celebration of wholeness beyond division.

Two streams merge before me, their waters braiding into one fluid dance. My feet sink into cool mud as lotus perfume floods my senses. A single blossom unfurls beside me, its petals embodying both receptive softness and fierce reaching toward light.

Energy surges through my limbs, masculine power and feminine grace flowing as one current. My arms spiral upward, fingertips trailing light through misty air. My body remembers this dance beyond duality, moving with Hapi's fluid grace between all forms of expression.

Starlight glimmers in indigo depths. The morning breeze carries temple songs. Sacred waters pulse beneath my feet, drumming a rhythm that transcends all boundaries. My heart beats with this ancient knowing - that true power lies in the dance between polarities.

Laughter bubbles up from my core, joining the river's song. Lightning dances through my veins. My hands paint ribbons of light across the dawn sky as I flow with Hapi's eternal dance, embracing the full spectrum of my being.

Sacred Reflection: Dancing Between Worlds

Rest in a quiet space where you feel both held and free. Let your pen flow like river water:

Touch a moment when you felt complete harmony between your fierce strength and tender softness. How did your body express this wholeness? Which colors painted your world? What music played in your heart?

Remember a time when you transcended expected boundaries, moving with perfect fluidity between different aspects of yourself. How did this freedom feel in your cells? Which scents, sounds, textures accompanied this dance?

Place your hands on your heart center. Feel its rhythm pulsing like the Nile's flow. What emerges when you release the need to be either/or? Let your words spiral between polarities, finding their own balance.

Recall an experience where water spoke to your soul - perhaps ocean waves, morning dew, or summer rain. How did this encounter reshape your understanding of flowing between forms? What whispers of wisdom did the waters share?

Draw or write about your own inner dance between masculine and feminine energies. Which movements express your wholeness? How does your unique light shine when all aspects of your being merge in harmony?

Close by capturing the sensation of pure fluidity - that moment when all labels dissolve and only radiant presence remains.

The Quantum Dance of Blossoming: A Sacred Journey

The lotus emerges from primordial depths, its unfolding an exquisite demonstration of quantum reality. Each petal's movement creates ripples through the field of infinite possibility, just as your own blossoming sends waves through the cosmic ocean of consciousness. For Decades J. Krishnamurti taught: "The Observer is the Observed." In this sacred dance, you become both the artist and the artwork, the dancer and the dance itself.

Consider how the universe mirrors your own transformation. At the subatomic level, particles exist in a state of superposition, embodying infinite possibilities until the moment of observation crystallizes one into reality. Your consciousness works in much the same way - each thought, each intention, each moment of awareness collapses waves of potential into manifest form.

Wave-particle duality reveals the paradox at existence's heart - you are simultaneously fixed and flowing, form and emptiness, individual and universal. The quantum field surrounds and interpenetrates your being, a vast ocean of creative potential from which all forms arise. Within this field, entanglement weaves invisible threads between all beings, connecting your personal blossoming to the flowering of universal consciousness.

Immersion: The Quantum Lotus Dance

The air around you vibrates with possibility. Feel how it caresses your skin, carrying messages from the quantum realm. Notice the play of light and shadow, each photon a dancer in the cosmic choreography. Let your awareness expand until you sense the atomic dance within each cell of your body, the electromagnetic field that surrounds you, the quantum soup from which reality emerges moment by moment.

Your breath becomes a bridge between worlds. Each inhalation draws in particles that have traveled through stars, each exhalation sends your essence rippling out through the quantum field. Your thoughts create waves in the fabric of reality, your presence affects the cosmic dance in ways both subtle and profound.

Enter now the Quantum Lotus Dance. Feel yourself as pure potential, a superposition of all possible states of being. The power of uncollapsed probability waves flows through you. You exist simultaneously as seed and flower, beginning and culmination, the entire journey of transformation held in a single eternal moment.

Direct your awareness through your being like a beam of light illuminating hidden potentials. Watch how observation transforms the possible into the actual, how your conscious presence shapes energy into form. Every moment of intentional awareness catalyzes new patterns of manifestation.

Feel the threads of entanglement that connect you to all of existence. Your transformation sends ripples through the entire fabric of reality. The universe responds to your blossoming with a symphony of synchronicities, a dance of mutual awakening that transcends space and time.

Let your highest potential crystallize in the field of your awareness. New patterns organize themselves in your energy field, drawing form from the infinite ocean of possibility. Experience the joy of conscious creation as your quantum flowering expresses itself through every aspect of your being.

Integration Practice: Anchoring the Quantum Dance

Stand firmly in your embodied presence, feeling the quantum field that interpenetrates physical form. Move with deliberate awareness, sensing how each gesture affects the fabric of reality. Let your body become a living expression of quantum principles - fluid yet precise, individual yet connected, manifest yet filled with infinite potential.

Place your hands upon your body's core centers - heart, solar plexus, belly. Direct quantum awareness through each center like light flowing through a prism. Feel new patterns crystallizing in your field, quantum frequencies anchoring themselves in your flesh and bones.

In the pages of your journal, let quantum wisdom flow through your pen. Describe the dance between observer and observed, the interplay of possibility and manifestation, the symphony of synchronicities that accompanies your transformation. Map the territory of your quantum flowering with words that bridge seen and unseen realms.

Express your quantum experience through creative acts that marry heaven and earth. Move as though your body were made of light. Create art that captures quantum frequencies. Let sound emerge that resonates with the music of the spheres. Design symbols that speak the language of universal unfolding.

Carry this quantum awareness into each day's unfoldment. Notice how your field affects every interaction, how synchronicities bloom in your footsteps, how reality reshapes itself in response to your conscious presence. Document the evidence of entanglement that appears in your life, the signs that confirm your place in the cosmic dance.

Remember always: you are a quantum being, your consciousness a creative force in the universe. Each moment of awareness plants seeds of transformation in the fertile field of reality. Your blossoming is both deeply personal and universal, an essential note in the symphony of existence. Dance your quantum dance with joy, knowing that your flowering contributes to the awakening of all beings.

Let this practice illuminate the bridge between potential and manifestation, between quantum and everyday awareness, between individual awakening and collective transformation. The dance continues, eternal and ever-new, and you are both its choreographer and its most beloved expression.

The Alchemy of the Kitchen: Where Nourishment and Transformation Converge

The air crackles with the sizzle of onions hitting hot oil, their pungent aroma mingling with the sweet perfume of simmering spices. Laughter echoes through the sun-drenched kitchen, a chorus of voices harmonizing with the rhythmic chopping of knives and the clatter of pots and pans. This is a crucible of transformation, a place where simple ingredients are alchemized into culinary masterpieces, where nourishment and love intertwine.

Growing up, our kitchen was a realm of mystery and magic, a place where my mother and aunts, those masterful alchemists of the culinary arts, wove their spells with effortless grace. The air thrummed with the intoxicating scents of cardamom, cumin, and cinnamon, each spice a vibrant hue in the symphony of aromas that filled our home. I, a wide-eyed child perched on a rickety stool, watched in awe as their hands danced over cutting boards and simmering pots, transforming humble ingredients into feasts that nourished both body and soul.

This bustling kitchen, with its warmth and laughter, became my first school of transformation. It was here that I learned the art of alchemy, not just in the culinary sense, but also in the deeper sense of transforming the ordinary into the extraordinary, the mundane into the magical.

Years later, in a tiny Moscow kitchen, the steam rising from a massive pot of borscht mingled with the laughter of three babushkas, their eyes twinkling with mischief as they guided my hands through the sacred ritual of Russian cooking. Words were scarce, but our shared laughter bridged all language barriers, creating a symphony of connection and shared joy.

As I peeled beets, their earthy scent mingling with fragrant dill, I felt a spark ignite within me, a warmth spreading through my being. It was the Heartfire Ray awakening, a primal energy that pulsed in harmony with the act of creation. Each chop of the knife, each stir of the wooden spoon, became a brushstroke on the canvas of transformation.

From the bustling streets of Cairo to the serene temples of Yamagata, kitchens became my classrooms, each one a portal to a different culture, a different way of expressing love and nourishment through food. The sizzle of garlic in olive oil transported me to sun-drenched Mediterranean shores, while the delicate dance of chopsticks over steaming bowls of ramen revealed the meditative heart of Japanese cuisine.

My own kitchen blossomed into a sanctuary of transformation, a place where limitations became invitations to creativity. Jars of spices lined the shelves like talismans, each one holding the memory of a journey, a lesson learned. Here, a handful of neglected vegetables could be transformed into a feast fit for kings, a testament to the abundance that springs from the heart.

As I stirred a bubbling pot, feeling the warmth seep into my bones, I realized the true alchemy wasn't in the food itself, but in the act of creation, in the love poured into every dish. This was how I expressed my deepest emotions, my gratitude for life, my connection to the divine. The kitchen became a canvas for my radiant blossoming, a place where I could create beauty and nourishment from whatever life provided.

The Alchemy of the Kitchen: Journaling Prompts for Transformation

- Recall your earliest kitchen memory. What sounds, smells, and textures rise from that moment? Who was there? What emotions stir as you remember?
- Write about a dish that connects you to your ancestors. How did you learn to make it? What stories and wisdom are wrapped within its preparation?
- Describe a time when cooking transcended mere food preparation and became a sacred act. What shifted in that moment? How did it feel in your body?
- Earth: What ingredients ground you? Which foods make you feel most connected to the land?
- Water: How does the flow of cooking move through you? When do you feel most fluid and intuitive in the kitchen?
- Fire: Where does passion ignite in your culinary creation? What dishes make your spirit flame with joy?
- Air: How does breath and space play a role in your kitchen alchemy? What lightness do you bring to your cooking?
- Describe a time when food bridged cultural or language barriers. What understanding emerged through shared nourishment?
- Write about a dish you've transformed through experimentation. How did limitations birth creativity?
- Remember a meal that healed more than hunger. What medicine did it carry? How did love flow through its preparation?
- Map your kitchen's energy. Where does magic happen? Which spots hold special power?
- What talismans and tools carry stories in your culinary temple? Choose one and trace its journey to you.
- How does your kitchen reflect your soul's seasons? What changes when you approach cooking as a ceremony?

- Describe your kitchen choreography. How does your body move when fully immersed in cooking?
- What rhythms and rituals ground your culinary practice? Which gestures feel like prayer?
- Where do you find meditation in mundane kitchen tasks? How does chopping, stirring, or kneading become sacred?
- How has cooking taught you about abundance? When has "not enough" become "more than plenty"?
- What wisdom have your kitchen failures revealed? How has imperfection nourished growth?
- In what ways does your cooking nurture spirit as well as body? How do you infuse food with intention?

After exploring these prompts, create a personal kitchen blessing or manifesto. Include:

- Your intentions for this sacred space
- The wisdom you wish to embody here
- The nourishment you choose to create and share
- The magic you commit to cultivating through your culinary alchemy

Immersion: The Alchemist's Kitchen

Step into the heart of your own culinary haven, a sanctuary where the aromas of spices mingle with the warmth of your creative spirit. This is not just a kitchen; it's an alchemical laboratory, a place where transformation simmers and bubbles, where the ordinary ingredients of your life are transmuted into something extraordinary.

Feel the smooth coolness of the countertop beneath your fingertips, the worn wood of the cutting board, the comforting weight of a well-loved knife in your hand. Inhale the fragrant symphony of spices – the earthy warmth of cumin, the fiery kiss of chili, the sweet whisper of cinnamon.

Each aroma carries a memory, a story, a connection to cultures and traditions that have shaped your culinary journey.

As you chop vegetables, their vibrant colors, a feast for the eyes, listen to the rhythmic percussion of your knife against the board, a steady beat that synchronizes with the pulse of your creative energy. Feel the heat of the stove radiating through your body, igniting a spark of inspiration within.

The sizzle of onions in the pan becomes a melody, the bubbling of a pot a harmonious counterpoint. Taste the sweet tang of tomatoes, the earthy depth of mushrooms, the vibrant zest of lemons. Each flavor is a note in the symphony of your creation, a testament to the alchemy of transformation.

As you stir a simmering sauce, envision the ingredients merging and transforming, their individual flavors blending into a harmonious whole. This is the magic of the kitchen, a reflection of your own journey of self-discovery, where seemingly disparate parts of your being come together to create something new and beautiful.

This is your alchemy, your unique expression of creativity and love. It's a dance between intuition and intention, a playful exploration of flavors and textures, a celebration of the senses. It's a way of nourishing not just your body, but also your soul, connecting you to the rich tapestry of your heritage and the vibrant expression of your authentic self.

Integration Practice: The Alchemist's Kitchen:

The Five Elements of Culinary Alchemy

- Begin by purifying your kitchen space with sound - ring a bell, shake a rattle, or simply clap your hands in each corner. Let the vibrations clear and elevate the energy. Light a candle to invoke the transformative power of fire.

1. Earth Connection (15 minutes)

   - Create an altar on your counter with items representing earth energy: crystals, herbs, sea salt
   - Stand barefoot if possible, feeling grounded through your feet
   - Hold each ingredient you'll use, connecting to its origin in the earth
   - Thank the soil, sun, rain, and hands that brought it to you
   - Set intentions for how this food will nourish body and spirit

2. Water Activation (10 minutes)

   - Fill a bowl with pure water
   - Add a pinch of salt and a blessing
   - Use this sacred water to:
     o Wash your ingredients mindfully
     o Clean your hands with intention
     o Sprinkle your workspace for purification

Notice how water transforms throughout cooking - steam rising, liquids reducing, flavors melding

3. Fire Transformation (Throughout cooking)

   - Before lighting your stove, honor the element of fire
   - Observe how heat transforms each ingredient
   - Notice the alchemical stages:
     o Nigredo (blackening) - when onions caramelize
     o Albedo (whitening) - when sauces clarify
     o Rubedo (reddening) - when dishes come to full maturation

Let the physical heat mirror your inner transformative fire

4. Air Integration (Between steps)

- Practice conscious breathing as you cook
- Notice the aromas rising - inhale their stories and wisdom
- Create space between actions for inspiration to enter
- Allow intuition to guide adjustments and additions
- Share the fragrances with your space, letting them purify and enliven

5. Spirit Infusion (Final stage)

- Before serving, pause in gratitude
- Hold your hands over the completed dish
- Infuse it with your highest intentions and love
- Speak a blessing that aligns with your spiritual practice
- Acknowledge the alchemy that has occurred - in the food and in you

Daily Integration:

- Keep a kitchen grimoire recording your alchemical discoveries
- Note which spices correspond to different intentions
- Track how phases of the moon affect your cooking
- Document kitchen synchronicities and magic
- Write down dreams or visions that come while cooking

Weekly Practice:

- Choose one meal to prepare as a full alchemical ceremony:
- Set aside uninterrupted sacred time
- Create ambiance with music, incense, or candlelight
- Move through each element consciously
- Document the entire process in your grimoire
- Share the blessed food mindfully

Monthly Rhythm:

- Deep clean and re-consecrate your kitchen space

- Refresh altar items and blessings
- Review grimoire notes for patterns and insights
- Plan a special feast honoring the season
- Share kitchen wisdom with fellow alchemists

The Lemon Tree Heartbeat: Awakening the Inner Fire

The scent of ripening lemons hung in the Giza air, a sharp sweetness that lingered even after I'd clambered down that gnarled old tree in my grandmother's tiny garden. My pockets bulged with treasures – smooth pebbles, a discarded feather, imagined remnants of ancient civilizations. My knees bore the scrapes of adventure, a badge of honor in my young eyes.

They'd scolded me gently, reminding me that little girls should be more composed. But their eyes held a glimmer of pride, recognizing the untamed spirit that flickered within me. It was an echo of the desert's boundless energy, the same joy that pulsed through my veins as I wove tales of the pigeons' secret lives or felt their wings fluttering against my outstretched palms on the rooftop of Teta's, my grandmothers house.

It was here, under the familiar Cairo Giza sky, that I first sensed the stirring of what I'd later understand as my Heartfire Ray. Just as the lemon tree defied the arid soil, my spirit began to blossom. My grandmother's quiet strength and the boundless dreams that took flight amidst those rooftop chickens kindled a warmth within me – a spark of creation that would grow into a radiant force.

In that moment, perched high in the branches, I was pure potential. The thrill of discovery, the simple joy of climbing a tree meant for boys – these were the first petals of my blossoming self, reaching towards the sun.

The Lemon Tree Heartbeat: Sacred Remembering Prompts

Awakening the Inner Fire: A Journey Through Memory

- Return to a moment when you first felt untamed joy stirring within. Where were you? What sensations lived in your body? How did the world feel different in that moment?
- What "trees meant for others" did your spirit long to climb? How did you navigate between society's expectations and your inner fire?
- Remember a time when nature spoke directly to your wild heart. What messages did it whisper? How did your body respond to this wild calling?
- What precious objects filled your childhood pockets? Choose one and write its story - not just what it was, but what magic it held for you
- Who were your early animal companions? How did they help awaken your inner fire?
- What "ancient civilizations" did your imagination discover in ordinary places? Describe one of these magical realms in detail
- Who first recognized your untamed spirit? How did they show their silent understanding?
- Write a letter to someone who tried to "compose" your wildness - what would you tell them now about the importance of that inner fire?
- What elder's quiet strength helped kindle your own? How did they teach you without words?
- When did you first feel the heat of your creative force? What did it urge you to make, say, or do?
- What "forbidden" spaces called to your adventurous heart? How did exploring them shape who you've become?
- Remember a moment when you felt absolutely free in your body. What unlocked this liberation?

- Close your eyes and let these sensory memories flow:
- The texture of rough bark under small hands
- The particular quality of light through leaves
- The taste of sun-warmed fruit
- The sound of wind in high branches
- The scent of childhood gardens
- What stirs in your body as these memories surface? Where do you feel the echo of that early joy? Let your writing emerge from this embodied place.
- What early dreams still pulse in your veins?
- How does your inner fire express itself now?
- What parts of your wild spirit are ready to be reclaimed?
- Where does your heart still long to climb?
- Write a scene that captures the exact moment you first felt your inner fire stirring. Include:
- The physical sensations in your body
- The emotions flowing through you
- The environment around you
- What you somehow knew in that moment, even if you couldn't name it
- How that spark has carried forward into your life
- How do you nurture your inner fire today?
- What practices help you reconnect with that original wild joy?
- What would your childhood self want you to remember about staying untamed?
- How can you honor both the composed and wild aspects of your being?

Closing Ritual

After writing, stand or sit in sunlight if possible. Place one hand on your heart, the other on your belly. Feel the warmth of your own inner fire. Speak aloud:

"I honor the wild joy that lives in me
I celebrate the fire that lights my way
I thank the child who kept the flame
I commit to letting my spirit stay untamed"

Immersion: Awakening the Heartfire

The sun-drenched meadow beckons, wildflowers swaying in the warm breeze. Ancient trees stand sentinel in their sacred grove, branches whispering earth's deepest secrets. Moonlight bathes the rooftop garden, stars hanging low enough to touch.

A magnificent tree rises at the center, its branches reaching skyward in welcome. This Tree of Life pulses with ancestral wisdom, roots weaving deep into earth's mysteries, leaves dancing with ancient stories.

The bark feels rough against your palms, each groove and whorl telling tales of seasons passed. The solid trunk radiates strength, stability flowing upward through your arms. Your feet find perfect purchase on gnarled roots, body remembering this primordial climbing dance.

Warmth builds in your core as you ascend, the Heartfire Ray awakening. This primal spark has lived within always, waiting for this moment of kindling. Pure creative force flows through your veins, passionate potential rising with each handhold gained.

The climb transforms awareness. Liquid sunlight courses through your body. Tree wisdom merges with bone and blood, its ancient power becoming yours. Each breath draws in more expansive possibility, your energy field merging with the tree's vibrant life force.

Leaves rustle encouragement as you reach higher, arm muscles singing with determination. The world below dissolves into pure energy. Colors sharpen, sounds crystallize, air crackles with electric potential. Every cell awakens to life's interconnected web, the dance of creation moving through all things.

A perfect perch awaits among high branches, the tree's embrace both nurturing and energizing. This sanctuary holds you in perfect balance between earth and sky. Visions arise naturally, passion ignites spontaneously, possibilities spiral outward in ever-widening circles.

Integration Practice: Anchoring the Flame

1. Physical Anchoring

- Place both hands over your heart center
- Feel the warmth building between your palms
- Let this heat sink into your chest
- Sense your heartbeat syncing with earth's pulse
- Notice where else this warmth flows in your body

2. The Symphony of Senses

Touch Awareness:

- Feel the lingering sensation of bark on your palms
- Experience the pressure dance between soft and firm grip
- Notice temperature variations between sun-warmed and shaded bark
- Sense the living pulse beneath rough surface
- Feel the tree's strength resonating through your hands

Sight:

- Hold the vision of sunlight weaving through leaves
- Track the dance of light and shadow
- Notice how perspective shifted with height
- See the pathways that opened before you
- Observe the visual rhythm of branch patterns

Sound:

- Listen for the echo of rustling branches
- Feel sound waves moving through your body
- Notice how tree songs changed with height
- Experience the harmony between breath and wind
- Sense the vibration of ancient wood

Scent:

- Breathe in the memory of wood and wild air
- Notice how aromas shifted between ground and crown
- Experience the mingling of earth and sky scents
- Feel how fragrance guides spatial awareness
- Sense the chemistry of transformation

Taste:

- Notice any flavors arising from this experience
- Sense how taste connects to full-body memory
- Experience the subtle essences of height
- Feel the mingling of inner and outer air
- Savor the nectar of awakened Heartfire

3. Movement Medicine

- Stand and let your body sway like a tree in wind
- Allow your arms to reach up like growing branches
- Let your feet root deeply into the earth
- Move in ways that express your awakened Heartfire
- Experience the body's memory of climbing rhythm
- Feel the dynamic balance of weight shifting between limbs
- Sense the muscular engagement of upward reach
- Notice the dance between stability and mobility
- Experience the fluid coordination of hands and feet

4. Creative Expression

- Draw or paint the tree that called to you
- Write a love letter to your awakened Heartfire
- Create a sound that expresses your inner flame
- Shape this energy with clay or natural materials
- Move, dance, or gesture your transformation

Immersion: The Sacred Chamber: A Dance of Inner Fire and Divine Partnership

The Sacred Chamber pulses with possibility. A warmth builds naturally in the chest, an ancient ember awakening. This Holographic Heartfire beats in harmony with another presence - the divine breath of the Neteru stirring the flames higher.

Heat spirals outward, touching every cell with living light. As the warmth expands, Sekhmet's lioness heart beats in rhythm with yours, her fierce love amplifying the fire. Colors dance at the edge of perception - royal purples deepening to cosmic blue, gold fracturing into rainbow prisms. Isis's wings cradle this transformation, her presence a catalyst for the body's awakening luminescence.

Waves of warmth ripple through time itself. The body holds all ages at once - the child's wonder alive in the fingertips, present strength grounding through the feet, future wisdom flowing through the crown. Tehuti's quicksilver intelligence shimmers through these timestreams, illuminating the sacred patterns that connect all moments of being.

The child-self dances through the bones, bringing forgotten flexibility and spontaneous joy. Horus's playful spirit joins this dance, his falcon energy lifting childhood dreams to new heights. Present-self anchors in the heart's steady beat, a rhythm of gathered strength and earned wisdom, while Hathor's golden resonance enriches each pulse with divine love.

Future-self radiates from the third eye, sending ripples of possibility through the field of becoming. Ma'at's feather brushes the brow, her touch revealing the perfect order hidden within seeming chaos. Each version of self resonates with its own frequency, creating a symphony where human potential and divine grace harmonize as one song.

Threads of living light extend from the central flame, weaving connections through the body's holographic field. The Neteru's presence enriches these filaments - Nephthys guarding the depths where cellular memories stir, Isis midwifing the birth of future possibilities, Osiris transforming old patterns into new life.

The space around the body becomes a multidimensional temple, each direction holding another facet of self and its corresponding divine aspect. Forward reveals paths of possibility blessed by Horus's far-seeing vision. Behind holds gifts of experience witnessed by Anubis's careful gaze. Above connects to higher wisdom through Nut's star-strewn body. Below grounds in earth's ancient knowing through Geb's eternal embrace.

At the center point, where the Heartfire burns brightest, human wisdom and divine presence dance as one flame. Heat builds to a celestial fever, expanding beyond physical form. The body becomes a prism, refracting this unified light into infinite rays. Each beam carries a note in the symphony of becoming - a perfect collaboration between inner knowing and divine support.

This is the sacred alchemy - not losing oneself in divine presence, not rejecting divine aid out of pride, but dancing in the space between, where human potential and divine grace meet in endless creation.

Integration Practice: The Sacred Dance of Self and Neteru

1. Body Temple Activation

   - Place one hand on heart center (inner flame)
   - Other hand rests where Neteru presence feels strongest
   - Allow these energies to pulse and merge naturally
   - Feel how divine presence amplifies inner knowing
   - Notice where this unified force wants to move or express

2. Directional Anchoring Create a living compass of integrated wisdom:

   - East: Face rising sun, feel Horus sharp clarity merging with your own vision
   - South: Sekhmet's fire dancing with your inner flame
   - West: Osiris's depth calling to your soul's hidden wisdom
   - North: Geb's solidity grounding your earned knowing. Let body move between directions, weaving these unified energies

3. Sacred Sound Weaving

   - Begin with your own heart tone
   - Allow Neteru frequencies to join naturally
   - Notice how these sounds braid together
   - Let this harmonic collaboration guide movement
   - Dance the song of unified being

4. Daily Touchstones for Partnership Dawn:

   - Kindle inner flame with first breath
   - Invite divine amplification
   - Move from this merged awareness

Noon:

   - Pause to feel where guidance flows naturally

- Notice how inner wisdom and divine support interplay
- Adjust course based on this unified knowing

Dusk:

- Gather the day's teachings
- Honor both personal growth and divine assistance
- Dream into next level of collaboration

5. Creative Expression Choose one:

- Paint with both hands - dominant hand expressing inner wisdom, other channeling divine guidance
- Move letting inner impulse lead, then divine energy respond
- Tone personal sound and let divine frequencies join in
- Journal with alternating voices of self and Neteru

6. Partnership Practices

- Create altar that honors both inner flame and divine presence
- Establish rituals that engage both wisdoms
- Design personal gestures for accessing unified field
- Develop unique ways of checking inner knowing against divine guidance

7. Environmental Anchors Place reminders of this sacred partnership in your space:

- Objects representing inner wisdom
- Symbols of Neteru connection
- Items that embody the merged energies
- Sacred geometric patterns showing unified fields

Remember: This is not about choosing between self and divine, but dancing in the fertile space where both meet. Let this partnership unfold organically, guided by the wisdom of heart and the grace of spirit.

The highest purpose of this integration is not to reach some final state, but to remain fluid in the eternal dance between personal truth and divine amplification. Each moment offers new opportunities to explore this sacred collaboration.

Trust both your inner knowing and the helpful presence of the Neteru. Together they create something greater than either alone - a living bridge between human potential and divine grace.

Immersion: The Lioness and the Cat: A Dance of Multi-Dimensionality

The scorching desert wind whips around you, its searing caress against your skin carrying grains of sand that sting like tiny embers. The air is thick with the scent of sun-baked earth and exotic spices, punctuated by the distant, primal roar of a lioness that reverberates through your very bones. As you shield your eyes from the blinding sun, the sky above transforms into a canvas of fiery hues - streaks of molten gold and burning orange painting the heavens, mirroring the intensity of the transformation that awaits you.

Before you looms a towering sandstone temple, its weathered facade telling tales of ancient power and forgotten wisdom. Two imposing lioness statues guard the entrance, their eyes seeming to follow your every move. These are no mere stone carvings; their gaze holds an otherworldly intelligence, timeless and fierce. You can almost feel the weight of their witness as you approach, your heart pounding in a mixture of awe and trepidation.

The very air around the temple crackles with energy, like the buildup before a lightning strike. This is the sanctuary of Sekhmet, the lioness goddess whose wrath once scorched the earth. Her presence is palpable, a force of nature barely contained within the temple walls. Yet beneath the searing heat of her power, you sense something else - a current of healing, of protection, of rebirth. It calls to you, beckoning you to step into the fire of transformation.

As you cross the threshold, the world outside falls away. The oppressive heat of the desert is replaced by a hushed coolness that raises goosebumps on your arms. The silence is so profound it seems to have a weight of its own, broken only by the soft padding of your bare feet on smooth stone. Flickering torchlight casts dancing shadows on walls covered in intricate hieroglyphs. As your eyes adjust to the dim interior, the symbols seem to writhe and shift, as if trying to whisper their ancient secrets directly into your soul.

The air is heavy with the mingled scents of incense and myrrh, their exotic fragrance transporting you across time and space. Underlying these refined aromas is something more primal - the musky scent of lion, a reminder of the raw power that dwells here. Each breath you take feels charged with potential, as if the very act of inhaling is filling you with divine energy.

In the heart of the chamber, bathed in a soft golden light that seems to emanate from nowhere and everywhere at once, stands a statue of Sekhmet. Her lioness head is crowned with the solar disk, her body radiating an aura of strength that makes you want to fall to your knees in reverence. But it's her eyes that capture you - fierce yet compassionate, they bore into your very being. In that gaze, you feel utterly exposed, every strength and weakness, every triumph and failure laid bare. Yet instead of judgment, you feel a spark of recognition, as if Sekhmet sees in you a reflection of her own divine fire.

Suddenly, the solid walls of the temple seem to ripple and dissolve like a mirage. The cool stone beneath your feet gives way to damp earth, and you find yourself transported to the lush banks of the Nile. The contrast is shocking - from arid desert to teeming life in the blink of an eye. Your senses are overwhelmed by the symphony of nature - the gentle lapping of water against the shore, the rhythmic croaking of frogs, the rustling of papyrus reeds swaying in the breeze. The air is thick with humidity, carrying the sweet perfume of lotus blossoms that promises renewal and rebirth.

From the dense reeds emerges a creature of impossible grace - a sleek black cat, its fur gleaming like polished onyx in the moonlight. Its eyes are twin emerald flames, holding a wisdom and mischief that marks this as no ordinary feline. This is Bastet, goddess of joy, fertility, and the domestic realm. Where Sekhmet radiates fierce power, Bastet exudes a gentler strength - the strength found in laughter, in creation, in the bonds of love and family.

Bastet regards you with a tilted head, her tail swishing in silent invitation. As you follow her along the riverbank, you feel the cool mud squishing between your toes, grounding you in the primal energy of the earth. The full moon hangs low and heavy in the sky, bathing everything in silvery light that lends an air of magic to the landscape. Each step feels like a dance, your body moving in harmony with the rhythms of nature that surround you.

The cat goddess leads you to a hidden clearing where a circle of women sit around a crackling fire. Their voices rise and fall in a hypnotic chant, weaving a tapestry of sound that seems to shimmer in the air. As you draw closer, you see that they are literally weaving - their hands moving with practiced grace over looms that glow with an inner light. The threads they work with are no ordinary fibers, but seem to be spun from moonbeams and starlight.

As you join the circle, a profound sense of belonging washes over you. These women are strangers, yet in their faces you see reflections of yourself - the wide-eyed wonder of your childhood self, the hard-won wisdom of your future crone. You are connected to an ancient lineage of women who have walked this path before you, their strength flowing into you like sap rising in a tree.

The fire's warmth seeps into your bones, igniting a corresponding flame within your heart. It burns away doubt and fear, leaving behind a pure, radiant joy. You feel a sudden urge to create, to express the boundless love and power that courses through you.

Bastet guides you to the center of the circle, where a pool of water shimmers, its surface as still and reflective as a mirror. As you gaze into its depths, the starry sky above is reflected with perfect clarity. But then the image shifts, and you find yourself looking at your own reflection - yet not as you are now. The face that looks back at you is radiant with inner light, eyes sparkling with divine fire, lips curved in a smile of serene confidence. This is you as you truly are, stripped of all illusion and self-doubt - a being of infinite potential and power.

Encouraged by Bastet's gentle nudge, you step into the pool. The cool water embraces you, washing away the last vestiges of who you thought you were. As you submerge yourself fully, you feel a profound shift - as if you are being unmade and remade on a cellular level. When you emerge, gasping and reborn, you feel as if you could move mountains with a thought, or create universes with a smile.

A warm hand on your shoulder startles you, and you turn to find Sekhmet standing beside you, her presence both terrifying and comforting. "Embrace your multi-dimensionality," she says, her voice a gentle rumble that resonates through your entire being. "You are both the lioness and the cat, the fire and the grace, the protector and the creator. In accepting all facets of yourself, you become whole. Now go forth, and let your light illuminate the world."

As the sun begins to rise, painting the sky in soft pinks and golds, you feel the immersion fading. Yet the wisdom and power you've gained remain, humming in every cell of your body. You are forever changed, carrying within you the fierce strength of Sekhmet and the joyful sensual creativity of Bastet. You step into your full potential, to blossom in radiant glory, and to weave your unique thread into the grand tapestry of existence.

Integration Practice: Dancing Between Fierce and Gentle

Sacred Space Creation:

- Find a quiet space where you can move freely
- Light two candles - one red/gold for Sekhmet's fire, one silver for Bastet's moonlight
- Optional: Have a mirror, some water in a bowl, and earthy/musky incense

1. Body Awakening

Begin standing, feet planted firmly on the earth. Close your eyes and take three deep breaths:

- First breath: Feel Sekhmet's desert heat
- Second breath: Feel Bastet's cool river mist
- Third breath: Feel them merge within you

2. The Dance of Duality

Move through these paired positions, spending several breaths in each:

- Lioness Pose: Strong, fierce, protective stance
- Cat Pose: Fluid, graceful, playful movement
- Roaring Power: Express Sekhmet's strength
- Purring Peace: Embody Bastet's gentleness

Let your body naturally flow between these energies, finding your own rhythm.

3. Voice Work

Create sacred sound expressing both aspects:

- Sekhmet's roar: Let out powerful sounds
- Bastet's song: Hum or softly chant

Allow these voices to weave together, finding harmony between fierce and gentle.

4. Mirror Gazing

Look into a mirror or bowl of water:

- See Sekhmet's fire in your eyes
- Find Bastet's grace in your smile
- Witness how both energies dance in your face

Speak to your reflection: "I am both fierce and gentle, protective and playful, warrior and creator."

5. Integration Journaling

Write responses to:

- Where do I need Sekhmet's fierce protection in my life?
- Where can Bastet's playful grace serve me?
- How do these energies already express themselves through me?
- What new possibilities open when I embrace both?

6. Daily Practice

Choose a simple way to carry these energies:

- Wear red/gold and black/silver together
- Create a gesture combining strength and grace
- Set up a small altar honoring both aspects

- Choose a word or phrase that captures your multidimensional nature

Close by placing one hand on your heart (Bastet) and one on your solar plexus (Sekhmet). Feel their energies merge in your center as you affirm:

"I am the lioness and the cat
Fierce protector and gentle creator
In my wholeness I find my power
Through my integration I shine my light"

The Nile's Embrace: Sisterhood on Sacred Waters

Under a canopy of stars so brilliant they set the indigo sky ablaze, we gather on the sun-warmed deck. The air hangs heavy with the heady scent of night-blooming jasmine, mingling with the earthy aroma of the river – fertile silt and hidden depths creating an intoxicating perfume of infinite possibility. The rough texture of weathered wood beneath our bare feet grounds us as we share our stories.

Words flow as freely as the Nile itself – tales of triumph that make our hearts soar, of heartbreak that echoes in our collective soul, of dreams yet unfulfilled that spark a fire in our eyes. With each syllable uttered, each knowing glance exchanged, the invisible threads connecting us grow stronger, weaving an unbreakable tapestry of sisterhood.

As we approach the temple of Philae, sanctuary of the goddess Isis, a palpable energy charges the air. Goosebumps rise on my skin despite the warmth. The island materializes from the mist like a mirage, its pillars glowing softly in the pre-dawn light, their weathered surfaces holding memories of countless devotees. We disembark in reverent silence, the only sound the soft splash of water against stone steps worn smooth by time.

Before the invisible sacred shrine of Isis, we form a circle without speaking, our hands instinctively linking. Palms press together, fingers intertwine – cool and warm, smooth and calloused, each unique touch a testament to our individual journeys. The power of the goddess seems to flow through us like an electric current, igniting our individual Heartfire Rays. The warmth in my chest expands, fueled by the collective energy, until I feel I might burst with radiant light.

Our bodies begin to sway, moving to a music that resonates in our very marrow. It's a dance of becoming – arms undulating like lotus stems reaching through murky depths, torsos unfurling like petals greeting the sun. The stone beneath our feet seems to pulse with ancient rhythms. Tears flow freely, salty droplets mingling with beads of perspiration. Joy and release intermingle as we surrender to the transformative power of this sacred space and our shared presence.

In this transcendent moment, we are more than thirteen individuals. We are a living, breathing mandala of feminine power, each of us a vibrant petal in a grand cosmic lotus. The boundaries between us blur like watercolors bleeding together. I feel my own blossoming magnified a thousandfold through the collective energy of our circle. My senses heighten – I can almost taste the metallic tang of transformation in the air, hear the silent roar of millennia of women's wisdom crashing over us like a wave.

As we continue our journey down the Nile, the imprint of that sacred dance remains etched in our bodies and souls. Each temple we visit becomes a new crucible for growth. Every site offers a chance to shed old layers like a snake sloughing off its skin, embracing the radiant beings we are becoming.

The river itself mirrors our transformation. Its surface shimmers with ever-changing patterns of sunlight and shadow, unchanging in its essence yet perpetually in motion. Like the Nile, we are ancient and newborn with every passing moment, carrying the wisdom of ages while remaining open to the infinite possibilities that lie ahead.

This journey reveals the true power of sisterhood in the process of radiant blossoming. Like lotuses growing together in a sacred pool, we support each other's growth – roots intertwined, stems reaching upward in unison. Our collective beauty far surpasses what any of us could achieve alone. The Nile's embrace has woven us into a tapestry of shared transformation, each thread essential, the whole infinitely more radiant than its parts.

Sacred Waters: Journaling Your Journey of Connection

- Recall a moment when you felt deeply connected to others in a profound way. What elements created that sacred container?
- What natural settings help you access your deepest truth and wisdom? Like the Nile, what bodies of water, mountains, or landscapes call to your soul?
- When have you experienced the power of collective energy? How did it differ from solitary practice?
- Who are the spiritual companions on your path? How do they mirror different aspects of your own becoming?
- What ancestral wisdom flows through your lineage? How do you honor those who walked this path before you?
- How has gathering in a sacred circle (of any gender) transformed your understanding of yourself?
- What old layers are you ready to shed? Like a snake releasing its skin, what no longer serves your growth?
- How does your body want to move when you feel most spiritually connected? What gestures or movements express your soul's yearning?
- When have you felt your personal transformation amplified by the energy of community?

- Like the Nile's ever-changing surface, how do you balance consistency and flow in your spiritual practice?
- What ancient wisdom resonates most deeply in your heart? How do you integrate timeless teachings with your modern life?
- In what ways are you both student and teacher on the path? How do you receive and share sacred knowledge?
- How do you support others in their blossoming while staying rooted in your own growth?
- What unique gifts do you bring to your spiritual community? How does your presence enhance the collective?
- Where do you find strength in unity while honoring individual paths?
- What sacred sites (physical or metaphorical) have shaped your spiritual journey?
- How do you create and maintain sacred space in your daily life?
- What rituals help you connect with divine presence and your own inner wisdom?

End your journaling session by:

1. Drawing or describing your own sacred mandala of connection
2. Writing a blessing for fellow seekers on the path
3. Creating a simple ritual to honor both solitary and collective aspects of your journey

The Nile's Lotus: Awakening the Inner Khepri

The cool night air of the Nile caresses your skin, carrying the sweet, intoxicating scent of lotus blossoms. You stand on the deck of the gently swaying dahabiya, the wooden planks solid beneath your feet. Twelve women form a circle with you, their presence electric with shared purpose. The full moon hangs low and heavy, its silver light transforming the river's surface into a field of dancing diamonds.

Warmth builds in your palms, subtle at first like dawn's earliest rays, then growing steadily stronger. This is the awakening of shared energy, ancient and profound, pulsing through your being. The moist river air fills your lungs, each breath drawing you deeper into this sacred moment.

The waters before the boat begin to churn. A massive lotus bud breaks the surface, its form radiating inner light. Though its petals remain closed, power emanates from within, charging the air with electric potential. The air grows thick with anticipation, charged with the electric potential of imminent creation.

The lotus begins to unfurl before your inner eye. Its petals open slowly, revealing layer upon layer of iridescent beauty. The scent intensifies, filling your senses with the perfume of creation itself. From the very center of the blossom, a golden light emerges.

This light takes form, coalescing into the shape of a magnificent scarab beetle - Khepri, the early manifestation of Ra, god of the rising sun. His carapace gleams with all the colors of dawn, and his presence fills you with a sense of renewal and infinite potential.

As Khepri rises from the lotus, feel an answering stirring within your own body. A warm, tingling sensation begins at the base of your spine - your root chakra awakening. This is your inner Khepri, your personal force of creation and transformation, beginning its ascent.

The energy rises, slowly at first, like sap moving through the stem of a lotus. It passes through your sacral chakra, igniting your creative and sensual energies. The warmth intensifies as it reaches your solar plexus, filling you with a sense of personal power and purpose.

As the energy continues ascending through your heart chakra, feel an overwhelming sense of love and connection - to your sisters in the circle, to the Nile, to all of creation. Let tears of joy flow freely as divine love fills your being.

The rising energy reaches your throat chakra, awakening the urge to voice your truth, to sing the song of your soul. Gentle sounds may naturally emerge - a soft hum, a whispered tone, an exhale of wonder. The very stars seem to vibrate in harmony.

As the energy fills your third eye chakra, let visions arise naturally. See yourself as you truly are - a divine being of light, capable of incredible transformation. Past, present and future merge in this eternal moment of becoming.

Finally, the energy reaches your crown chakra, bursting forth in a fountain of light that connects you directly to the cosmos. In this moment, you are one with Khepri, one with the Nile, one with all that is. You are both the creator and the created, the lotus and the beetle, the river and its source.

Feel the warmth gathering in your creative center, the place from which you birth new ideas, new aspects of yourself, new ways of being in the world. This sacred space pulses with infinite potential.

Integration Practice: Anchoring the Lotus Light

1. After completing this immersion, take time to integrate the experience:

2. Rest quietly for a few moments, allowing the energies to settle into your being

   - In your journal, capture your journey through:
   - The sensations you experienced in each chakra
   - The visions or insights that arose
   - The gifts or wisdom received from Khepri
   - A symbol or drawing that represents your transformation

3. Create a simple daily practice to maintain this connection:

    - Place a lotus image or scarab symbol on your altar
    - Take three breaths each morning imagining the golden light rising
    - Touch each chakra point while remembering this journey
    - Speak a word or phrase that emerged during the experience

4. Honor your transformation through:

    - Creating or choosing a piece of art that captures this awakening
    - Writing a poem or song expressing your inner Khepri
    - Making a small offering to the forces of renewal
    - Sharing your experience with a trusted friend

Quantum Entanglement of Cultures

Just as subatomic particles can become entangled, instantly affecting one another across vast distances, so too can cultures become intertwined in ways that transcend traditional notions of exchange and influence. This quantum entanglement of cultures speaks to a deeper, more instantaneous form of connection - one that ripples across the globe, shaping our collective consciousness in profound and often unexpected ways.

Threads of Light: A Filmmaker's Blossoming

The grand hall of the Dubai Film Festival buzzed with anticipation, the air thick with perfume and nervous energy. My heart pounded a wild rhythm as I stood backstage, seven years of work distilled into the film about to premiere. I closed my eyes, and for a moment, I was back in the sun-baked desert, the voices of Bedouin women echoing in my ears, their trust a precious gift woven into every frame of "Nomad's Home."

The lights dimmed, plunging the hall into darkness. As the first images flickered to life on the screen, I held my breath. Each scene was a memory relived - the rough texture of tent fabric, the aroma of sage-laced tea, the glint of sunlight on intricate embroidery. Time stretched and compressed, until suddenly the credits rolled and applause erupted like a sandstorm.

Trembling slightly, I stepped into the spotlight to accept the award. Its weight in my hands was proof that this journey - the endless pitches, the cultural barriers that seemed insurmountable - had been worth every moment. Words of gratitude spilled from my lips, my voice thick with emotion as I acknowledged the Bedouin women who had opened their lives to my camera.

The celebration that followed was a sensory whirlwind. One of Egypt's most popular indie musicians took the stage, their melodies intertwining with the intricate patterns of Bedouin textiles I could still see when I closed my eyes. As I swayed to the music, surrounded by the excited chatter of fellow filmmakers and new admirers of Bedouin culture, I felt something shift within me. It was as if every cell in my body was expanding, reaching towards some new, bright possibility.

Months later, I found myself in the grand theater of the Yamagata International Documentary Film Festival. The realization that "Nomad's Home" was competing alongside works by directors like Terrence Malick sent a thrill of disbelief through me. Yet what truly set this experience apart wasn't the competition, but what had come before.

Days earlier, I had stood atop Yamagata's most sacred mountain with a Shinto teacher, mist curling around us as we deposited prayers gathered from around the world. The wind whispered through ancient trees, and for a moment, I felt connected to something vast and timeless.

When I shared this experience with the Yamagata audience before the screening, the atmosphere in the theater shifted palpably. As "Nomad's Home" played, I sensed the audience wasn't just watching a film about Bedouin women, but experiencing it through the lens of our shared spiritual encounter.

The journey continued, each screening a unique alchemy of place and people. In Ramallah, heated debates about art and resistance stretched into the night, the passion in people's voices a stark contrast to the cool stone walls around us. At the FESPACO film festival in Burkina Faso, sweat trickled down my back as we waited for a sputtering projector to be repaired, the audience's patience in the sweltering heat a humbling testament to the power of storytelling.

Now, standing on the rooftop of the Goethe Institute in Cairo, these memories swirled around me as "Egyptian Jeanne d'Arc" came to its conclusion. The air crackled with emotion, sobs and laughter mingling with the distant honking of cars. A young woman pushed through the crowd, wrapping me in a fierce embrace that spoke louder than words.

As one of Egypt's most respected indie filmmakers led a passionate Q&A, I felt a profound sense of homecoming. This wasn't just a screening; it was a collective reckoning with our recent past, our uncertain future. The rooftop hummed with voices, each person eager to share their story, to see themselves reflected in the struggles and triumphs on screen.

As the night drew to a close and the last attendees drifted away, I stood alone, gazing out over the city that had inspired it all. The cool night breeze carried the scent of jasmine and diesel, a fitting mixture for this complex, beautiful place. I realized then that this journey wasn't ending, but transforming. Each person who had engaged with these films - from the elderly Kazakh man gesturing animatedly to a young Egyptian woman in Astana, to the tearful audience members in New York - was now part of this continuing story.

The first light of dawn began to paint the Cairo sky, and I felt a familiar stirring of excitement. This wasn't an end, but a new beginning, with countless stories yet to be told, countless connections yet to be made. The revolution that had inspired "Egyptian Jeanne d'Arc" was still echoing in hearts and minds around the world. And I, heart wide open, was ready for whatever came next.

Journaling Prompts: Weaving Your Cultural Tapestry

Find a quiet moment and open your journal. Let these questions guide you into exploring your own experience of cultural quantum entanglement:

- What cultures flow through your veins? Consider not just your heritage, but the cultural influences that have shaped your way of seeing, thinking, creating. How do these different streams merge and dance within you?
- Recall a moment when cultural boundaries dissolved - perhaps while experiencing art, sharing food, or connecting deeply with someone from a different background. What shifted in your understanding? How did this experience change you?
- What art, music, stories or traditions from cultures not your own have touched you most deeply? How have they become part of your own creative voice?
- Where do you find yourself serving as a bridge between different worlds? What unique gifts emerge from your position at these cultural crossroads?
- What stories are you carrying that long to be shared across cultural boundaries? How might your own creative expression serve as a thread connecting different worlds?

- When have you felt most aware of being part of humanity's greater tapestry? How did this awareness change your sense of purpose or possibility?
- What new forms of cultural connection are awakening in you now? What next steps do you feel called to take in fostering deeper cross-cultural understanding?
- Write a letter to yourself about the cultural bridges you dream of building. What connections do you wish to nurture? What boundaries do you feel ready to transcend? What beauty might emerge from these new entanglements?

The Library of Sacred Memory: Walking with Seshat

Warmth spreads across your skin as you enter an ancient library. The air carries the scent of honey, papyrus, and starlit wisdom. Your bare feet find cool, smooth stone beneath them, each step sending tiny ripples of energy up through your body.

The space opens endlessly around you, filled with soft golden light. Before any sight or sound reaches you, you feel Seshat's presence - ancient, wise, yet somehow familiar as your own heartbeat. The divine scribe's energy fills the vast chamber, making the air itself shimmer like sun on water. Her leopard cloak ripples with living starlight, each spot a window into another time, another story.

Scrolls and books float gently in the luminous air, some ancient as creation, others fresh as tomorrow's dreams. Seshat's presence guides you forward without words, her energy weaving with yours like threads in a tapestry. Through her essence, you begin to understand - these aren't just stories, they're the living wisdom of all existence.

A particular scroll calls to you, its energy resonating with your deepest self. As your fingers touch parchment, Seshat's wisdom flows through you. The scroll unfurls and suddenly you're swimming in the river of your own becoming:

The first time you felt truly seen. That moment courage bloomed in your heart. Every triumph, every tear, every transformation streams through you like sunlight through stained glass. You experience each memory with new depth - through Seshat's eyes, even the smallest moments shine with sacred significance.

Tears of recognition roll down your cheeks, each drop catching light like a newborn star. Through Seshat's presence, you understand how every experience has woven itself into the magnificent tapestry of your becoming. Her energy holds you gently as past and present dance together, showing you the beauty of your own unfolding.

An iridescent feather materializes in your palm - Seshat's gift, a bridge between worlds. Though light as a breath, it carries the weight of infinite knowing. As the familiar world returns, you feel her wisdom settled into your bones. The sacred library lives within you now, accessible through the feather's touch.

Integration Practice: Anchoring Cosmic Wisdom

1. Sacred Grounding

   - Hold Seshat's feather (or visualize it) over your heart
   - Feel its vibration aligning with your heartbeat
   - Let its rhythm ripple through your entire being

2. Body Memory

   - Trace where you felt each sensation during the journey
   - Notice which parts still hum with cosmic energy
   - Map these awakened points in your journal

3. Wisdom Integration Create three containers in your journal:

- Past Wisdom: Record memories that surfaced
- Present Truth: Note current revelations
- Future Seeds: Document potential futures glimpsed

4. Creative Expression Choose one way to anchor this experience:

- Draw symbols that emerged
- Write a poem in the language of the Records
- Move your body to express cosmic rhythms
- Create a sound that captures the library's essence

5. Daily Practice Select one simple way to maintain connection:

- Touch the point where the feather rested
- Whisper a word received in the Records
- Draw a symbol of cosmic connection
- Feel the library's pulse in quiet moments

Close by placing both hands over your heart, feeling the merge of cosmic and personal rhythms. You carry the Records within now - let their wisdom flow naturally through your daily life, informing choices and illuminating paths with divine light.

Remember: This gateway remains accessible. Return whenever guidance is needed, letting Seshat's presence and the Records' wisdom support your continuous unfolding.

Dancing with Sothis: Awakening Celestial Light

In the vast night sky above ancient Egypt, one star burned brighter than all others - Sothis, celestial manifestation of Isis herself. When this brilliant blue-white star appeared on the pre-dawn horizon, the Nile's life-giving waters began to rise, marking the season of renewal and abundance. More than just a celestial marker, Sothis embodied the sacred bridge between heaven and earth, channeling divine radiance into earthly form.

The priests and priestesses of ancient Egypt understood Sothis as the cosmic source of inner illumination. Her light, they taught, could awaken the divine radiance within each human being. Through her, the macrocosm of celestial forces and the microcosm of human consciousness merged in sacred union. Her annual rising reminded them that each soul contains this same capacity for radiant transformation.

To work with Sothis is to remember our own inner starlight, our capacity to bridge worlds and channel divine radiance. She calls us to recognize ourselves as living constellations, each cell a star contributing to our unique pattern of light. Through her blessing, we awaken to our role as channels between heaven and earth, carriers of celestial frequencies into earthly form.

The Sothis Dance: Awakening Your Inner Star

The night air shimmers with stellar frequencies. Above, Sirius blazes with impossible brightness, her blue-white radiance piercing the veil between worlds. Your skin tingles with celestial electricity as Sothis' light bathes the earth in waves of divine power.

Feel your feet connecting deeply with the earth as starlight streams down from above. Each cell in your body begins to awaken, remembering its divine origin. You are made of stardust, each atom forged in cosmic fire. Let this knowing ripple through your being.

Sothis' light intensifies, penetrating every layer of your existence. Your cells begin to pulse and glow like tiny stars, creating constellations throughout your body. Energy centers illuminate one by one, each a sun in your inner galaxy. The light builds and builds until you become a human aurora, colors dancing through your energy field.

Notice how this light moves in fractal patterns - spirals within spirals, waves within waves. Each small awakening creates ripples that contribute to larger transformations. You are a living mandala of light, continuously unfolding into greater radiance.

The boundaries of your form begin to dissolve as your personal field of light merges with the greater field of cosmic radiance. You are simultaneously infinitely vast and perfectly contained, a unique node in the cosmic web of light. Sothis' presence fills you completely, awakening ancient memories of your stellar origins.

In this expanded state, watch the pattern of your soul's journey emerge. See how each small moment of growth, each challenge transformed into light, has contributed to your soul's magnificent unfolding. You are a living fractal of divine consciousness, expressing celestial light in your unique human form.

Integration Practices

1. Daily Light Activation

   - At first light, face the eastern horizon where Sirius rises
   - Breathe in stellar light through your crown, filling each cell
   - Tone the sound "Soh-this", feeling it amplify your inner radiance
   - Bless and drink water charged with morning sunlight

2. Fractal Growth Reflection Create a star map of your transformation:

   - Place a central star representing your core light
   - Add smaller stars for moments of micro-blossoming
   - Connect these into constellations of larger transformation
   - Notice the patterns that emerge in your soul's light journey

3. Celestial Connection Ritual

   - Gather with others under the night sky

- Form a circle and link hands, creating a living constellation
- Take turns speaking your star blessing: "I am [name], a living light of Sothis"
- Feel the group field amplify each person's inner radiance
- Close by toning together, creating harmony between earth and sky

Immersion: The Cosmic Lotus Unveiling

The air fills with electric possibility, tiny stars dancing through every breath. Golden light streams from every pore, creating a shimmering cocoon of radiance. This divine warmth seeps into bones, transforming flesh into weightless, luminous potential.

Cool, silky water embraces bare feet at the edge of a vast cosmic river. Its surface swirls with stardust and liquid light, each ripple creating a symphony of colors beyond earthly perception. The universe's melody resonates through blood and bone - haunting, beautiful, awakening ancient memories in the core of being.

From celestial waters rises a giant lotus bud, its closed petals pulsing with inner radiance. Shadows and light dance across the river's surface in sacred geometries. The bud's energy pulls like a cosmic magnet, calling to the soul's deepest knowing.

Night-blooming jasmine mingles with indefinable cosmic essence on the cool breeze. Above, Nut's presence takes breath away - her form a living tapestry of stars and galaxies stretching across infinity. Her celestial wisdom flows directly into cells, confirming truth: this moment contains all that has been, all that is becoming.

Each step toward the lotus sends ripples through spacetime. The living water reflects a kaleidoscope of soul memories - courage found in a trembling voice, love's infinite discovery, every challenge transformed into light. Hard-won wisdom and cultivated love sparkle in each wavelet.

Hands meet lotus buds, warmth flowing like sunlight through meridians. The surface feels like silk woven from solar flares, vibrating with pure potential. Divine presence gathers - Hathor's creative radiance shimmering the air with infinite possibilities, her starlit joy illuminating new pathways of becoming.

Cosmic waters purr with Bast's playful power, ripples of feline grace circling the lotus. Her essence awakens sensual wisdom, reminding cells how to dance with joy. Sekhmet's heat builds like a summer storm, fierce pride igniting internal fires. Each goddess's energy amplifies the unfolding transformation.

The first petal opens with celestial chimes, releasing waves of light that wash through body and soul. This radiance carries the echo of first awakening - power recognized, potential glimpsed, beauty remembered. Joy overflows in tears that evaporate into newborn stars.

Each successive petal releases new aspects of blossoming self. Compassion expands the heart to cosmic proportions. Creativity ignites the mind into kaleidoscopic visions. Wisdom flows like a river connecting all moments of existence. Strength roots deeply into unshakeable truth.

The cosmic river mirrors this emergence, reflection revealing pure light barely contained in human form. As inner petals approach, vulnerability and power pulse in equal measure. Isis's presence surrounds like wings of light, her protective love creating sacred space for deepest unfolding. Myrrh-scented grace infuses every breath with infinite potential.

Drawing in the breath of cosmos itself, the final petals unfurl. Pure radiance explodes upward, piercing heaven's veil. All boundaries dissolve - lotus and light, river and sky become one unified field of consciousness. Every molecule vibrates with creation's frequency as understanding floods through - each experience has served this magnificent blooming.

The cosmic lotus floats fully opened, its heart a swirling galaxy of potential. From its center emerges a golden seed, pulsing with universes waiting to be born. Tehuti's wisdom flows without words as the seed passes to waiting palm - both infinitely heavy with possibility and light as divine promise.

The familiar world returns transformed. The cosmic lotus lives within now, eternally unfolding. The seed of infinite potential rests in palm and heart, bridging completed blossoming to coming creation. Every cell hums with music of the spheres, ready to birth new worlds into being.

This threshold moment contains all endings and beginnings. The coolness of cosmic waters, the warmth of divine light, the sacred seed's tangible power - all testify to completion and commencement. Radiant Blossoming flows naturally into Sacred Seeding, the eternal dance continues.

V. Sacred Seeding

Isis, Weaver of Legends, let your story guide our hand,
In honoring your struggles, may our own find reprimand.
Through trials faced with courage, a path of healing appears,
For within shared wisdom, we conquer our deepest fears.
Isis, Source Eternal, from your strength our spirits rise,
Suffering transformed, may we illuminate the skies.
Inspired by your example, with compassion and with grace,
We shall become the weavers of a world where love finds its place.

The Dreamer's Seed

The cool, damp earth clings to my bare feet as I stand at the edge of the Nile. Pre-dawn mist swirls around me, blurring the line between water and sky. I close my eyes, breathing in the rich, loamy scent of the river bank. In this moment, suspended between night and day, I feel the weight of a tiny seed in my palm – a single blue lotus, its potential thrumming against my skin.

My mind drifts back to the little girl I once was, huddled under blankets with a flashlight, scribbling fantastical worlds in the margins of her schoolbooks. I can almost hear the whispers of those around me: "Such a dreamer. When will she learn to face reality?"

A smile tugs at my lips. If only they could see me now.

The mist begins to lift as the first rays of sunlight pierce the horizon. I open my eyes, watching as the Nile comes alive with color. There, bobbing gently on the water's surface, a sea of blue lotuses unfurls their petals to greet the dawn. My breath catches in my throat. These flowers, once nearly lost to Egypt, now bloom in abundance – a testament to the power of persistence, of nurturing even the smallest seed of hope.

I think of my son, his fierce determination to create a more just world mirroring the lotus's journey from mud to radiant blossom. I recall the faces of the 13 women who joined me on this Nile pilgrimage, each of us carrying our own seeds of transformation. Together, we witnessed our collective awakening, as powerful and beautiful as the lotuses before us.

The tiny seed in my hand pulses with renewed energy. This, I realize, is the true essence of Sacred Seeding. It's the dreams that refused to die, even in the face of near-death experiences. It's the visions that manifested into award-winning films, carrying messages of hope across the globe. It's the concept of the Holographic Being, born from countless hours of contemplation, now a beacon of connection and amplified potential.

I kneel at the water's edge, gently placing the lotus seed on the surface. As it floats away, carried by the current, I whisper an invocation: "May this seed, like every dream we dare to nurture, find fertile ground. May it grow strong, breaking through the murky depths to reach the light. And may it remind all who see it that within each of us lies the power to bring a piece of heaven to Earth."

Rising, I feel a surge of energy course through me. The sun now bathes the landscape in golden light, illuminating the canyons, deserts, and mountains that have shaped my journey. I've been blessed to witness this Earth in all its raw beauty, and even more blessed to play a part in its unfolding story.

As I turn to leave, a gentle breeze carries the fragrance of lotus blossoms. It whispers of quantum possibilities, of moments where time bends and dreams take tangible form beneath our fingertips. I smile, knowing that the greatest revolutions often begin with the smallest of seeds.

To you, beloved traveler, I offer this truth: Nurture the blue lotus seed within your own heart. Let it draw strength from the very challenges that seek to overwhelm it. Reach towards the sun, breaking through doubt and chaos to bloom in radiant possibility. For in your dreams, in your relentless hope, lies the power to illuminate not just your own path, but to become a lighthouse guiding us all towards a more beautiful world.

The journey of Sacred Seeding begins now. What dreams will you plant today?

Seeds of Dreams: Sacred Seeding Journal Prompts

- What dreams did you nurture in secret as a child, perhaps under blankets with a flashlight or in the margins of your notebooks?
- When were you told to "face reality" instead of following your dreams? How did those moments shape you?
- What visions have refused to die within you, persisting even through life's challenges?
- Like the lotus breaking through murky depths, what dreams are currently pushing through obstacles toward the light?
- Where do you feel most connected to the Earth's raw beauty? Describe this place in vivid sensory detail.
- What "seeds" of transformation are you currently carrying? List both small hopes and grand visions.
- Like the Nile's fertile banks, what environments nurture your dreams? What conditions help your visions take root?
- Who are the 13 people (or however many resonate) that form your circle of transformation? How do you support each other's growth?
- What seeds of change have you already planted in the world? Include both realized dreams and those still growing.

- How have your challenges become fertile soil for growth? Describe how difficulties have strengthened your vision.
- What messages of hope do you carry that could illuminate paths for others?
- Like the lotus seeds floating on the current, what dreams are you releasing into the world? What do you hope they will become?
- Write your own invocation for the seeds you're planting. Begin with "May this seed…"
- What quantum possibilities are awakening in your life? Where do you sense time bending toward new potential?
- How are you becoming a "lighthouse" for others? What light do you shine into the world?
- What piece of heaven are you called to bring to Earth?
- What seeds will you plant today?

Immersion: The Overture of Sacred Seeding: A Cosmic Symphony

A single, crystalline note pierces the veil of existence, its purity shattering the boundaries between you and the cosmos. The vibration ripples through you, a lightning strike of divine resonance igniting every cell, every atom of your being. Your skin tingles, your breath catches, as darkness shimmers and transforms before your eyes into an ocean of luminous threads, each one pulsing with life and infinite potential.

The cosmic loom materializes, its vastness so overwhelming that your mind struggles to comprehend its scale. Colors explode into being with an intensity that transcends sight – you taste the deep indigos of infinite wisdom on your tongue, feel the radiant golds of divine inspiration warming your skin, breathe in the vibrant greens of perpetual growth. Each hue sings its own melody, a harmony so complex and beautiful that tears spring unbidden to your eyes.

Your bare feet sink into the cool, silken sand at the shore of the celestial Nile. Its waters mirror the dance of stars above, each ripple a gateway to untold possibilities. The gentle lapping of waves against the shore syncs with your heartbeat, grounding you in this liminal space between worlds. You are both infinitesimally small and cosmically vast, a perfect paradox embodied.

A warm zephyr caresses your skin, carrying the intoxicating fragrance of night-blooming lotus and sun-kissed earth. But this is more than just scent – as you breathe in, you inhale the very essence of time itself. Memories that are not your own flood your consciousness – the birth of stars, the rise and fall of civilizations, the quiet courage of countless beings across eons. The accumulated wisdom of the universe flows through you like honey, sweet and golden.

Your fingertips come alive, crackling with creative potential. As you reach out, cosmic threads respond to your touch, bending and swirling in a joyous dance that defies physics. Colors blend and separate, forming patterns of breathtaking complexity. A laugh bubbles up from deep within you as exhilaration courses through your veins. You are not merely observing this grand performance – you are composer, conductor, and instrument all at once.

The cosmic symphony swells, each note resonating in perfect harmony with your soul. Strands of light coalesce before your eyes, taking shape with a beauty that transcends earthly understanding. A lotus of cosmic proportions unfurls its petals, each one a vivid, living chapter of your journey. You see yourself emerging from the fertile darkness of Primal Mud, seeking Light with unwavering determination, ascending through challenges that forged your spirit. As the final petal opens, revealing your Radiant Blossoming, constellations burst into life around you. Each star pulses in time with your heart, a seed of possibility you've nurtured through your transformation.

The voice of creation itself joins the melody, so deep and profound that it vibrates in your very marrow. It calls to you, not in words, but in a language your soul has always known. As you open your mouth to respond, to add your unique note to this grand composition, understanding dawns with the brilliance of the first light of creation.

This – this moment of perfect union between your individual journey and the cosmic dance – is Sacred Seeding. Your personal transformation alchemizes into the power of co-creation. Every thought that crosses your mind, every emotion that stirs your heart, every action you take becomes a brushstroke on the infinite canvas of reality.

The Neteru gather around you, their presence a symphony of divine energies that amplifies your own. Nut arches overhead, her star-studded body a reminder of the vast potential within you. Geb's solid presence beneath your feet offers unwavering support. Their eternal embrace resonates within you, a reminder of the sacred union of heaven and earth in your own being. Ra's solar radiance illuminates the path before you, while Sekhmet's fierce roar awakens your inner warrior. Ptah approaches, his eyes alight with the fire of creation, and gently guides your hands towards the threads of the cosmic loom.

As your fingers brush the shimmering strands, you feel the weight of your entire journey – every triumph, every tear, every moment of hard-won wisdom. Each thread you touch hums with infinite potential, eager to be woven into the grand tapestry of existence.

The universe itself seems to hold its breath in anticipation. Infinite possibilities stretch before you, awaiting your touch to spring into being. What magnificent worlds will you seed into existence? What dreams, nurtured in the secret chambers of your heart, will you now bring forth into dazzling reality?

The overture reaches its zenith, and in this eternal moment, you recognize your true nature. You are the composer, your life experiences the notes. You are the conductor, your choices and intentions the guiding baton. And you are the very music itself, your being an essential thread in the cosmic symphony.

Take a deep breath, beloved co-creator. Feel the power coursing through you, the wisdom of ages at your fingertips, the love of the universe supporting your every move. The grand movement of Sacred Seeding begins now.

What will you create?

The Symphony of Sacred Seeding: A Vibrational Integration Practice

Find a space where you can make sound freely. You'll need:

- A clear glass bowl filled with water
- A crystal or singing bowl (if available) or any object that can create a pure tone

Core Practice: Weaving Your Cosmic Note (30 minutes)

1. Finding Your Crystalline Note (10 minutes)

- Stand barefoot, grounding like you did on the celestial shore
- Begin humming softly, letting your voice explore different tones
- When you feel resonance in your cells, you've found your note - it will create tingles or vibrations in your body
- Hold this note, feeling it ripple through you like that first crystalline sound
- Let the note gradually grow stronger, imagining it shattering boundaries between worlds

2. Water Symphony (10 minutes)

- Place your hands on either side of the water bowl

- Continue sounding your note, watching how it affects the water's surface
- Observe the patterns forming - these are your cosmic threads made visible
- Vary the intensity and watch how different vibrations create different patterns
- Let your note interact with the water until you see a pattern that feels complete

3. Weaving With Sound (10 minutes)

- Keep your hands by the water but now move them as if weaving on the cosmic loom
- Your voice becomes the shuttle, weaving between dimensions
- Let your note rise and fall like waves on the celestial Nile
- When you feel the presence of the Neteru, allow their frequencies to join your song
- Your voice will naturally create harmonics - these are the colors you tasted becoming sound

The Completion

- As your symphony reaches its natural conclusion, place one hand in the water
- With the other hand over your heart, sound one final sustained note
- Feel it connecting the water's patterns to your own creative potential
- The water now holds your vibrational signature - your unique thread in the cosmic weave

Divine Dialogue

Connect with the Neteru who approached you:

- What message did Nut whisper about potential?
- How did Geb's support feel through your feet?
- What did Ra illuminate in your path?
- How did Sekhmet's roar transform you?
- What did Ptah reveal about creation?

The patterns you've created in the water are a physical manifestation of your cosmic seeding vibration. Each time you return to this practice, observe how your patterns evolve as your creative power grows.

The California Awakening: Seeds of Cosmic Collaboration

The California sun beat down, a fiery furnace igniting our creative spirits. We were a motley crew, artists and seekers, drawn together by a shared yearning to explore the interconnectedness of art, nature, and the ancient wisdom of the Neteru.

Our journey began in the Mojave Desert, amidst the twisted limbs of Joshua trees, their spiny arms reaching towards the heavens like ancient hieroglyphs etched against the endless blue canvas. The air crackled with a primal energy, the silence a symphony of whispers carried on the desert wind. Here, in this land of stark beauty and ancient whispers, we set our intentions, our hearts pounding with the rhythm of our creative quest.

Our trusty van, a chariot of dreams and aspirations, became our vessel, carrying us across California's diverse landscapes. Each vista unfolded like a scroll painting come to life – the rugged peaks of the Sierra Nevada, their snow-capped summits piercing the clouds, mirroring the challenges and triumphs of our own inner landscapes; the crystal-clear waters of Lake Tahoe, reflecting the azure sky, whispering of the boundless depths within our souls.

And then, we entered the realm of the redwoods, those ancient giants that stood as silent sentinels, their towering trunks adorned with intricate patterns of bark and moss, whispering tales of resilience and ancient wisdom. The air, thick with the scent of damp earth and fragrant needles, awakened a primal connection within us, a sense of belonging to something far greater than ourselves.

The female dancer, her limbs flowing like water, embodied the threefold aspect of the feminine – Hathor's joy and sensuality, Sekhmet's fierce power, and Bastet's playful grace. Her laughter echoed through the trees, mingling with the rustling leaves and the murmuring streams, a symphony of creative expression.

She twirled and leaped, her movements as unpredictable as the wind, her energy as radiant as the sunbeams that filtered through the canopy. Her laughter echoed through the ancient grove, a playful invitation to embrace the fullness of life, to dance with abandon, to celebrate the sensual beauty of the body.

The male dancers, their strength and agility a testament to the masculine principle, channeled the energies of Horus, the falcon-headed god of vision, and Anubis, the jackal-headed guardian of the underworld. Their movements were a dance of light and shadow, a celebration of the duality that exists within each of us.

They moved with a focused intensity, their bodies sculpted by years of training, their spirits attuned to the ancient rhythms of the earth. Their eyes, sharp and alert, scanned the forest floor, seeking the hidden pathways, the subtle signs that guided their steps. Their hands, strong and steady, reached out to touch the rough bark of the redwoods, drawing strength from the ancient wisdom of the trees.

Together, the dancers wove a tapestry of movement and energy, their bodies a living testament to the power of the Neteru. They became conduits for the divine, their dance a sacred ritual that honored the interconnectedness of all things.

As we filmed their movements, capturing their grace and power on camera, we felt a profound shift in our own awareness. The boundaries between art and nature, between the human and the divine, began to dissolve. We were no longer just observers; we were participants in this sacred dance, co-creators with the universe, weaving a tapestry of beauty and transformation.

Within this sacred grove, we danced with the Neteru, our bodies becoming vessels for their divine energies. The female dancer, her movements fluid and graceful, embodied the threefold aspect of the feminine – Hathor's joy and sensuality, Sekhmet's fierce power, and Bastet's playful grace. Her laughter echoed through the trees, mingling with the rustling leaves and the murmuring streams, a symphony of creative expression.

We built labyrinths of stones, each one a spiral pathway leading towards the center of our being, a metaphor for the journey of self-discovery and transformation. We walked these paths with reverence, our footsteps echoing the whispers of the ancients, our hearts open to the wisdom that awaited us at the center.

We discovered a redwood with a hollow at its base, a natural womb where we choreographed a scene of rebirth. A dancer emerged from the darkness, unfurling like a new shoot reaching for the light, her movements a testament to the resilience of the human spirit and the transformative power of the Primal Mud.

As we immersed ourselves in this creative process, the boundaries between art and nature, between the human and the divine, began to dissolve. We became one with the landscape, our movements echoing the whispers of the wind, our voices harmonizing with the rustling leaves and the murmuring streams. We were no longer just artists; we were co-creators with the universe, weaving a tapestry of beauty and transformation.

The culmination of our journey was a short film, a tapestry woven from the threads of our experiences, a symphony of movement, music, and visual poetry. It was a celebration of the interconnectedness of all things, a testament to the transformative power of art, and an offering to the Neteru who had guided us on our path.

As we shared our creation with the world, we felt the ripple effect of our collective energy, the seeds of our inspiration taking root in the hearts of others. We had not just created art; we had participated in the sacred act of seeding the world with beauty, wisdom, and the transformative power of the Lotus-Born Heart.

Seeds of Creative Collaboration: Reflection Prompts

- What landscapes have awakened your spirit? Describe a place where you felt the boundaries between human and divine dissolve.
- Like the Joshua trees reaching toward heaven, what aspects of your creativity yearn upward?
- When have you felt the "primal energy" of a place crackling through your being? What emerged from that connection?
- Which natural settings become your creative sanctuaries? How do they shape your artistic expression?
- When have you moved beyond being an observer to become a participant in something greater than yourself?
- How does your body want to express the threefold feminine energies within you?
  - Hathor's sensual joy
  - Sekhmet's fierce power
  - Bastet's playful grace
- Where do you find the balance between focused intensity and fluid grace in your creative practice?

- What emerges when you let your body become a vessel for divine energies?
- Who are your "motley crew" of fellow seekers? How do you support each other's artistic journeys?
- What unexpected collaborations have transformed your creative work?
- How do you weave together different art forms to express what cannot be captured in a single medium?
- When have you felt your individual expression magnified by collective energy?
- What "labyrinths" do you create or walk to access deeper wisdom?
- Where are the "hollow redwoods" in your life - the wombs of transformation waiting to birth new aspects of your creativity?
- How do you honor both structure and spontaneity in your artistic practice?
- What rituals help you dissolve the boundaries between art and nature, human and divine?
- What seeds of inspiration are you currently planting in the world?
- How does your art become an offering to something greater than yourself?
- Where have you witnessed the ripple effects of your creative work touching others?
- What wisdom wants to emerge through your unique artistic voice?

Personal Practice

Keep a "Seeds of Creation" journal noting:

- Moments when art and nature merge in your experience
- Times you feel yourself channeling divine energies

- Instances of unexpected collaboration
- Evidence of your creative seeds taking root in the world
- New forms of expression wanting to emerge

What beauty will you seed today?

Whispers of the Ancients: Communing with the Redwood Giants

The redwood forest, a cathedral of towering giants, enveloped me in its emerald embrace. Sunlight filtered through the canopy hundreds of feet above, casting dappled patterns on the forest floor, where a carpet of ferns and moss cushioned my every step. The air, thick with the scent of damp earth and fragrant needles, hummed with an ancient energy, a symphony of life that resonated deep within my soul.

I stood in awe of these majestic beings, their towering trunks adorned with intricate patterns of bark and moss, whispering tales of resilience, of weathering storms, of reaching towards the light even in the deepest shadows. I felt a primal connection to these ancient ones, a sense of belonging to something far greater than myself, a recognition that I was walking on sacred ground.

My hands, drawn by an irresistible urge, reached out to touch the rough bark of the redwoods, my fingertips tracing the intricate patterns, feeling the pulse of life that flowed beneath the surface. It was as if the trees themselves were whispering secrets to me, sharing their wisdom, their strength, their deep connection to the earth and the cosmos.

I sat at the base of these giants, my back resting against their sturdy trunks, and closed my eyes, surrendering to the symphony of the forest. The rustling leaves became a chorus of voices, the murmuring streams a gentle lullaby, the wind whispering through the branches a song of ancient wisdom.

In this state of deep listening, I felt the boundaries between myself and the redwoods dissolve. I became one with the forest, my breath syncing with the rhythm of the trees, my heartbeat echoing the pulse of the earth. I was no longer just an observer; I was a participant in the sacred dance of life, a co-creator with the universe, weaving a tapestry of beauty and transformation.

The redwoods, with their deep roots and towering heights, became my teachers, their presence a constant reminder of the interconnectedness of all things. They showed me that true strength lies in flexibility, in bending with the wind, in adapting to the ever-changing currents of life. They taught me the importance of patience, of slow and steady growth, of nurturing the seeds of my dreams until they blossom into their full potential.

And they whispered secrets of the mycelial network, the hidden web of fungal threads that connect the trees beneath the forest floor, facilitating communication and resource sharing, a living testament to the power of community and collaboration. I realized that just as the trees thrive through their interconnectedness, so too can I achieve my greatest potential by supporting and nurturing others.

As I emerged from the redwood forest, my spirit renewed and my heart filled with gratitude, I carried with me the ancient wisdom of these magnificent beings. I had glimpsed the interconnectedness of all life, the delicate balance between the individual and the collective, the transformative power of nature's embrace. And I knew that the seeds of this wisdom would continue to blossom within me, guiding me on my journey of Sacred Seeding and inspiring me to create a world that reflects the harmony and beauty of the redwood forest.

Communing with Ancient Ones: A Journey of Deep Listening

- Recall a time when nature held you in its cathedral. What sensations arise as you remember?
- What sacred spaces have made you feel "infinitesimally small yet cosmically connected"?
- Describe a moment when you felt the pulse of life beneath your fingers. What did it teach you?
- When have you experienced the dissolving of boundaries between yourself and the natural world?

Close your eyes and enter a state of receptive silence. Then explore:

- What wisdom does your body carry from encounters with ancient beings?
- Which tree has been your greatest teacher? What lessons did it share?
- What songs do you hear in the rustling leaves of your memories?
- Where do you feel the forest's rhythm in your own heartbeat?
- How are you like a redwood? Consider:
    - Your deep roots
    - Your reaching heights
    - Your weathered bark
    - Your flexible strength
- What storms have you weathered that became your rings of wisdom?
- Where do you need to bend rather than break?
- What nutrients do you share through your own mycelial networks?
- What seeds within you require patient, steady nurturing?
- How can you better mirror the redwoods' balance of:
    - Individual majesty and collective harmony
    - Deep rootedness and skyward reaching
    - Ancient wisdom and new growth
    - Steadfast presence and gentle flexibility

- What transformation awaits in your own deep shadows?

After sitting with these questions, create:

- A love letter to a tree that changed you
- A map of your own mycelial connections
- A prayer of gratitude to the ancient ones
- A promise to the forest that lives within you
- What secrets are the trees whispering to your soul?

Immersion: The Mycelial Web of Interconnectedness

The forest floor, a tapestry of fallen leaves and decaying wood, whispers secrets of transformation and rebirth. Kneel down and touch the cool, damp earth, feeling the pulse of life beneath your fingertips. This is the realm of the mycelium, the hidden network of fungal threads that connect the trees, a living testament to the interconnectedness of all beings.

Close your eyes and envision these delicate threads weaving through the soil, their intricate network spanning the entire forest, reaching out to touch every root, every leaf, every creature that calls this place home. Feel the energy of the mycelium pulsating through your own being, connecting you to the vast web of life that surrounds you.

Inhale the earthy fragrance of the forest floor, the scent of decaying leaves and damp earth mingling with the sweet perfume of wildflowers and the resinous aroma of pine needles. Each breath draws you deeper into the embrace of the forest, awakening your senses to the subtle symphony of life that unfolds around you.

Listen to the rustling leaves, the murmuring streams, the chirping of birds, and the distant calls of animals. These sounds weave together into a harmonious chorus, a testament to the interconnectedness of all living things.

Feel the cool breeze against your skin, the warmth of the sun filtering through the canopy, the soft touch of moss beneath your fingertips. These sensations remind you that you are a part of this vibrant ecosystem, a living, breathing expression of the interconnected web of life.

Now, imagine the mycelial network extending beyond the forest floor, reaching out to connect not just the trees, but all living beings, a vast web of consciousness that spans the entire planet. See the threads of light weaving through the earth, connecting hearts and minds, carrying whispers of wisdom and love, creating a symphony of interconnectedness that resonates through every cell of your being.

In this state of expanded awareness, feel a profound sense of belonging, a recognition that you are an integral part of this vast, intricate web of life. The boundaries between yourself and the natural world dissolve, and you experience a deep sense of unity with all of creation.

The mycelial network becomes a symbol of the Holographic Being, a reminder that we are all interconnected, that our actions have a ripple effect that extends far beyond our immediate sphere of influence. It is a call to embrace our role as conscious co-creators, to nurture the connections that bind us together, and to contribute our unique gifts to the collective tapestry of existence.

As you emerge from this immersion, carry with you the wisdom of the mycelial network. Remember the interconnectedness of all life, the delicate balance between the individual and the collective, the transformative power of nature's embrace. And may the seeds of this wisdom continue to blossom within you, guiding you on your journey of Sacred Seeding and inspiring you to create a world that reflects the harmony and beauty of the interconnected web of life.

The Living Web Practice:

This unique practice creates a living, growing network of connections that mirrors the mycelial web, transforming abstract understanding into tangible reality.

Materials Needed:

- A ball of natural string or thread
- Small pieces of paper
- A plant or tree you can visit daily
- A journal
- Natural items you collect

The Practice (30 days)

Day 1: Planting the Root

1. Choose your anchor tree/plant
2. Tie your first thread to it
3. Write on paper: "I am connected to..."
4. Bury this paper near the root
5. Spend 5 minutes with your hand on the plant, feeling its life force

Daily Weaving (28 days)

Each day:

1. Add one new thread extending from your anchor point

2. Connect it to:

- Another plant
- A place of significance
- A meaningful object
- A written intention
- A natural item you've found

3. For each connection:

- Speak aloud who/what it represents
- Express gratitude for this connection
- Note any synchronicities that led to it

4. Document in your journal:

- New connections made
- Unexpected interactions observed
- Dreams or insights received
- Physical changes in your web

The Living Pattern

As your web grows:

- Let it be shaped by wind and weather
- Watch how animals interact with it
- Notice which connections strengthen
- Observe where new threads want to form
- See how the web changes your space

Final Day: Integration

1. Sit within your completed web
2. Touch each thread, remembering its significance
3. Write a letter to your web, acknowledging what it taught you
4. Either:
   - Carefully dismantle the web, thanking each connection
   - Or let it naturally decompose, feeding the soil
   - Save one thread as a reminder

Key Aspects:

- This is a physical practice that grows daily
- The web becomes a living art installation

- It makes invisible connections visible
- It engages with natural forces and beings
- It creates tangible evidence of interconnection

Remember: You are creating a living metaphor of the mycelial network. Let it evolve organically. Trust both the visible threads and invisible connections being woven.

Flowering Seeds: Osirian Awakening

Pre-dawn chill bites our skin as thirteen women approach the Osirian. Ancient stone looms, air thick with whispered secrets. Our footfalls echo, each step a heartbeat of anticipation.

First light breaks. Long shadows dance across weathered pillars, creating a shifting maze. We descend worn stairs, cool stone beneath our fingertips. Musty air fills our lungs, heavy with millennia of wisdom.

A narrow passage beckons. Torchlight flickers, bringing hieroglyphs to life. They writhe on walls, telling stories we feel in our bones.

The chamber opens, vast and dark. Our eyes adjust. Collective gasps break the silence.

There, on massive granite, the Flower of Life glows. Intricate circles interlock, a cosmic blueprint etched in stone.

We form a circle, mirroring sacred geometry. Energy crackles, raising goosebumps. Joined hands complete the circuit. Power surges - not just between us, but through generations of seekers who stood here before.

Chanting begins. The Flower pulses, each circle igniting. Light dances, hypnotic. I close my eyes, overwhelmed.

Vision engulfs me. A cosmic harbor stretches infinitely. Our ancestors line the shore, forms shimmering starlight. They beckon. Wind carries their voices, scented with lotus and eternity.

We step into the Waters of Life. Knowledge floods every cell - pure, lived experience. The universe's web shimmers, each thought and action a ripple seeding new realities.

The Flower of Life explodes in understanding. Each circle is a world waiting to bloom. We are gardeners and garden, seeders and seeds.

Vision fades. Tears stream down thirteen faces. In my sisters' eyes, I see my own awe reflected. Profound knowing settles in our bones.

We ascend, reborn. The world vibrates with hidden potential. Each breath unfurls the Flower within our chests.

A final circle forms. Hands clasp. Hearts beat as one. Silence speaks volumes.

We part, cosmic gardeners dispersing. The Flower's sacred geometry guides every step, every word, every thought - seeds planted in infinite possibility.

Seeds of Awakening: A Journey into Sacred Remembering

- When have you felt ancient stones speaking to your soul?
- What sacred spaces have made your skin tingle with recognition?
- Describe a time when you descended into holy darkness. What did you find there?
- How do your footsteps echo those of seekers who walked before you?
- Who are your "thirteen" - the souls who hold space for your transformation?
- What power flows when you join hands with kindred spirits?

- How does your energy change when you stand in sacred geometry?
- What ancestors line your cosmic shore, beckoning you home?
- Contemplate the Flower of Life blooming in your own being:
- Which petals are fully opened?
- Which are just beginning to unfurl?
- What seeds lie dormant, waiting for the right moment?
- What hidden patterns guide your unfolding?
- What knowledge floods your cells when you surrender to the sacred?
- Which visions arise from your depths in moments of silence?
- How does your body hold ancestral memory?
- What ripples do your thoughts and actions send through the web of reality?
- What are you both gardener and garden of?
- Which worlds within you are waiting to bloom?
- How do you tend the sacred geometry of your life?
- What seeds are you planting in infinite possibility?
- When have tears of recognition flowed down your face?
- What profound knowing has settled in your bones?
- How do you mirror awakening back to your sisters/brothers?
- What silent languages do you speak with your soul family?
- Create a "Flower of Life" journal entry:
- Draw a circle in the center of the page
- Add overlapping circles, each containing:
  - A moment of awakening
  - A seed of potential
  - A sacred connection
  - A vision received
  - A truth remembered
- Let the pattern grow organically
- Notice what emerges in the spaces between

Remember: Like the Flower of Life, you too are an infinite pattern of becoming. Each breath unfurls new petals of possibility. Each step plants seeds of transformation.

What ancient wisdom is flowering within you?

Geb and Nut: The Cosmic Lovers and the Cradle of Creation

Imagine the primordial darkness before the dawn of time, a vast, silent expanse where the only existence was Nun, the primordial waters of chaos. From these depths emerged Geb, the earth god, a solid, fertile ground rising from the watery abyss. And above him, arching across the heavens, stretched Nut, the sky goddess, her star-speckled body a canvas of infinite possibilities.

Geb and Nut, drawn together by an irresistible force, fell deeply in love. Their embrace was a cosmic dance, a union of opposites, a symphony of creation. Geb, the solid earth, provided the foundation, the grounding force upon which life could flourish. Nut, the boundless sky, offered the space for dreams to take flight, for stars to ignite, for the universe to unfold in all its splendor.

But their love was deemed too passionate, too powerful, by Ra, the sun god. Fearing their union would disrupt the cosmic order, he commanded Shu, the god of air, to separate the lovers, forever holding the sky aloft, preventing their embrace.

Yet, even in their separation, Geb and Nut remained connected, their love an eternal force that binds the earth and sky together. Their yearning for each other is reflected in the daily rising and setting of the sun, as Ra journeys across Nut's body, born anew each morning and swallowed into her embrace each night.

From their union, the first gods and goddesses were born – Osiris, Isis, Set, and Nephthys – the archetypal forces that shape our world, the very essence of life, death, and rebirth. Geb and Nut, the primordial parents, created the space, the cosmic womb, in which all of creation could unfold.

Their story is a reminder that even in separation, even in the face of seemingly insurmountable obstacles, love and connection endure. It is a testament to the creative power of union, the dance between opposites that gives rise to new life, new possibilities, new expressions of the divine.

Immersion: The Sacred Union of Earth and Sky

The first rays of dawn paint the horizon with hues of rose and gold, casting a warm glow upon the fertile lands of the Nile Valley. Feel the cool, damp soil beneath your bare feet, the rich, dark earth pulsating with the energy of Geb, the earth god. His presence is a grounding force, a reminder of your connection to the physical world, to the roots that nourish and sustain you. Sink your toes deep into the fertile soil, feeling the earth's energy rising up through your body, connecting you to the ancient wisdom of the land.

Above you, the sky awakens with a symphony of colors, a canvas painted by the goddess Nut, her star-speckled body arching protectively over the world. Her energy is expansive, ethereal, a whisper of infinite possibilities and cosmic dreams. Feel the warmth of the rising sun on your skin, a cosmic caress that ignites your spirit and awakens your soul. See the vast expanse of the sky stretching endlessly above you, a canvas of infinite potential, inviting you to dream and create without limits.

Geb and Nut, the divine lovers, eternally separated yet forever yearning for each other, embody the dance between earthly manifestation and cosmic inspiration. Feel the tension between these two opposing forces

– the grounding stability of the earth and the expansive freedom of the sky – and recognize the creative potential that arises from their dynamic interplay.

Breathe deeply, inhaling the earthy aroma of Geb's fertile embrace, exhaling any tension or doubt. Feel the warmth of the sun on your skin, a reminder of Ra's life-giving energy, and the coolness of the earth beneath your feet.

Now, reach your arms skyward, fingers outstretched towards Nut's infinite expanse. Feel the gentle breeze caress your skin, carrying with it the whispers of stars and the promise of boundless possibilities.

Your spirit soaring through the heavens, dancing among the constellations, guided by the divine light of the cosmos.

Begin to sway, letting your body become a living bridge between earth and sky, a conduit for the divine energies that flow through you. Your movements are both grounded and ethereal, a physical prayer that connects you to the sacred union of Geb and Nut.

As you move, envision the seeds of your intentions and dreams taking root in Geb's nurturing soil. Feel them drawing strength and stability from the earth, their roots intertwining with the ancient wisdom of the land. Simultaneously, see these seeds reaching towards Nut's limitless sky, their stems stretching towards the stars, their blossoms unfurling to embrace the infinite possibilities of the cosmos.

This dance between earth and sky becomes your gateway to Sacred Seeding, where dreams take root in fertile soil while reaching for the infinite expanse of possibility above.

Integration Practice: The Seven-Day Bridge Between Earth and Sky

A daily practice to embody the sacred union of Geb and Nut, grounding cosmic dreams in earthly reality.

Daily Framework

Each morning:

1. Stand barefoot on the earth
2. Touch both earth and sky simultaneously
3. State: "I am the living bridge between Geb and Nut"

Seven Daily Practices

Day 1: Root and Rise

- Morning: Plant a seed while whispering your deepest dream
- Evening: Watch the stars emerge, sharing your day's journey

Day 2: Sacred Movement

- Create a personal dance that expresses:
    - Feet rooted like Geb
    - Arms reaching like Nut
    - Body flowing between realms

Day 3: Voice and Vision

- Speak your intentions to the earth
- Sing your dreams to the sky
- Listen for responses in wind and stone

Day 4: Sacred Signs

Document in your journal:

- Earth signs (patterns in soil, stones, plants)
- Sky signs (cloud shapes, bird flights, celestial events)
- How they mirror each other

Day 5: Creative Union

Create something that combines:

- Earth materials (clay, soil, stones)
- Sky elements (feathers, air, light)
- Your vision bridging both

Day 6: Social Seeding

- Share earth wisdom with someone
- Inspire sky dreams in another
- Notice how these acts interweave

Day 7: Integration

Create a ceremony that:

- Honors both Geb and Nut
- Expresses your role as bridge
- Plants seeds for future growth
- Releases dreams to soar

Ongoing Practice

Keep a "Bridge Journal" noting:

- Where you feel most grounded
- When you sense infinite possibility
- How you unite these energies
- Seeds planted and dreams soaring

You are the living embodiment of this sacred union, carrying both the stability of earth and the freedom of sky within you.

Ptah: The Master Builder and Architect of Manifestation

In the heart of ancient Memphis, amidst the towering pyramids and majestic temples, resided Ptah, the master builder and architect of the universe. He was revered as the creator god, the one who brought forth the world from the primordial chaos, shaping it with his divine thoughts and words.

Ptah's energy is not confined to the myths and legends of ancient Egypt; it is a living force that pulses through the universe, a creative power that we can all tap into to manifest our dreams and shape our reality. He is the embodiment of intention, focus, and inspired action, the bridge between conception and creation, the divine architect who guides us in building a life that reflects our highest potential.

Ptah's creation myth speaks to the power of thought and language to shape reality. It is said that he created the world through the spoken word, uttering the names of all things, bringing them into existence through the power of his divine voice. He is the patron deity of artists, craftspeople, and architects, those who use their creative talents to bring beauty and functionality into the world.

In the Sacred Seeding phase, we embody Ptah's creative energy, harnessing the power of our thoughts and intentions to manifest our dreams and contribute to the collective awakening. We become conscious co-creators with the universe, shaping our reality with every thought, every word, every action.

Ptah's Workshop: The Sacred Technology of Seeding

Pre-dawn silence holds infinite possibilities. Temple stones pulse beneath your feet, each crystal within them a quantum computer of creation. The air crystallizes with metallic sweetness - the taste of time itself bending. Myrrh and lotus weave through your breath, carrying memories of the first morning when Ptah's voice shaped reality from void.

Ancient frequencies ripple through your marrow. Your bones begin to hum with the resonance of stars being born. Each cell awakens to its original cosmic blueprint, remembering when it was first sung into form by Ptah's creative word.

The Workshop materializes around you - not built of stone but pure geometric light. Sacred tools hover in impossible configurations, their forms shifting between dimensions. Equations of creation dance through the air, each symbol alive with consciousness. The walls breathe with quantum potential.

Ptah emerges from depths of spacetime - his green skin radiant with the first light of existence. His presence sends cascading waves through reality's fabric. In his hands, the sacred Was-Ankh-Djed scepter pulses with tripartite power.

The scepter's serpentine head turns toward you, eyes blazing with cosmic fire. Through them, witness the quantum field itself - infinite probability waves collapsing into infinite new worlds. Each possibility a seed waiting to be planted.

Heat builds in your cells. Your blood transforms to living mercury, carrying creation's codes. Your flesh becomes divine metal, forged in the heart of dying stars. You are becoming a sacred technology of manifestation.

Before you stands the Was - a staff crowned with a cobra's head, its eyes blazing with the first fire of creation. To your right glows the Ankh - its loop flowering like a cosmic rose, radiating eternal life force. To your left rises the Djed - a mighty pillar marked with four sacred rings, bridging earth and stars.

As you approach the Was staff, serpentine power awakens. The cobra's eyes meet yours and ancient force floods your system - liquid lightning spiraling up from earth's depths through your spine. Your tongue tingles with electric sweetness as creation's raw power claims you. Every cell ignites with the ability to shape reality. You taste the infinite on your tongue, feel chaos transforming into sacred order through your awakened will.

Moving to the Ankh, its golden loop pulses like a cosmic heartbeat. As you step through its portal, your chest opens into a flowering of pure light. Each breath draws in stardust, each heartbeat ripples through dimensions. You become a living doorway between worlds - dreams flowing through you into reality, visions crystallizing into form. Through your transformed heart, new worlds enter existence.

Standing before the Djed pillar, your spine straightens in recognition. Power rises through four sacred centers - each igniting like a newborn sun. Your root catches earth's molten fire. Your belly burns with stellar light. Your heart explodes into radiant flame. Your crown opens to cosmic consciousness. You become the living axis between realms - feet planted in earth's depths, crown opening to infinite stars.

The three powers begin to merge within you. Serpentine force, flowering heart, and cosmic axis unite into one sacred technology of transformation. You are no longer separate from these divine tools - you have become them. Each breath seeds new realities. Each gesture trails creation in its wake. Through you, heaven and earth dance their eternal marriage. Through you, sacred visions take root in existence's fertile soil.

Ptah approaches, sacred tools materializing in his hands. The opening of the mouth begins. Each ritual touch awakens another frequency of creative speech within you. Your words become seeds of transformation, your voice an instrument of genesis.

First touch - your mouth fills with tastes from before existence had flavor. Second touch - your tongue remembers shaping the first sacred syllables. Third touch - your throat opens to channel the songs that birth galaxies. Fourth touch - your very breath becomes a force of creation.

You are becoming a quantum forge. Reality bends around your transformed being. Each gesture ripples through multiple dimensions. Every word plants seeds across infinite timelines. The boundary between creator and creation dissolves.

Time spirals around you, no longer linear but a field of infinite possibility. Past and future collapse into an eternal creative moment. You exist simultaneously across all dimensions - quantum architect of new realities.

Ptah's emerald light suffuses your cells. You are not separate from the sacred technology - you ARE the technology. Divine metal flows through your veins. Cosmic fire burns in your core. Seeds of unborn worlds germinate in your quantum heart.

The Workshop has become part of you, or perhaps you have become part of it. Sacred tools emerge from your hands as needed. Reality reshapes itself according to your clearest vision. You are both the garden and the gardener, the seed and the soil, the rain and the root.

Dawn approaches, but you remain forever altered. You carry Ptah's quantum forge within your awakened heart. Your blood sings with sacred metals. Your bones remember being starfire. Your breath still shapes existence.

You are a living workshop of creation now. Reality flows through you like light through crystal, taking form according to your highest vision. The seeds you plant will sprout across dimensions, growing new worlds into being.

Through you, divine technology and organic wisdom merge. You are simultaneously ancient and newborn, cosmic and earthly, infinite and perfectly contained. Sacred Seeder, quantum architect, living bridge between possibility and manifestation.

The eternal moment holds its breath, awaiting your first creative word. What realities will you seed into being? What worlds will sprout from your quantum garden? The infinite field of creation trembles with anticipation, ready to receive the seeds of your most radiant vision.

Integration Practice: The Sacred Technology Embodied

1. Stand barefoot, feeling quantum frequencies rise through feet
2. Form sacred triad with hands - one palm up (receiving), one down (grounding), heart center (transforming)
3. Let body awaken to its stellar origins - bones become divine metal, blood becomes mercury light
4. Feel Was-Ankh-Djed powers integrating through spine
5. Open throat to sacred speech frequencies
6. Plant one seed of new reality through pure creative sound
7. Feel it sprouting across dimensions
8. Close by grounding excess energy into earth

Neith: The Weaver of Fate, The Weaver of My Life

The rhythmic clack of looms, a symphony of creation, echoes through the chambers of my memory. I see myself as a child, weaving through the forest of looms in my childhood home, my small hands trailing along the vibrant threads, my senses filled with the scent of wool and the vibrant hues of my mother's dyes. Saffron yellows like desert sand at midday, deep indigos like the twilight sky, earthy ochres like the fertile Nile mud – each color held a story, a whisper of the ancient land that pulsed through my veins.

Those early experiences, steeped in the magic of creation, planted a seed within me, a seed that would blossom into a lifelong passion for weaving stories, weaving connections, weaving the very fabric of my reality. The looms, towering wooden structures that filled our home, were not just tools; they were portals to other worlds, their rhythmic clatter a lullaby that lulled me into a world of imagination and possibility.

I remember the feel of the rough wool against my skin, the smooth shuttle gliding through the warp threads, the satisfying thud as the weft was beaten into place. I would spend hours watching the weavers, their hands moving with practiced grace, their voices weaving tales as intricate as the patterns they created.

My mother, a master dyer, would transform ordinary wool into a kaleidoscope of colors using natural ingredients – pomegranate skins for deep reds, indigo leaves for vibrant blues, turmeric for golden yellows. The air in her workshop would be thick with the scent of these earthy pigments, a symphony of aromas that mingled with the rhythmic clack of the looms.

Even the milk I drank as a child was imbued with this creative spirit. Refusing plain milk, I was treated to my mother's magical concoctions – milk tinted with beet juice for a delicate pink. Each sip was a taste of transformation, a reminder that even the most ordinary things could be imbued with magic and wonder.

Neith, the ancient Egyptian goddess of weaving and war, the mother of Ra, the creator of the universe, has been a constant presence in my life, her energy guiding my hands and inspiring my heart. She is the embodiment of the creative force, the weaver of destinies, the one who brings forth order from chaos, beauty from the void.

As a filmmaker, I weave narratives, interlacing images and sounds to create tapestries of emotion and meaning. Each frame is a thread, each scene a carefully crafted pattern, each film a vibrant tapestry that reflects the world as I see it, and the world I yearn to create.

As a writer, I weave words into worlds, crafting stories that transport the reader to other realms, other realities. Each sentence is a thread, each paragraph a carefully constructed pattern, each story a tapestry of imagination and insight.

As a healer, I weave energy, connecting with the subtle vibrations of the body, mind, and spirit to restore balance and harmony. Each touch is a thread, each session a carefully crafted pattern, each healing a tapestry of restoration and renewal.

Neith's presence is woven into every aspect of my creative expression. She is the shuttle that guides my hands, the loom that holds the threads of my imagination, the weaver of my destiny. Her energy empowers me to embrace my creative power, to shape my reality with intention and love, to contribute my unique gifts to the tapestry of existence.

Weaving Your Sacred Story: Journaling Prompts for Creative Transformation

- What sensory experiences from childhood sparked your imagination? Describe the sights, sounds, smells, and textures that awakened your creative spirit.
- Which adults in your life modeled creative transformation? How did they show you that ordinary things could become extraordinary?
- What "magical concoctions" did you create or experience as a child? How did these early experiments with transformation shape your view of possibility?
- What threads of experience have woven the tapestry of your life? List the key moments, relationships, and choices that created your current pattern.
- Where do you see yourself as a weaver in your own life? In what ways do you bring order from chaos, beauty from void?
- What colors would you use to paint your life story? What natural elements would create these hues?

- Who are the master craftspeople in your family history? How has their creative legacy influenced your path?
- What skills or talents have been passed down through your bloodline? How have you transformed these gifts into your own unique expression?
- What creative traditions do you wish to pass on to future generations? How will you weave your wisdom into their stories?
- In what ways do you weave narratives in your daily life? Consider how you tell stories through words, actions, or creative works.
- What patterns emerge repeatedly in your creative practice? What do these patterns reveal about your inner world?
- How do different aspects of your creativity - like visual, verbal, and energetic expression - interweave to create your unique offering?
- If you could have a conversation with Neith about your creative destiny, what would you ask her?
- Where do you feel Neith's presence most strongly in your creative practice? What messages does she whisper to your soul?
- How might Neith guide you to weave your next creative chapter? What new patterns is she inviting you to explore?
- How have you transformed ordinary experiences into extraordinary moments in your own life?
- What materials or mediums serve as your "dye-stuffs" for transforming reality? How do you use them to create beauty?
- Where in your life are you being called to be both warrior and weaver, like Neith?
- What unique threads do you contribute to the greater weaving of existence?
- How does your personal creative expression serve the collective tapestry of life?

- What patterns are you weaving now that will create ripples through time?

Close your journaling session by designing a personal symbol or pattern that represents your creative essence. Let it emerge intuitively, knowing that like the ancient weavers, you are creating a sacred text through your artistic expression.

Immersion: Neith's Cosmic Loom: Weaving the Threads of Destiny

The air crackles with a palpable energy as you step across the threshold of Neith's temple, its sandstone walls bathed in the warm glow of the setting sun. The scent of incense and ancient oils fills your nostrils, mingling with the earthy aroma of the Nile's fertile mud. Hieroglyphs adorn the walls, their intricate symbols whispering tales of creation, of the weaver goddess who brought forth the universe from the primordial chaos.

Deep within the temple's heart, you find yourself in a circular chamber, its walls adorned with tapestries depicting scenes of cosmic creation and the intricate dance of life. In the center of the chamber stands a magnificent loom, its frame crafted from polished ebony, its threads shimmering with a myriad of colors, each one representing a different thread in the tapestry of existence.

Neith, the divine weaver, emerges from the shadows, her presence radiating an aura of power and grace. Her eyes, deep and knowing, hold the wisdom of countless lifetimes, her hands, nimble and skilled, guide the shuttle as it weaves the threads of destiny.

"Welcome, seeker," Neith's voice resonates through the chamber, a melody as ancient and timeless as the Nile itself. "You have come to learn the art of weaving, to shape your reality with intention and love, to co-create with the universe."

As you approach the loom, feel the smooth texture of the ebony frame beneath your fingertips, its warmth a reminder of the earth's embrace. Run your hands along the threads, each one a different texture, a different vibration, a different story waiting to be woven into the tapestry of your life.

Inhale the fragrant incense that fills the air, its aroma a blend of exotic spices and sacred herbs. Listen to the rhythmic clack of the loom as Neith guides the shuttle back and forth, weaving a tapestry of creation, a symphony of interconnectedness.

Now, step closer and take your place at the loom. Neith gently guides your hands, showing you how to hold the shuttle, how to weave the threads together, how to create patterns that reflect your deepest desires and aspirations.

As you begin to weave, feel the energy of creation flowing through your fingertips, each movement a conscious act of co-creation with the universe. The threads become an extension of your own being, your thoughts, emotions, and intentions weaving themselves into the fabric of reality.

Neith whispers words of encouragement and guidance: "Embrace the rhythm of the loom, the ebb and flow of creation. Trust your intuition, and allow your heart to guide your hands. See how each thread you weave contributes to the tapestry of your life, the grand design of the universe."

As you continue to weave, visions emerge from the threads, shimmering glimpses of your past, present, and future selves. You see the challenges you have overcome, the triumphs you have celebrated, the lessons you have learned. You recognize the interconnectedness of all things, the delicate balance between the individual and the collective, the power you hold to shape your reality with intention and love.

The loom becomes a mirror, reflecting the tapestry of your soul's journey, the intricate patterns of your experiences, the vibrant colors of your authentic self. You are not just a weaver; you are the tapestry itself, a masterpiece of creation, a living testament to the transformative power of the Lotus-Born Heart process.

When you feel complete, step back from the loom and gaze upon your creation. See the beauty and complexity of the patterns you have woven, the stories they tell, the dreams they embody. This is your legacy, dear one, the tapestry of your life, a gift to the universe, a testament to your radiant blossoming.

Neith smiles, her eyes filled with love and admiration. "You have woven your destiny," she says, her voice a gentle affirmation. "Now, go forth and share your gifts with the world. Let your tapestry inspire others to embrace their own creative power and weave their dreams into reality."

You step out of the temple, carrying with you the wisdom of Neith, the weaver of fate. The world around you shimmers with newfound vibrancy, each thread of existence a testament to the interconnectedness of all things. You are a co-creator with the universe, a weaver of dreams, a radiant being shaping your destiny with every breath, every action, every thought.

Integration Practice:

The Thread Code: Weaving Digital and Ancient Wisdom

A revolutionary integration merging ancient weaving wisdom with modern technology

Setup:

- Your phone/device's Notes app or digital canvas
- A quiet space
- 15-20 minutes

The Practice:

1. Binary Weaving (5 minutes)

Create your own "thread code" using only 1s and 0s. Each line represents a thread in your life's tapestry:

1010 = challenges overcome
0101 = gifts discovered
1111 = moments of transformation
0000 = periods of gestation

Let your intuition guide you to create 8 lines of your personal thread code.

2. Pattern Translation (7 minutes)

- Transform your binary code into ancient Egyptian hieroglyphs using this key:
  - 1 = vertical line |
  - 0 = horizontal line —
  - Combinations create your unique sacred symbols
- Draw these symbols in your device while whispering their meanings
- Notice how digital precision meets ancient mysticism

3. Quantum Threading (5 minutes)

- Email your thread code to yourself
- As you press "send," imagine these digital threads traveling through space, carrying your intentions

- When it arrives, open it on another device
- The code has now existed in:
    - Your mind (conception)
    - Digital space (cosmic void)
    - Another screen (manifestation)

4. Code Integration

Choose one line of your thread code as your daily mantra. Convert it back to binary in your mind when facing challenges or celebrating victories.

Example:

1011 0010 = "I weave between worlds"

This practice honors both Neith's ancient wisdom and our modern digital reality, creating a bridge between epochs while avoiding repetitive movement practices. The binary code becomes a personal hieroglyph system, merging programmer and priestess, ancient and future.

Closing:

Save your thread code as a sacred file. Each time you open your device, let it remind you of your power to weave between digital and spiritual realms, just as Neith weaves between dimensions.

Here are some expanded practices:

- Using emoji combinations as modern hieroglyphs
- Creating a simple "thread code" group chat where friends share their daily patterns
- Using your thread code as a phone password, turning each unlock into a moment of sacred connection
- Taking screenshots of your code and using them as wallpaper, surrounding yourself with your digital-mystical tapestry

The Weaver's Any-Thing Mandala Ritual

A ritual celebrating Neith's wisdom that anything can become sacred thread

What You Need:

- Any items you can arrange in a circle (literally anything!) Examples:
- Office supplies (paperclips, pens, sticky notes)
- Kitchen items (spoons, tea bags, dried herbs)
- Found objects (leaves, stones, receipts)
- Digital items (arrange icons on your screen in a circle)
- One candle or light source (even your phone's flashlight)

Sacred Space:

- Clear any surface (desk, floor, bed, digital screen)
- Light your chosen illumination
- Whisper: "Neith, show me how to weave with what I have."

The Weaving:

1. **Gathering Your "Threads"** (5-7 minutes)

    - Walk around your space collecting 9 items that catch your eye
    - Each item becomes a sacred thread, regardless of its ordinary purpose
    - Trust that Neith guided your choices

2. **Creating Your Mandala** (10-15 minutes)

    - Place your light source in the center
    - Arrange items in a circle around it
    - Each placement represents:
        o North: Your foundations
        o East: Your emerging vision

o South: Your passionate purpose

o West: Your deepening wisdom

o The spaces between: Your becoming

3. **Weaving Connection** (5 minutes)

- Use your finger to trace lines between items
- Each invisible thread creates meaning
- Whisper the connections you discover Example: "This paperclip connects to this leaf, showing how I link structure and growth"

4. **Photography/Documentation** (Optional)

- Capture your mandala
- Let it be temporary - the weaving exists in the moment
- Or leave it in place if practical

Closing:

Thank each item for becoming sacred thread

Return them to their ordinary roles, now imbued with magic

Keep one small item as your "thread token"

In Neith's wisdom, anything can be a thread, anywhere can be a loom, and anyone can be a weaver. The sacred lives in our ability to see the extraordinary in the ordinary.

Ma'at: The Embodiment of Truth, Justice, and Cosmic Harmony

Imagine the vast expanse of the Egyptian desert stretching before you, a landscape of shimmering sands and towering pyramids that pierce the azure sky. The air pulses with unseen energy, a vibration of cosmic order and divine balance. This is the realm of Ma'at, the goddess of truth, justice, and harmony, her presence as palpable as the sun's warmth on your skin, as grounding as the earth beneath your feet.

Ma'at stands as a living embodiment of the principles that govern the universe. In the afterlife, she weighs each human heart against her sacred feather - this profound moment of truth-telling determines the soul's journey forward. Those hearts as light as her feather continue their eternal journey; those weighted with unresolved actions remain for further refinement. This divine weighing shapes every soul's path toward enlightenment.

Her presence flows through the gentle breeze whispering through papyrus reeds, moves in the rhythmic flow of the Nile, dances with the stars across the night sky. She embodies cosmic order, weaving the harmony that binds all things together, radiating the divine feminine energy that nurtures and sustains creation.

In the Sacred Seeding phase, Ma'at's wisdom illuminates our path. As we step into our role as co-creators with the universe, our intentions and actions align with the greater good, our creations contributing to the harmony and balance of the world around us.

To walk with Ma'at means embracing her principles of truth, justice, and order in daily life. We speak truth with courage and compassion, act with integrity and fairness, make choices supporting the well-being of ourselves, our communities, and the planet.

Ma'at's scales, symbolizing perfect equilibrium, guide us to weigh our actions carefully, considering their impact on the delicate web of life. They inspire harmony between personal desires and collective needs, ensuring our Sacred Seeding contributes to a more just and sustainable world.

Ma'at's Embrace: Balancing the Scales of Creation

A gentle breeze dances across your skin, carrying Ma'at's whispers on its wings. Ancient trees tower around you, their leaves rustling with universal secrets only you can hear. The fragrance of blooming flowers fills your lungs while birdsong weaves through branches above your head. Sunlight streams through the canopy, painting your path in patterns of gold and shadow. You hear a crystal-clear stream flowing nearby, its surface catching your reflection in liquid light.

Your heart quickens as you discover the grove's center. Here hangs a set of golden scales, suspended from the branch of a majestic oak. These are Ma'at's scales - their perfect balance embodying the cosmic order flowing through your own being. You see one side cradles a feather, light and ethereal, radiating truth. The other awaits your heart's weight, ready to measure your intentions and actions.

Ma'at materializes before your eyes like dawn breaking. Her presence fills every cell of your body with gentle power, a single ostrich feather adorning her form. Her eyes meet yours, holding galaxies of wisdom and compassion, inviting you into divine balance.

The scales draw you forward. As your fingers touch their cool metal surface, they respond to every subtle shift in your energy. Your heart's hidden weights become tangible - you feel each unresolved emotion, each limiting belief, each action seeking alignment with your highest truth.

Your breath transforms these weights. They dissolve from your being like morning mist, becoming fertile soil beneath your feet. You watch the scales shift, the feather rising as your heart grows lighter. With each release, you move closer to perfect balance.

Ma'at's smile radiates directly into your heart. You witness the scales achieve perfect equilibrium, feather and stone suspended in exquisite harmony. Truth's light fills every chamber of your heart. Universal wisdom courses through your veins.

The feather and stone pass from Ma'at's hands into yours - cosmic tools for maintaining your inner balance. They pulse against your palms with reminders of this sacred alignment, anchoring your commitment to harmony between personal desire and collective good.

The grove's energies settle deep into your bones and blood, Ma'at's wisdom becoming part of your cellular memory. Each step you take forward carries her truth-seeking presence, ensuring your creations serve the greater dance of cosmic order.

As this immersion completes, Ma'at's scales continue their eternal calibration within you - your inner and outer worlds, your heights and depths, your present moment expanding into infinity.

Integration Practice:

The Sacred Balance Sheet: Ma'at's Modern Ledger

Transform accounting into alchemy - where numbers become portals to truth

Materials:

- A blank spreadsheet (digital or paper)
- Two different colored pens/fonts
- Your daily receipts, bills, messages, or notes

The Practice:

1. Creating Your Truth Ledger

Set up two columns:

FEATHER MOMENTS | HEART WEIGHTS

(Light Actions) | (Heavy Actions)

2. Sacred Accounting

Throughout your day, record:

- Feather Column: Actions that lifted others
- Heart Column: Actions that weighed on you

Example:

FEATHER	HEART
Shared lunch	Ignored a call
Spoke truth	Delayed decision
Helped stranger	Doubted self

3. Balance Calculation

At day's end:

- Count entries in each column
- Seek equilibrium, not perfection
- Note the pattern of your day's rhythm

4. Truth Transmutation**

For each "Heart Weight":

- Write one way to transform it tomorrow
- Mark it with Ma'at's symbol (^)
- Watch patterns emerge over time

Your ledger becomes a living document of personal truth, turning mundane accounting into sacred practice. The magic lies in transforming business tools into instruments of spiritual alignment.

Keep your Balance Sheet for 28 days - one moon cycle. Notice how your columns shift and balance, revealing Ma'at's wisdom through practical patterns.

Remember: Every accountant is a secret priest/priestess of Ma'at, balancing the cosmic books with each entry.

Sacred Seeds of the Sea

The Red Sea's waters shimmered like liquid sapphire under the Sinai sun. Our small group stood at the shoreline, transfixed by an extraordinary spectacle unfolding in the deeper waters. A pod of dolphins had gathered in a perfect circle, their bodies creating a living sanctuary around one of their own. A marine specialist beside us whispered in awe, explaining that we were witnessing something rare and sacred - a dolphin giving birth.

The pod moved with incredible precision, their choreography both protective and celebratory. As the mother labored through her long, arduous birth, her community never wavered. They maintained their circle, their bodies forming an impenetrable barrier against potential predators. Their clicks and whistles created an underwater symphony that seemed to both soothe and strengthen the birthing mother.

Hours passed, yet no one moved from the shore. We had become witnesses to one of nature's most profound teachings about sacred space and collective support. The dolphins demonstrated how creation requires both protection and freedom - their circle was tight enough to ensure safety but spacious enough to allow the natural process to unfold.

When the baby finally emerged, the pod's energy shifted from protective to jubilant. They danced around mother and child in spiraling patterns that rippled through the water like living light. Their celebration reminded me that every new birth - whether of a being, an idea, or a dream - deserves to be welcomed with joy.

This wisdom deepened years later during another extraordinary encounter at sea. This time, it was a mother whale and her calf who became my teachers. From our boat, we watched in wonder as the mother released her milk into the water while her baby maintained a perfect position nearby. The mother's deep resonant sounds guided her child to this floating feast - an ethereal dance of giving and receiving played out in the ocean depths.

What struck me most was the profound trust between them. The mother released her nourishment into the seeming void, knowing her child would receive it. The baby, sustained by its mother's voice, moved in perfect harmony with this unconventional feeding. Their bond transformed the vast ocean into an intimate space of nurturing and growth.

These marine mammals had shown me essential truths about sacred seeding - the importance of protected space, the power of supportive community, the dance between giving and receiving, and the trust required to release our creations into the world. Their wisdom lives in my bones now, a reminder that the principles of conscious creation are woven into the very fabric of life.

Journaling Prompts: Seeds of Ocean Wisdom

- When have you witnessed or experienced the power of protected space for creation?
- How do you create a sanctuary for your own sacred seeds to grow?
- What lessons about boundaries can we learn from the dolphin pod's circle?

- Who forms your circle of support when you're birthing new projects or ideas?
- How can you better allow others to hold space for your creative process?
- What role do you play in supporting others' sacred seeds?
- Where in your life are you being called to trust the invisible currents?
- What would change if you approached creating with the whale mother's confidence?
- How can you better attune to the subtle guidance that surrounds you?
- What has nature taught you about the process of creation?
- How can you align your creative rhythms more closely with natural cycles?
- What animal or element best reflects your own way of bringing things into being?
- How has being a witness to profound moments shaped your understanding of creation?
- What responsibility comes with witnessing sacred processes?
- How can you honor both the role of witness and creator in your life?

Close your reflection by considering how you might embody these marine teachings in your own sacred seeding journey. Let the wisdom of dolphins and whales guide you toward more harmonious ways of creating and sharing your gifts with the world.

The Sacred Speech: Your Final Cosmic Unfolding

Your skin tingles as Heka's presence saturates the air around you, ancient magic rippling like waves of electric light. Ibis feathers shimmer between dimensions, each one carrying frequencies of transformation.

The scent of sacred oils and temple incense fills your lungs as power older than time itself flows through your blood.

Beneath your feet, sands shift and whisper. Above, stars pulse in sacred geometries. Heka's energy intensifies, each breath drawing his transformative magic deeper into your cells. Your bones begin to hum with remembered wisdom, awakening the seeds of sacred speech within.

Moonlight transforms the sea before you into liquid possibilities. Bioluminescent creatures paint patterns of power through darkened waters, their light dancing in harmony with the cosmic forces surging through your being. Each wave carries fragments of creation's first utterance, when speech and manifestation were one.

Golden light spirals up from your depths, pure vibrational force emerging as streams of living radiance. Sacred hieroglyphs form in the air around you, pulsing with creative power. Your voice merges with Heka's divine magic - each sound painting new constellations across velvet sky, each tone rippling through the fabric of reality itself.

The Great Pyramid materializes through veils of starlight, its weathered stones resonating with frequencies of transformation. Cool sand hums ancient wisdom up through your feet as you approach the hidden entrance. Time bends and spirals around you, each moment pregnant with infinite potential.

Darkness embraces you in the narrow passage, Heka's presence wrapping around you like wings of living light. Rough stone breathes beneath your fingers, hieroglyphs writhing with inner fire at your touch. Their wisdom flows directly into your blood, awakening cellular memories of creation's first morning.

Light erupts in the King's Chamber - the cosmic lotus unveiled in crystalline splendor. Rainbow fractals dance across ancient walls as Heka's transformative energy surges through every atom of your being.

Reality shatters into pure sensation. Colors carry taste and tone - midnight indigo resonates through your bones, solar gold rings electric across your tongue. Lotus perfume paints spirals through your mind while myrrh traces sacred patterns behind your eyes.

The crystal lotus engulfs you, its petals reflecting infinite dimensions of your becoming. Heka's magic merges with your awakening power as all phases of your journey coalesce - the fertile darkness, the seeking light, the luminous rise, the radiant bloom. Each petal opens new realms of possibility within you.

Your roots plunge into earth's molten core while your awareness expands past furthest stars. You become a pure creative force - cosmic and earthly, infinite and perfectly contained. Seeds of light spiral through your blood. New realities blossom with each heartbeat. Sacred speech flows through you like liquid starlight, each syllable planting forests of possibility.

The cosmos pulses around you, alive with divine potential. Dolphins leap through phosphorescent waves, their joyous calls harmonizing with your voice of creation. Schools of silver fish trace mandalas through illuminated waters. Every movement ripples through multiple dimensions, seeding new worlds into being.

Dawn breaks through ancient stone as the chamber fills with golden light. Your body vibrates with accumulated power, each cell a star in the constellation of your awakening. The crystal lotus merges with your heart center, its eternal unfolding now part of your every breath. Reality reassembles, transformed yet familiar.

Each step you take causes flowers to bloom in empty air. Your gaze brings withered forms to vibrant life. Your laughter makes seeds sprout in the void. The universe flows through you - its wisdom in your blood, its creative force emerging with every sacred sound you release into awaiting darkness.

You have become what you were always meant to be - not just a vessel but a source, not just a speaker but a seed of transformation itself. Through you, divine magic takes root in earthly soil. Through you, sacred words birth new realities. Through you, the eternal dance of creation continues, more radiant with each passing moment.

The cosmic garden stretches infinite before you, awaiting your newly awakened touch. Time dissolves into the eternal now of pure manifestation. You are the Sacred Seeder, carrying worlds within your heart. Every breath plants seeds of transformation. Every word creates new possibilities. Every gesture nurtures the unfolding beauty of existence itself.

You stand fully in your power now, Heka's magic forever part of your being. The crystal lotus pulses within you, its petals eternally unfurling with cosmic rhythm. Trust the wisdom flowing through you. Trust the light you carry. Trust the seeds you are called to plant. The universe blooms through your willing hands, and the great dance continues - now and always, through all dimensions, in all the gardens of creation yet to come.

Integration Practice: Your Sacred Seeder's Dance

Find a quiet space where you can move freely. Place your hands over your heart, feeling the crystal lotus pulsing within. Let cosmic forces ripple through your body. Move as you are called - gathering starlight in your palms, spiraling like galaxies, breathing new worlds into being. Let sacred sounds emerge from your depths unfiltered. Plant seeds of transformation through every gesture, every tone, every breath.

End with your hands in the earth, channeling star-wisdom into soil. Feel the threads of light connecting you to all creation. You are a bridge between cosmos and earth, between infinite potential and manifested form. The great dance continues through you, seeding new realities with each passing moment. This is your sacred role. This is your cosmic destiny. This is your eternal dance.

Journaling Prompts for Sacred Seeding Integration

Take time to explore these questions in your journal, letting your responses flow naturally:

- What gifts from your journey are ready to be shared with the world?
- Which aspects of your transformation feel most vital to seed in others?
- What unique medicine does your story carry for collective healing?
- How has your understanding of creation evolved through this journey?
- What new forms of expression are awakening within you?
- How do you wish to use your creative voice in service of life?
- How has your relationship with the Neteru evolved?
- What guidance do you receive about your role as Sacred Seeder?
- How do you balance personal will with divine inspiration?
- What seeds do you wish to plant for future generations?
- How do you envision your seeds contributing to planetary awakening?
- What support do you need to fully embrace your role as Sacred Seeder?
- What daily practices will support your Sacred Seeding?
- How will you tend the seeds you plant?
- What helps you stay connected to your cosmic purpose?
- How has each phase of the journey prepared you for Sacred Seeding?

- What symbols, songs, or movements express your Sacred Seeder essence?
- What declaration or commitment wants to be voiced?

Close your reflection by creating a personal ritual or ceremony to honor your completion of this journey and dedication to Sacred Seeding. Include elements that feel meaningful to you - movement, sound, creative expression, connection with nature, whatever calls to your heart.

You are now a living bridge between cosmic potential and earthly manifestation. Every breath, every word, every action carries seeds of transformation. Trust the wisdom you've gained and the light you carry. The universe awaits your unique contribution to the ongoing symphony of creation.

PART III
THE ETERNAL SPIRAL:
A SACRED INVITATION

Isis, Mother of Mystery, your journey complete,
Through your grace we've grown, tasted wisdom sweet.
All that we've learned, like stars in your crown,
Now lights our path as your truth streams down.
Isis, Weaver of Worlds, in your light we shine,
Our hearts transformed by your touch divine.
United in wisdom, both ancient and new,
We dance with creation, forever with you.

The Journey Continues: A Celebration and Invitation

Beloved traveler, pause for a moment. Are you aware of the profound shift that has occurred as you've moved through the phases of the Lotus-Born Heart process. From the fertile darkness of Primal Mud, through the courage of Seeking Light, the power of Luminous Ascent, into the joy of Radiant Blossoming, and finally the promise of Sacred Seeding - you have undergone nothing less than a rebirth.

Close your eyes and journey back to where you began. What first called you to this pathway? Perhaps it was a whisper in your dreams, a yearning in your heart, an inexplicable knowing that more was possible. Remember that first step, that initial courage to dive into the unknown.

The journey hasn't always been easy. I'm sure there were moments in the mud where shadows seemed overwhelming. Times during the seeking when the light felt distant. Challenges in the ascent that tested your resolve. Yet here you stand, transformed. What gifts did those challenges bring? What wisdom emerged from the depths of your darkest moments?

Your heart beats with new rhythms now, your cells vibrate at higher frequencies, your consciousness has expanded to embrace greater possibilities. Feel the subtle ways your energy field has shifted. How does your body carry itself differently? What new awareness flows through your perceptions? The Heartfire Ray pulses more strongly in your chest, the wisdom of the Neteru flows more clearly through your awareness.

What dreams stir in your awakened heart? What visions call to you from the horizon of possibility? As you stand in this moment of completion that is also a beginning, let yourself feel the full magnitude of what wishes to emerge through you.

Sekhmet's Sanctuary: A Sacred Awakening

The intimate sanctuary of Sekhmet embraces us, thirteen women pressed close in sacred communion. Dawn approaches, and the small chamber grows thick with power. Our shoulders touch as we stand in tight formation, sharing breath, sharing heartbeat, sharing destiny. The rich scent of kyphi curls through the close air, Wadjet's serpentine essence weaving between our bodies.

Sekhmet's presence saturates every molecule of her compact domain. Her lioness head form radiates such fierce intensity that the air shimmers around her golden-crimson form. First light filters through the narrow entrance, catching ancient pigments that pulse in rhythm with our gathered hearts. The heat of thirteen bodies transforms the sanctuary into a crucible of unfolding.

Our voices begin low, a whisper of prayer growing into a lioness purr. The sound builds upon itself in the small space until limestone walls vibrate with our combined power. Each gesture in the close quarters becomes precise, intentional - hands rising to hearts, feet planted on worn stone, spines arching in devotion. The intimacy amplifies every sound: rustling linen, clinking carnelian, bare feet on ancient floors.

Sekhmet's power moves through us like wildfire, the close quarters intensifying her essence until every woman glows from within. Our Ka bodies expand beyond physical constraints, rising through the roof to dance with the emerging sun. The small chamber contains universes as our voices rise in ecstatic praise. We become Sekhmet's living flames, our combined radiance illuminating the ancient stones with codes of awakening. One by one, we emerge from the sanctuary, reborn in Sekhmet's fierce grace. The morning sun blazes overhead as we move with purpose toward the temple courtyard.

The intimate sanctuary of Sekhmet still resonates in our bones as thirteen women step onto the gently swaying deck of our floating temple. The Dahabiya rocks beneath our feet, cradled in the eternal waters of Nun. Sunset approaches, painting the Nile in hues of amber and rose. The air shivers with possibility as we arrange ourselves around the crystal grid laid out on weathered wooden planks still holding memories of ancient celebrations.

The river's breath mingles with our own as we position the sacred geometry of crystals - amethyst points marking cardinal directions, rose quartz hearts forming an inner circle of love, clear quartz pillars channeling pure light. At the center, a massive diamond-clear crystal lotus awaits, ready to merge the powers of air and water, heaven and earth. The gentle rocking of the boat creates subtle movements in the crystal formation, as if the grid itself breathes with the river's rhythm.

Sekhmet's fire still blazes in our blood, but here it meets the cooling waters of Nun, creating sacred steam that rises around us like incense. Our bare feet sense the river's pulse through the wooden deck, while our Ka bodies reach toward the lightening sky. The women beside me radiate their unique frequencies - some carrying Sekhmet's warrior flame, others flowing with Isis's healing waters, still others humming Hathor's celestial songs.

A sistrum begins to chime, its metal discs catching light as its sound merges with the river's song. The crystals respond, each stone amplifying the harmony of metal and water. The air thickens as our cellular memories awaken, ancient priestess wisdom rising from the depths of our DNA like bubbles ascending through sacred waters. Our bodies sway with the boat's gentle motion, our robes catching the evening breeze like sails.

The crystal lotus begins to spin, powered by the merged forces of fire and water we carry. The rotation creates tiny whirlpools of energy, spiral patterns that mirror the river's own mysteries. Through our inner vision, we see strands of light connecting each woman, forming a living matrix of consciousness that extends below the water's surface and up into the brightening sky. The warrior fire from Sekhmet's sanctuary transmutes into pure creative power, cooled and transformed by Nun's ancient wisdom.

A priestess raises her voice in a tone that carries both Sekhmet's roar and the river's eternal song. One by one, we add our notes to the harmony, weaving a tapestry of sound that ripples across the water's surface in sacred geometric patterns. Fish leap in response, their scales flashing like additional facets in our crystal mandala. The grid blazes brighter, its light reflecting and refracting off the water in countless directions.

We move as one being now, thirteen priestesses unified in the eternal dance of creation, our movements guided by the river's flow. The boat becomes a living temple, its gentle rocking keeping time with our ceremony. Wisdom flows through our combined consciousness like the current beneath us. Visions cascade through our awareness - ancient river ceremonies where priests and priestesses merged with Nun's creative power, future Earth awakened to its full potential, sacred geometries forming and dissolving like patterns on the water's surface.

The crystal lotus shoots a pillar of light skyward while simultaneously sending a beam deep into the river's heart. Our circle connects water ceremonies across time and space, past and future priestesses joining our song. Through our unified field, we sense the larger pattern forming -

our floating temple, one point of light in a planetary grid of awakening. The Nile itself sings through the crystals as ancient knowledge activates in its waters.

In this moment of perfect coherence, we exist as both individual and collective, unique drops in an infinite ocean. The frequency of awakening broadcasts through our combined field into the river's memory, rippling outward to all waters of Earth. Even the evening breeze seems to pause in reverence of the energies we weave.

As the sun crests the western bank, our ceremony stabilizes. The crystal grid hums with transformed power, the lotus at its center now singing with the voice of the river. Each woman glows with actualized potential, carrying codes of awakening in every cell. We gather the crystals with reverence, knowing they have become vessels of water wisdom.

Our embraces feel like waves meeting, words falling away before the magnitude of our communion. The deck still rocks with residual energy as we prepare to carry these frequencies into the world. We have been forged in Sekhmet's fire, transformed by crystal light, and baptized in Nun's sacred waters. The seeds we plant today will flower across dimensions, calling humanity to remember its fluid, eternal nature.

The sistrum sounds once more, its chime merging with the river's song. Our circle spirals outward like ripples from a stone dropped in still water, carrying codes of transformation to every shore. We move as living flames tempered by sacred waters, as crystal light flowing with divine purpose, as priestesses of the eternal river. The great remembering unfolds through us, wave by wave, breath by breath, heartbeat by heartbeat. The awakening continues, and we flow on.

Where Ancient Wisdom Meets Quantum Reality: The Holographic Being

Quantum physics now confirms through its most rigorous experiments what mystics intuited through millennia of inner exploration - reality far surpasses our wildest dreams. As modern measuring devices pulse with unexpected readings, ancient stone chambers and sterile laboratories alike reveal a profound truth that dissolves the imagined boundary between science and spirit. Moonlight streams through temple windows, illuminating an understanding that bridges the gap between empirical measurement and mystical wisdom.

Consider how the mere act of observation affects quantum particles. Consciousness itself influences what manifests in physical reality. This "observer effect" validates what temple initiates always knew - we live in a responsive universe that engages with awareness itself. Just as J. Krishnamurti taught: "The Observer is the Observed."

Like light itself - which behaves as both particle and wave - you exist as both form and infinite potential, your consciousness dancing between defined reality and pure possibility. Each intention ripples through the quantum field like a stone dropped in still water, sending waves of possibility in all directions.

Deep in the quantum realm, particles that once interacted remain instantly connected across any distance. This quantum entanglement reveals how everything exists in a profound relationship. Your own transformation sends ripples through this entangled cosmic web. When you shift your consciousness, you affect the entire field. The butterfly effect becomes literal - small changes creating profound effects throughout the interconnected system.

Perhaps nowhere do we see these quantum mysteries more playfully manifested than in the eternal enigma of lost socks. Like particles that seem to vanish into parallel dimensions, socks have a way of slipping between worlds - not truly lost, but exploring other realities, gathering wisdom from unseen realms. Or perhaps, like enlightened beings, they've simply transcended their paired existence, choosing instead to dance solo through the infinite possibilities of the cosmos. Every lost sock creates potential for sacred mismatch, every vanished mate opens the door for unexpected partnership. They demonstrate quantum principles in the most ordinary of settings - disappearing and reappearing as if through quantum tunneling, existing in multiple states of possibility until observed, their very absence creating ripples of transformation through the fabric of daily life. These humble teachers of whimsy and wisdom remind us that what appears missing might simply be gathering magic in dimensions beyond our sight.

Inside each neuron in your brain, tiny protein structures called microtubules achieve quantum coherence - a state where particles vibrate in perfect synchrony. In deep meditation, your brain waves synchronize with Earth's own resonant frequency - the Schumann resonance pulsing at 7.83 Hz. You enter expanded states where past, present and future merge into an eternal now.

Your heart generates the body's strongest electromagnetic field, measurable up to several feet away. This toroidal field creates a bridge between personal and universal energy fields. Each emotion sends specific frequencies rippling through this field, affecting quantum probability patterns. Love becomes a tangible force, reorganizing reality at the subatomic level.

Within every cell of your body, DNA coils in a sacred spiral, its crystalline structure serving as an antenna receiving and transmitting information through quantum channels. Your ten trillion cells form a living internet of light, where biophotons - tiny sparks of coherent light - create communication networks faster than neural pathways.

The water in your cells arranges itself in geometric patterns mirroring the architecture of space-time. This structured water responds instantly to consciousness, storing and transmitting information through quantum fields. Your body becomes a programmable liquid crystal matrix, consciousness shaping reality through living geometry.

Like a hologram where each fragment contains the complete image, you exist as a living hologram - each part containing the pattern of the whole. Every cell contains your complete DNA. Each drop of ocean holds the taste of all waters. Every point in space-time contains information about the whole universe. Your individual awakening ripples through the entire cosmic hologram, contributing to humanity's collective emergence.

Modern science now validates what mystery schools taught for millennia. We live in a conscious, holographic universe where everything connects through quantum channels. Your awakened presence engages directly with this living field of infinite potential. Each breath, each intention, each moment of expanded awareness sends ripples through the cosmic web, transforming both self and world in an eternal dance of unfolding.

The Lotus-Born Heart Process: A Group Journey

Throughout this journey - from Primal Mud through Sacred Seeding - each phase builds upon the last, deepening our capacity for transformation and growth.

While this work can be powerful in solitude, something remarkable happens when we gather in groups. The energy amplifies, insights deepen, and transformations that might take years alone can unfold more quickly together. Like a circle of candles burning brighter than one flame, each person's presence strengthens the whole.

Experienced guides help create a safe container for this work, supporting each person's unique journey while nurturing the group's collective growth. Their steady presence helps participants navigate new territories of awareness with confidence.

The effects continue long after our gatherings end. Participants carry these experiences into their daily lives, supported by practices they can continue on their own or in community. Each person's transformation contributes to our shared journey of awakening to greater human potential.

The Final Quantum Immersion: The Sacred Emergence:

This final integration seals all quantum shifts cultivated through the Lotus-Born Heart journey. Find your sanctuary - perhaps a meditation room perfumed with sacred oils, or a hidden corner of nature where earth's pulse beats strong. The solid ground beneath offers unwavering support as you begin.

Take several deep, conscious breaths. Feel weight settling into bones, breath flowing like river currents, heart drumming ancient rhythms. Each exhale releases another layer of tension, grounding essence deeper into flesh. The air around you grows thick with presence, shimmering with otherworldly light.

Frankincense and myrrh spiral through golden rays, mingling with the primal scent of fresh river clay. This ancient perfume speaks directly to cellular memory - every molecule in your body recognizes this fragrance from the first moments of creation. The walls of ordinary reality dissolve into luminous mist. Beneath your feet, smooth stone emerges, worn by millennia of sacred ceremonies.

You stand at Khnum's threshold. Crystal lamps ignite along temple walls, their light liquid and alive. Hieroglyphs pulse with inner fire - not mere symbols but living portals into primal creation. Each glyph writhes with cosmic energy, telling the story of emergence from first waters. The air grows electric with creative potential.

The colossal wheel rises before you, black granite shot through with veins of living gold that pulse like blood vessels carrying divine light. It emerges from waters that somehow contain entire galaxies though you stand deep beneath earth. Each ripple reveals another dimension of possibility. The wheel's surface holds power accumulated through countless transformations, humming at frequencies that awaken dormant codes in your DNA.

Khnum materializes - his ram's horns spiral with fractal complexity, solar disk blazing above his brow. Through his hands flows pure creative force, each finger channeling specific frequencies of manifestation. The clay appears upon his wheel - primordial mud gathered from the cosmic Nile where existence birthed itself. Every particle shimmers with starlight while remaining deeply, essentially earthen.

Wadjet enters the chamber as serpentine royalty, her cobra hood flaring with rainbow iridescence. The temperature begins to fluctuate dramatically as she awakens mastery of internal flame. Heat ripples through your body in precise waves - first a flash like desert sun, then cool like predawn air, then white-hot like stellar core. Each temperature shift recalibrates your cellular structure at quantum levels.

Your spine undulates with new intelligence as Wadjet's wisdom activates each vertebra. The sensation begins at the base, a cool tingling that transforms into liquid fire as it rises. Each vertebra becomes a key in the cosmic lock, your skeleton transforming into crystalline light. The serpent fire dances through marrow and membrane, transmuting dense matter into luminous potential.

The clay rises past your solar plexus, each layer adding new frequencies of transformation. In your belly center, golden warmth explodes into a sun. Your heart erupts into a thousand-petaled lotus of living light. Your throat becomes a chamber of creative sound where worlds are sung into being.

Horus steps closer, his electric presence making every hair rise. His Eye blazes brighter until suddenly you perceive through divine sight. The crystalline matrix of evolution reveals itself - sacred geometries flowing like living rivers of light. You witness your own emergence across all timelines simultaneously - healer, warrior, sage, artist - each aspect contributing its wisdom to your present awakening.

Through your awakened pineal gland, corona light streams in rainbow cascades. Reality reveals itself as pure potential, unbound by form's limitations. The sacred tools arise - copper ribs humming creation's first songs, golden knives that carved original forms, crystal stones still holding the memory of polishing first light bodies. Each one offers its specific frequency, its unique contribution to your transformation.

Your hands float before your eyes trailing stellar fire. Through your palms pulses the heartbeat of distant suns. Your fingers weave unconscious patterns, each gesture releasing cascades of crystalline sound. Energy flows like auroral streams, painting new constellations with each movement. Your first breath in this transformed state floods lungs with living light - indigo depths of cosmic mystery, molten gold of solar fire.

You stand complete - a living synthesis of earth and starlight, matter and potential, form and infinite possibility. Through serpent wisdom, you perceive multiple dimensions simultaneously. Through Horus's sight, you read the patterns of creation. Through Khnum's blessing, you shape new realities. You are vast as galaxies yet precisely yourself, more powerful than imagined yet perfectly aligned with divine will.

The sacred wheel turns within you now, eternal potter's wisdom alive in your hands. You have emerged. You have awakened. You have remembered. Creation spirals onward, and you stand at its heart - both masterpiece and master artist, forever shaped while forever shaping anew.

As the power of Khnum's wheel still resonates through your being, something extraordinary unfolds. One by one, the Neteru who have guided your journey through the Lotus-Born Heart process begin to appear. Each brings their unique gift, their sacred essence, completing your transformation.

Isis steps forth with her wings of magic, while Sekhmet approaches radiating fierce power. Hathor's love fills the space as Tehuti holds wisdom's flame. Ma'at brings her perfect balance while Nut arches overhead, star-scattered and vast. Geb's earthen strength rises through your feet as Ptah speaks the words of creation.

These divine forces are no longer external - they have become living aspects of your own awakened nature. Your journey through the sacred spirals has woven their essence into your very being.

Deep in the Primal Mud, you discovered Khnum's creative power flowing through your hands. As you ventured forth Seeking Light, Horus's vision awakened in your eyes. Your Luminous Ascent blazed with Sekhmet's strength, transforming every challenge into fuel for growth. Through Radiant Blossoming, Hathor's love burst forth from your heart like divine flowers opening to cosmic sun. And in Sacred Seeding, you finally embodied Isis's magic, becoming a vessel through which creation dreams itself anew.

Final Integration Where All Patterns Dissolve

Now, in this final integration, all these forces merge within you. You stand complete - not seeking the gods, but embodying their divine qualities through your unique human form.

Find your sanctuary as twilight approaches. Light Egyptian frankincense, its smoke carrying memories of temple mysteries. Place a large bowl of water at the center, floating lotus or night-blooming jasmine atop its surface. Seven candles mark a spiral path around you. The air grows thick with possibility.

Begin by touching water to your third eye, heart, and palms. Feel how different your energy has become through this journey - more fluid, more radiant, more alive. Your cells pulse with accumulated light from each phase of transformation.

Ground deeply into earth, feeling the rich mud of beginning. Let your breath become river-deep, ocean-vast. Remember how it felt to trust the fertile darkness, to let yourself be shaped by unseen forces. Place your hands in cool clay or soil, awakening primal knowing in your palms.

Rise slowly, body undulating like a cobra. Let Wadjet's wisdom move through your spine, awakening each vertebra into living light. The serpent fire you've cultivated dances through your being. Temperature shifts ripple through your flesh - desert heat, moonlit cool, star-core radiance.

Begin to spiral with the candle light, each turn awakening another layer of transformation. Your feet remember every step of seeking - the desert pilgrimages, the temple initiations, the nights under infinite stars. Let your body move with all it has learned about crossing thresholds.

The Lotus Breath awakens naturally - inhaling light through every pore, exhaling radiance through your whole being. Your energy centers have become thousand-petalled galaxies of light. The boundaries between flesh and spirit grow translucent. You are becoming the living bridge you were born to be.

Dance your blossoming - not as metaphor but as embodied reality. Your arms are lotus petals opening to cosmic light. Your heart is a flower of infinite unfolding. The radiance you've cultivated spills over, too abundant to contain. Let joy move you, let ecstasy spin you, let love pour through you.

Close your eyes with Ma'at's perfect balance.

Now open them with Horus's piercing vision.

In this infinitesimal moment - where Isis weaves magic between worlds, where Tehuti holds the cosmic scroll, where Sekhmet's fire meets Hathor's love, where Bast dances through moonlit temples, where Khepri pushes dawn from night's depths, where Neith weaves fate's golden threads - EVERYTHING transforms.

Through Nut's starlit body and Geb's earthen power, no movement is needed.

Through Nephthys's deep stillness and Osiris's eternal knowing, no breath work is required.

Through Wadjet's serpent wisdom and Neith's weaving light, no visualizations are necessary.

Simply BE as Khnum's wheel eternally turns, where Ptah's creative force ignites, where Khepri rolls the sun across the sky, where all possibilities collapse into Nefertem's lotus dawn.

Your cells pulse with Sekhmet's flame and Isis's healing light. Your DNA spirals with Seshat's sacred geometry and Wadjet's kundalini fire. Your feet dance with Bast's liquid grace while Neith weaves your destiny's golden threads. Your consciousness spans galaxies through Nut while remaining perfectly grounded through Geb.

You've already undergone every initiation with Anubis as guide. You've already crossed every threshold with Horus lighting the way. You've already become what Khnum shaped from cosmic clay.

The final integration isn't seeking Isis - you ARE her magic.

Not calling Sekhmet - you ARE her power.

Not reaching for Hathor - you ARE her love.

Not channeling Tehuti - you ARE his wisdom.

In this recognition, reality reshapes itself as Ptah's living breath. Time reorganizes in Seshat's infinite scroll. Space responds like Sothis cosmic dance.

You are no longer becoming through Ma'at's scales - you ARE Ma'at's perfect truth.

Through Khnum's vision - you ARE the masterpiece.

Through Isis's knowing - you ARE the mystery.

Through Horus's sight - you ARE the awakened one.

The Neteru aren't separate forces to invoke - they are aspects of your true nature, now fully remembered, perfectly expressed through your unique human form.

Stand as Sekhmet's pillar of fire.
Dance as Hathor's cosmic joy.
Move with Bast's perfect grace.
Create as Ptah's living word.
Know as Tehuti's infinite mind.
Love as Isis's eternal heart.

Transform as Khnum's sacred vessel.
Weave as Neith's golden thread.
Rise as Khepri's eternal dawn.
BE as all forces merged in NOW.
Everything before was Anubis preparing the way.
Everything now is Horus revealing the truth.
Everything after is Nefertem's endless blossoming.
Walk through your life as Isis walking Earth.
Speak with Tehuti's creative power.
Touch with Sekhmet's healing fire.
See with Horus's divine sight.
Love with Hathor's infinite heart.
Create with Ptah's sacred sound.
Transform with Khnum's potter's skill.
Dance with Bast's liquid grace.
Weave with Neith's golden thread.
Rise with Khepri's dawning light.
The revolution spins through Nut's cosmic dance.
The integration flows through Geb's earthen power.
The symphony plays through Hathor's eternal joy.
You ARE Isis's magic.
You ARE Sekhmet's power.
You ARE Hathor's love.
You ARE Tehuti's wisdom.
You ARE Ma'at's truth.
You ARE Khnum's creation.
You ARE Bast's grace.
You ARE Neith's weaving.
You ARE Khepri's dawn.
You ARE.

Close by blessing the water with your new radiance. Touch it to your crown, third eye, throat, heart, solar plexus, sacral center, and feet - sealing these frequencies into your physical form. Drink a sip, taking the starlight into your very cells.

Closing Prayer

May my roots grow deep in wisdom's soil
May my leaves reach forth seeking sun
May my stem rise strong through life's waters
May my petals open to share beauty's light
May my seeds scatter hope on fertile ground
For the benefit of all beings
So it is, so it shall be

Awakening the Holographic Being: A Sacred Invitation

As the last shimmers of daylight danced across the Giza sands, beneath the eternal gaze of the pyramids, I stood at the stable's entrance - a restless sixteen-year-old, poised on the precipice of metamorphosis. The magnificent Arabian before me tossed his regal head, his mane catching the fading light like molten silver. Time itself seemed suspended, waiting with bated breath.

When my palm met the horse's warm, velvet nose, an electric spark ignited between us - two kindred spirits reuniting across the whirling currents of fate. His eyes held galaxies, reflecting the very starlight that thrummed through my veins. This was no chance encounter, but a rendezvous written in the stars.

Without hesitation, I swung into the saddle, my body remembering a timeless wisdom my conscious mind had forgotten. The moment my legs gripped his powerful flanks, the horse quivered beneath me, raw power contained in earthly form. Before my guide could speak, we surged forward - something primal and unbridled awakening within us both.

We raced across the shimmering dunes, reality blurring at the edges as we activated hidden codes in the sacred land. Through my wild body, I felt the pulse of limitless potential humming all around us. In that eternal moment, I remembered the secret, shape-shifting truth of our nature.

That sixteen-year-old girl still rides through my heart, showing the way forward into unlimited possibility. In the decades since, I have become a weaver of dreams - filmmaker, diplomat, healer, mentor, strategist. Each role a vibrant thread in the magnificent tapestry I now embody, a unified field of creative potential. This is the Holographic Being, beloved - a luminous convergence of your deepest gifts and most daring visions.

And you, beloved- what wild wisdom gallops through your dreams? What untamed possibilities await your courage to embrace them? Like a merchant in the timeless bazaar, you stand at the crossroads of who you've been and who you're becoming. The universe beckons with infinite potential.

The Nile flows eternal, its waters carrying whispers of transformation. In hidden temple chambers, CEOs and creatives, entrepreneurs and engineers gather in sacred silence, receiving transmissions that transcend time. Here, quantum physics meets ancient wisdom, where expanded consciousness catalyzes unprecedented innovation.

I've walked these pathways countless times, navigating between corporate boardrooms and temple sanctuaries, merging practical success with inner evolution. Through near-death experiences, artistic rebellion, and quantum revelations, I've learned to bridge worlds - translating mystical insight into tangible results, cosmic wisdom into strategic clarity.

The Akashic Records opened their cosmic library to me in a temple by the Nile, unlocking a practical technology for accessing higher intelligence. Each session becomes a strategic meeting with the universe itself, where visionaries receive guidance for next-level growth, where innovators download solutions beyond conventional thinking, where leaders access the quantum field of infinite possibility.

Sacred circles gather globally - scientists and shamans, executives and artists, their combined frequencies generating breakthrough insights. In these living laboratories, ancient wisdom meets future emergence. Whether beside the eternal Nile, in mountain temples, or through virtual space, these gatherings activate dormant potential.

For some, the path calls for deeper communion - one-on-one mentoring where transformation aligns your being into one magnificent frequency. Like a river gathering countless streams into its powerful flow, we weave together your talents, dreams, apparent failures, hidden gifts into a single coherent force. Having navigated from primal mud to luminous ascent while building international projects, I recognize the unique symphony waiting in each seeker. Together, we illuminate the path where your business acumen, creative passions, spiritual wisdom, and personal power merge into the Holographic Being - where every facet amplifies the whole, creating unprecedented possibility. Here, your entrepreneurial drive becomes spiritual practice, your creativity informs leadership, your setbacks reveal themselves as initiations.

The temples pulse with activation codes for next-level leadership. The desert holds silent wisdom about sustainable success. The Nile waters carry frequencies that purify limiting beliefs. Through modern miracle, these transformative experiences reach across space and time to those ready for revolution.

I stand at the threshold between worlds for those ready to claim their magnificence - whether leading organizations with higher purpose, innovating humanity's solutions, or embodying success that serves the greater good. Like that sixteen-year-old girl who dared to ride with wild abandon into her destiny, your moment beckons. Visit holographicbeing.com when your mind calculates the return on transformation and your heart confirms the call. Through this sacred hour, we'll explore pathways for unleashing your highest potential, letting your spirit run free across the eternal sands.

THE LOTUS-BORN HEART: A GLOSSARY OF TERMS

Abydos (Egyptian: Abdju)

Ancient Egyptian temple complex sacred to Osiris, considered one of Egypt's most ancient and sacred sites. Known as "the place of healing and resurrection," it houses the mysterious Osirion temple, believed to be connected to water from the primordial ocean Nun. The ancient Egyptians believed it contained the head of Osiris in its sepulcher, making it a major pilgrimage site for thousands of years. Its temple walls preserve the Flower of Life symbol and contain some of the most beautifully preserved reliefs in Egypt, including the famous King List. Home to seven shrines dedicated to Osiris and the unique structure of its Temple of Seti I demonstrates advanced knowledge of sacred architecture.

Akashic Records (Sanskrit: Akasha, meaning "sky," "space," or "aether")

The cosmic library containing all knowledge of past, present and future, described in various spiritual traditions worldwide. In Egyptian tradition, connected to the goddess Seshat, divine scribe and keeper of records. Believed to exist in a non-physical plane where every thought, action, and event that has ever occurred or will occur is encoded. Can be accessed through expanded consciousness, deep meditation, and divine connection. The concept appears in various forms across cultures - as the "Book of Life" in Judaism, the "Tablet of Destiny" in Mesopotamian tradition, and the "Memory of Nature" in Western esoteric teachings.

Ankh (Egyptian: ʿnḫ, meaning "life")

Sacred symbol representing eternal life, often called "the key of life" or "the key of the Nile." Combines the masculine tau cross with the feminine circular loop, representing the union of heaven and earth, spirit and matter. When held by Egyptian deities, it represents their power to give and sustain life. Its shape may have been inspired by the sunrise over the horizon or the tie of a sandal strap. Used in temple ceremonies to bestow divine life force and in healing practices. The loop at the top is said to represent the womb or the sun rising between mountains, while the cross below represents earthly existence or the spine.

Anubis (Egyptian: Anpu or Inpu)

The jackal-headed god of death, mummification, and rebirth, whose black coloring represents the fertile Nile soil and regeneration. Known as "He Who is Upon His Mountain" and "Lord of the Sacred Land," watching over necropolises from desert cliffs. Guides souls through the underworld and weighs their hearts against Ma'at's feather in the Hall of Judgment. Son of Nephthys and Osiris, he embodies precise care and protection during transitions. His jackal form may have developed from observations of wild dogs guarding cemetery grounds. Associated with the star Sirius and the summer solstice. In temple initiations, his energy assists in transformation through facing and integrating shadow aspects of the self.

Ba (Egyptian: bꜣ)

One of the five aspects of the soul in Egyptian spiritual anatomy, often depicted as a human-headed bird with arms, representing the soul's ability to transcend physical existence. The Ba was understood as the personality or animated character of a being - that unique essence which makes each individual distinct. During sleep or after death, the Ba could leave the body to travel between worlds, always returning to reunite with the physical form. This concept influenced later philosophical and religious ideas about the soul's nature. The Ba works in conjunction with other aspects of being: the Ka (vital force), Akh (transformed, immortal being), Ren (true name), and Sheut (shadow). In temple art, the Ba is often shown hovering over mummies or bringing air and nourishment to the deceased, symbolizing eternal life.

Bastet (Egyptian: Bast, Baast, Ubaste, or Baset)

Originally a fierce lioness goddess who later evolved into the more gentle cat goddess of Lower Egypt. Her main cult center was Bubastis ("House of Bastet"). As "Lady of the East" and "Eye of Ra," she protected the pharaoh and was seen as both nurturing mother and fierce defender. Her dual nature reflects the cat's domestic gentleness and hunting prowess. Sacred cats were mummified in her honor, and her festivals were famous for their joyous music and dancing. Bastet governed pleasure, sensuality, perfume, and sacred oils, while maintaining protective powers against evil spirits and disease. Her energy particularly supports women's mysteries, feminine power, and the integration of gentleness with strength.

Bes

Unique among Egyptian deities for being depicted frontally and as a dwarf with lion-like features. Despite his fearsome appearance, Bes was a beloved household god who protected through joy rather than force. His name may derive from the word "besa" meaning "to protect." Often shown brandishing knives and sticking out his tongue to ward off evil spirits, particularly those threatening children or women in childbirth. Associated with music, dance, and sexual pleasure, his image was carved on bedroom walls and furniture. Unlike most Egyptian gods, Bes was accessible to common people and honored in everyday life. His ability to transform fear through laughter represents a special kind of spiritual protection through joy and play.

Blue Lotus (Nymphaea caerulea, Egyptian: seshen)

Sacred flower central to Egyptian spirituality and creation mythology. Known scientifically as Nymphaea caerulea and called "seshen" in ancient Egyptian, this water lily opens with the rising sun and closes at night, symbolizing the eternal cycle of death and rebirth. According to creation myths, the first lotus emerged from Nun's primordial waters, containing the child-god who would become Ra. Its fragrance was believed to facilitate spiritual awakening and divine communion. Used in temple ceremonies, festivals, and as a ritual entheogen due to its mild psychoactive properties. The flower appears extensively in Egyptian art, often shown being offered to deities or emerging from Osiris's body. Its geometric pattern of unfoldment inspired sacred architecture and mathematical principles. The blue lotus represents the journey from darkness to light, from potential to manifestation.

Chi (Egyptian: Sekhem)

Universal life force energy known by different names across traditions: Prana in Sanskrit, Qi in Chinese, Mana in Polynesian, and Sekhem in ancient Egyptian. In Egyptian understanding, this vital force was particularly associated with the goddess Sekhmet, whose name means "power" or "might." This energy flows through all living things, can be cultivated through spiritual practice, and is fundamental to healing arts. The Egyptians understood this force as operating through specific channels in the body, similar to the meridian system in Chinese medicine. Through temple practices and sacred movements, this energy could be consciously directed for transformation and healing.

Dahabiya (Arabic: ذهبية, meaning "golden")

Traditional wooden sailing vessel used on the Nile since pharaonic times, named for its original golden decorative elements. These elegant boats combine practical river navigation with sacred design principles. The characteristic triangular sails were believed to catch not just wind but spiritual energies. Used historically by nobility and now for spiritual journeys, their design allows intimate connection with the Nile's sacred rhythms. The traditional layout includes spaces for meditation and ritual, while the gentle rocking motion facilitates altered states of consciousness. The dahabiya's unhurried pace allows deep attunement to the river's transformative power.

Dendera Temple (Egyptian: Iunet or Tantere)

One of Egypt's most beautifully preserved temple complexes, dedicated to Hathor as "Lady of Dendera." Famous for its celestial ceiling depicting astronomical alignments and zodiac symbols (now in the Louvre), the temple combines astronomical science with spiritual wisdom. The complex includes crypts containing important initiatory symbols and texts. Its walls feature images of Cleopatra VII and Caesarion. The temple's unique design includes healing chambers where sound and light were used for transformation. The columns, shaped like sistra (Hathor's sacred rattle), are believed to transmit specific vibrational frequencies. Underground crypts contain relief carvings that some interpret as depicting advanced technological knowledge. The temple's orientation and architecture create specific energy effects during solstices and equinoxes.

Djed Pillar (Egyptian: ḏd)

One of Egypt's most ancient and sacred symbols, representing stability, strength, and regenerative power. Often called "the backbone of Osiris," this pillar symbol appears in the earliest dynasties. Physically resembles a human spine with four vertebrae, symbolizing stability through four planes of existence. The raising of the Djed pillar was an important royal ceremony associated with resurrection and renewal. In temple architecture, Djed columns were positioned to create energy channels connecting earth and sky. The symbol integrates masculine stability with feminine regenerative power. On a spiritual level, represents the awakening of the spine's transformative energy (similar to kundalini in yogic tradition) and the alignment of physical, emotional, mental, and spiritual bodies.

Flower of Life

Sacred geometric pattern found etched into the walls of Abydos Temple, consisting of multiple evenly-spaced, overlapping circles arranged in a hexagonal pattern. This ancient design contains profound mathematical and symbolic wisdom, including the golden ratio, Fibonacci sequence, and platonic solids. Considered a template for creation itself, the pattern shows how all life emerges from one source through sacred geometric progression. Found in various cultures worldwide, but its presence in Abydos suggests deep Egyptian understanding of universal mathematical principles. Used in meditation and healing practices to align with creation's fundamental patterns. The complete pattern contains 19 overlapping circles enclosed by a larger circle, though some representations show different numbers of circles depending on the teaching level.

Geb (Egyptian: Gb, also Seb or Keb)

The earth god who, with his sister-wife Nut (sky), forms the primary duality of manifested creation. Often depicted lying beneath Nut, his body forming the earth's mountains and valleys. Known as "The Great Cackler" who laid the cosmic egg from which the sun first rose. Father of Osiris, Isis, Set, and Nephthys. His laughter was said to cause earthquakes, and his emotions affect earth's fertility. Sacred to him was the goose, whose honking was thought to have broken the silence of pre-creation. In temple practice, connecting with Geb's energy facilitates grounding, abundance, and attunement to earth's rhythms. His hieroglyph includes the symbol for inherited divine power.

Hathor (Egyptian: Ḥwt-Ḥr, meaning "House of Horus")

One of Egypt's most ancient and beloved Goddesses, whose worship spans the entire dynastic period. Her name means "House of Horus," referring to her role as the sacred space in which divine consciousness (Horus) dwells. Depicted either as a cow-headed woman or a woman with cow ears and horns holding a solar disk. Known by many titles including "Lady of the Western Mountain," "Golden One," and "Lady of the Stars." Associated with joy, love, beauty, dance, music, motherhood, and celestial wisdom. Her temples, especially at Dendera, were centers for healing through sound, light, and dreams. The sistrum (sacred rattle) and menat necklace are her primary ritual tools. Her seven Hathors were cosmic dancers who determined fate. Hathor's energy supports artistic expression, sacred sexuality, and the integration of sensual pleasure with spiritual awakening.

Heartfire Ray

A concept describing the unique spiritual signature or divine essence within each being. Like a specific frequency of cosmic light expressing through the individual heart center. Awakens gradually through spiritual practice, particularly in temple environments and sacred sites. Connected to the Egyptian understanding of the heart (ib) as the seat of soul, thought, and divine connection. The ray's activation brings heightened creativity, healing abilities, and clear purpose. Its frequency can be strengthened through specific breathing practices, sacred movement, and attunement to divine presence.

Heka (Egyptian: Ḥk³)

The deified power of magic itself, present at creation's beginning. More than just a deity, Heka represents the primal creative force that enables manifestation of divine will into physical reality. The word literally means "activating the Ka" or life force. Associated with the divine word's creative power and the force behind all ritual and transformative practices. In Egyptian understanding, Heka was a natural force like gravity that could be worked with through proper knowledge and practice. Temple texts describe specific words of power (hekau) that activate this force for various purposes.

Hieroglyphs (Greek: "sacred carved letters"; Egyptian: medu netjer, "divine words")

Sacred writing system whose symbols are believed to carry living power. More than just a writing system, hieroglyphs were seen as "divine words" capable of creating reality. Each symbol contains multiple levels of meaning - phonetic, symbolic, and energetic. The system includes ideograms, phonetic signs, and determinatives that specify meaning. Sacred scribes underwent intensive training not just in writing but in the magical properties of symbols. Temple hieroglyphs were thought to maintain cosmic order through their mere presence.

Holographic Being

This is a contemporary term created by the author to describe human beings as microcosms of the universe. According to this concept, each person contains and reflects all aspects of creation, just as each piece of a hologram contains the whole image. This idea appears in ancient Egyptian temple texts, which describe humans as being "made in the image of the gods" and containing all elements of creation within them. This understanding stems from direct mystical experiences where individual consciousness expands to encompass cosmic awareness, while still maintaining a sense of individual identity. The "Holographic Being" concept suggests that we live in an immersive, merged state of our unique frequencies, talents, skills, experiences, hidden potentials, and dreams and visions - all of which are interwoven reflections of the greater cosmic whole. This perspective points to the profound interconnectedness and multidimensional nature of human existence, aligning with the ancient Egyptian worldview of the individual as a microcosm of the universal macrocosm.

Horus (Egyptian: Ḥr or Hor, meaning "The Distant One")

One of Egypt's most ancient and complex deities, appearing in many forms throughout Egyptian history. The falcon-headed god represents divine consciousness, kingship, and clear spiritual vision. Born to Isis after she resurrected Osiris, his story represents the triumph of light over darkness and order over chaos. His eyes represent the sun and moon - the right (sun) symbolizing action and Ra's power, the left (moon) representing healing and Tehuti's wisdom. The injury and healing of his left eye became a central symbol of wholeness and healing. As divine king, Horus united Upper and Lower Egypt, symbolizing the integration of spiritual and material realms. Living pharaohs were considered earthly embodiments of Horus. His sharp vision represents spiritual discernment and the ability to perceive divine truth.

Isis (Egyptian: Aset or Iset)

One of Egypt's most powerful and enduring deities, whose worship spread throughout the ancient world. Her name "Aset" means "throne," symbolizing her role as the seat of divine power. Known as "Great of Magic" and "She of 10,000 Names," her magical abilities were considered unmatched. The story of her resurrection of Osiris through perfect love and powerful magic became a template for spiritual transformation. Her wings represent protective divine love, and she was often depicted nursing the pharaoh, symbolizing the transmission of divine wisdom. As mistress of magic (heka), she knows the secret name of Ra, giving her mastery over creation itself. Her mysteries were celebrated in temples throughout Egypt, particularly at Philae, her island sanctuary. The tyet or "Isis knot" symbol represents her protective and regenerative powers.

Ka (Egyptian: k³)

Essential spiritual component representing vital force or life energy. One of the five aspects of the soul in Egyptian spiritual anatomy. The Ka is born with a person but can survive death when properly nourished through offerings. Represented in hieroglyphs by upraised arms, suggesting the receiving and holding of life force. The Ka acts as an energetic double, connecting physical and spiritual realms. In temple practice, "activating the Ka" refers to awakening higher spiritual capacities. The ankh symbol is often shown being offered to the Ka, representing the transmission of divine life force.

Karnak Temple (Egyptian: Ipet-isut, meaning "Most Select of Places")

The largest religious complex ever built, developed over 2,000 years. Covers 200 acres and contains temples to various aspects of the Theban triad (Amun, Mut, and Khonsu). Its main axis aligns with the summer solstice sunrise. Features include the Great Hypostyle Hall with 134 massive columns representing the primordial marsh from which creation arose. Contains sacred lake for ritual purification, a unique chapel dedicated to Sekhmet, and various astronomical alignments. The complex was understood as a model of the universe itself, with each area corresponding to different aspects of creation.

Khepri (Egyptian: ḫprr)

The scarab-headed aspect of Ra representing self-generated renewal. His name means "He Who Comes Into Being," sharing roots with the word kheper (to become/transform). The scarab beetle, rolling its ball of dung across the sand, was seen as a symbol of the sun's journey and the soul's ability to regenerate itself. Morning manifestation of Ra, representing emergence from darkness into light. In temple texts, associated with spontaneous creation and transformation through divine will.

Khnum (Egyptian: Ḫnmw)

Ram-headed creator deity who shapes all living things on his potter's wheel. Known as "The Divine Potter" and "Builder of Builders." Associated with the source of the Nile at Elephantine. Shapes not only physical bodies but the Ka (spiritual double) of each being. Works with Heket, frog goddess of birth, to animate his creations with breath of life. His creative power is particularly associated with the flooding of the Nile and fertility.

Kom Ombo (Egyptian: Pr-Sbk, "House of Sobek")

Unique double temple honoring both Horus the Elder and Sobek. Architectural design precisely divided to honor both deities equally, with parallel sanctuaries, courts, and halls. Contains important medical and astronomical texts. The temple's duality represents the integration of seemingly opposing forces: light/dark, order/chaos, sky/earth. Ancient healing center containing surgical instruments depicted on temple walls.

Lotus-Born Heart Process

Contemporary spiritual framework based on ancient Egyptian temple teachings of transformation. Maps the soul's journey through five distinct phases, each corresponding to stages of the lotus's growth from mud to full bloom:

- Primal Mud: Represents gestation in fertile darkness, where potential gathers
- Seeking Light: Active quest for wisdom and understanding
- Luminous Ascent: Conscious rising toward greater awareness
- Radiant Blossoming: Full emergence and expression of inner light
- Sacred Seeding: Contributing to collective evolution

Ma'at (Egyptian: m³'t)

Goddess embodying cosmic order, truth, justice, and harmony. Her name literally means "that which is straight." Represented with an ostrich feather, which weighs against the heart in the judgment hall. More than just a deity, Ma'at represents the fundamental order and balance that maintains creation. Pharaohs were responsible for maintaining Ma'at through proper rule and ritual. Her principles guided Egyptian society at all levels, from cosmic order to personal ethics.

Neith (Egyptian: Nit or Neit)

One of Egypt's most ancient deities, worshipped since pre-dynastic times. Known as "Mother of the Gods" and "Opener of the Ways." Associated with creation, weaving, wisdom, and war. Her temple at Sais contained the saying: "I am all that has been, that is, and that will be. No mortal has yet been able to lift my veil." Depicted with crossed arrows or shuttle, representing her roles as hunter and weaver of fate.

Nut (Egyptian: Nwt)

Sky goddess whose star-studded body arches over the earth. Each evening she swallows the sun, which travels through her body to be reborn at dawn. Mother of Osiris, Isis, Nephthys, and Set. Often depicted on coffin lids, embracing the deceased into cosmic life. Her body represents the Milky Way, and she was understood as the cosmic mother from whom all celestial phenomena emerge.

Osiris (Egyptian: Wsir or Aser)

God of death, resurrection, and eternal life. Originally a divine king who brought civilization, he was murdered by his brother Set but restored to life through Isis's magic. His resurrection established the possibility of eternal life through spiritual transformation. Associated with the cycles of nature, particularly the flooding of the Nile and growth of grain. His green or black skin represents regeneration and fertile soil. As judge of the dead and lord of the underworld, he represents the soul's potential for eternal life through moral and spiritual development.

Luminous Ascent

The "Luminous Ascent" represents the third phase of the "Lotus-Born Heart" process, where the seeker's consciousness consciously rises toward greater light, wisdom, and spiritual understanding. This stage signifies a pivotal moment of illumination and expanded awareness, as the individual's inner energies become increasingly refined and aligned with the divine blueprint. The Luminous Ascent is akin to the lotus flower's stem extending upward, reaching toward the sun and the celestial realms. It is a time of profound revelation, where the veils of illusion thin and the seeker gains access to deeper insights, mystical currents, and the universal principles that govern creation. Through this ascent, the individual becomes an ever-brighter beacon, radiating the light of their transformed consciousness and preparing to fully blossom in the final stages of spiritual emergence.

Merkaba

The merkaba is a sacred geometric pattern composed of two intersecting tetrahedra (three-sided pyramids) that form a three-dimensional Star of David. This symbol is deeply rooted in ancient Egyptian mysticism, where "Mer" represents light, "Ka" represents the spirit or soul, and "Ba" represents the physical body and reality. The merkaba is viewed as a "light vehicle" that can facilitate consciousness travelling between dimensions and realms. It serves as a template for unifying the realms of spirit and matter, allowing an individual to transcend the limitations of the physical world and access higher planes of existence. The merkaba geometry is believed to harness and direct powerful spiritual energies, enabling transformation, ascension, and the expansion of one's awareness.

Mimasi

The mimasi, or "birth house," was a sacred space within ancient Egyptian temple complexes where divine birth rituals were performed. These ritual chambers were considered liminal spaces - thresholds between the mortal and divine realms. Within the mimasi, priests and priestesses would conduct ceremonies to facilitate the spiritual rebirth and transformation of initiates. This sacred space was imbued with potent energies that catalyzed inner awakening and the emergence of one's higher self. The mimasi represented a womb-like environment where the old self could die and the new, spiritually-enlightened self could be birthed through ritualized practices. It was a place of sacred transition, where the mundane merged with the mystical.

Mycelial Network

The mycelial network refers to the underground fungal systems that connect the roots of plants and trees. These intricate, interconnected webs beneath the soil surface are often used as a metaphor for spiritual interconnectedness. Just as the mycelium serves as a vast, unseen communication highway for the natural world, transmitting water, nutrients, and information between various organisms, the concept of the mycelial network symbolizes the unseen energetic and informational pathways that link all beings in the universe. This metaphor suggests that, like the mycelium, we are all fundamentally interconnected at the deepest levels of consciousness - that our individual identities are in fact aspects of a greater, cosmic whole. Exploring and honoring these unseen, mystical webs of relationship can foster a profound sense of unity, interdependence, and holistic understanding of our place in the grand tapestry of existence.

Neteru

The Neteru are the gods and goddesses of ancient Egyptian cosmology, representing the fundamental cosmic forces and principles that sustain the manifest world. These divine beings are viewed as transcendent, archetypal principles that govern the natural order, as well as immanent presences that are actively engaged in the daily affairs of humanity. Each Neter (singular of Neteru) embodies a specific aspect of the divine, such as Osiris representing death and resurrection, Sekhmet embodying solar power and healing, or Tehuti overseeing writing, knowledge, and the movement of celestial bodies. Together, the Neteru form a pantheon of inter-related forces that work in harmony to uphold creation. They are not seen as separate, anthropomorphic deities, but rather as facets of a greater, unitary divine consciousness that permeates and sustains all of existence. Honoring and aligning with the Neteru allows individuals to attune themselves to the fundamental laws and rhythms of the cosmos, facilitating personal and spiritual growth.

Nephthys

Nephthys is the sister of the goddess Isis in the ancient Egyptian pantheon, and is considered a funerary and transitional deity. As the sister and counterpart to Isis, Nephthys represents the hidden, mysterious aspects of the divine feminine. She is associated with the liminal spaces between life and death, guarding the sacred thresholds where transformation occurs. Nephthys assists in the process of death and rebirth, helping to release the old and usher in the new. Her domain includes the realms of darkness, the unconscious, and the unseen forces that underlie manifesting reality. Nephthys is often depicted as a woman with the hieroglyphic symbol for a palace or temple enclosure on her head, signifying her role as the guardian of sacred spaces and the keeper of hidden wisdom. Through invoking Nephthys, individuals can access the deeper, more elusive currents of the psyche, unlocking the mysteries that lie beyond the veil of the known.

Nile River

The Nile River holds a sacred, life-giving significance in ancient Egyptian cosmology and spirituality. As the longest river in the world, the Nile was revered as the source of all life and the conduit for the divine life force that flowed through the land of Egypt. The annual flooding of the Nile nourished the fertile soil, allowing the ancient Egyptians to cultivate abundant crops and sustain their civilization. Beyond its physical attributes, the Nile was seen as a metaphysical river that connected the earthly and spiritual realms, facilitating the cyclical renewal of creation. The waters of the Nile were believed to carry the potent energies of the gods, and were used in sacred rituals and temple ceremonies. In this way, the Nile river represented the ceaseless flow of divine providence that sustained both the material and metaphysical aspects of existence. Honoring and aligning with the Nile was essential for the ancient Egyptians, as it symbolized the underlying unity and perpetual regeneration at the heart of the cosmos.

Nut

Nut is the ancient Egyptian sky goddess, whose star-filled body arches over the earth, creating the celestial vault. She is the wife of Geb, the earth god, and together they represent the union of heaven and earth. Nut is depicted as a woman whose body is covered in stars, symbolizing her role as the great cosmic mother who gives birth to the sun, moon, and other heavenly bodies each day. As the sky goddess, Nut embodies the infinite possibilities and creative potentials of the universe. She is associated with transformation, rebirth, and the cyclical nature of existence. Nut swallows the sun each evening and gives birth to it anew each morning, representing the perpetual renewal of life. In this way, she is seen as the womb from which all creation emerges and the vast expanse into which all things eventually return. By honoring Nut, the ancient Egyptians sought to align themselves with the eternal rhythms and ever-renewing forces of the cosmos, fostering a deep sense of connectedness to the divine matrix underlying all of reality.

Osiris

Osiris is the central god of the ancient Egyptian pantheon, representing the eternal cycle of death and resurrection. As the lord of the underworld, Osiris presides over the transition from life to death, and is associated with the soul's journey through the afterlife. According to myth, Osiris was murdered by his brother Set, but was later restored to life through the magical workings of his wife, Isis. This narrative symbolizes the cyclical nature of existence, where endings give rise to new beginnings and the spirit transcends the limitations of the physical form. Osiris embodies the principle of transformation, demonstrating how even in the face of apparent destruction, there lies the potential for rebirth and regeneration. His story reminds us that death is not an end, but rather a necessary phase in the continuous unfolding of life. By aligning with the energies of Osiris, individuals can learn to navigate their own transitions with grace, trusting in the greater pattern of spiritual growth and evolution.

Papyrus

Papyrus is a water-dwelling reed plant that was extensively used in ancient Egypt for the production of paper-like writing material. Beyond its practical applications, papyrus holds deep symbolic significance within the Egyptian spiritual cosmology. As a plant that emerges from the primal waters, papyrus represents the process of manifesting form out of the formless void. It symbolizes the transition from the realms of pure potentiality into the world of tangible existence. The upright, columnar stems of the papyrus plant also evoke the principle of vertical ascent, suggesting humanity's capacity to rise above the material limitations of the physical plane. In temple rituals and sacred texts, the papyrus plant was often depicted alongside the lotus flower, indicating their shared role as emblems of divine creation and spiritual unfoldment. By honoring the sacred symbology of papyrus, the ancient Egyptians cultivated a reverence for the generative powers of nature and the mysteries of manifestation inherent in the fabric of existence.

Philae Temple

The Philae Temple complex, located on an island in the Nile River, was a renowned sanctuary dedicated to the goddess Isis in ancient Egypt. Often referred to as the "Pearl of Egypt," this sacred site was considered a preeminent center for the veneration of the divine feminine. The temples and shrines of Philae were imbued with the wise, nurturing energies of Isis, who was revered as the ultimate Mother Goddess, sorceress, and protector of the dead. Pilgrims from across the ancient world would journey to Philae to partake in the temple's mystical rites and rituals, seeking Isis's blessings, healing, and guidance on their spiritual paths. The Philae complex represented a powerful portal to the deeper, esoteric dimensions of Egyptian spirituality, where the veils between the physical and metaphysical realms were believed to thin. As a sanctuary for the sacred feminine, Philae served as a wellspring of divine wisdom, empowering individuals to reclaim the intuitive, regenerative aspects of their own consciousness.

Primal Mud

In the context of the "Lotus-Born Heart" process, the "Primal Mud" represents the first phase of spiritual transformation and inner awakening. This stage symbolizes the fertile, receptive darkness from which new life and possibility can emerge. The primal mud evokes the archetypal image of the primordial waters or "chaos" that precedes ordered creation - the formless, undifferentiated source from which all manifested forms eventually arise. It is a place of gestation, where the seeds of inspiration and rebirth lie dormant, awaiting the spark that will catalyze their flowering. By embracing the primal mud, individuals are invited to surrender into the unknown, to let go of rigid identities and structures, and to open themselves to the generative forces of the unconscious. This phase represents a necessary dissolution of the old in order to make way for the new, a shedding of the outmoded in service of a more authentic, spiritually-aligned way of being.

Ptah (Egyptian: Ptḥ)

Ptah is the ancient Egyptian god of craftsmanship, architecture, and the creative arts. As the divine craftsman, Ptah is believed to have brought the physical world into manifestation through the power of thought and speech. In Egyptian cosmology, Ptah is credited with conceiving the blueprint of creation within his mind, and then actualizing it through the utterance of sacred words and incantations. This principle of divine creativity manifesting in material form is a central tenet of the Ptah-centered belief system. Ptah represents the capacity of consciousness to shape and direct the fabric of reality, demonstrating how the unseen realms of mind and spirit can be channeled into tangible expression. By honoring Ptah, the ancient Egyptians sought to align themselves with the generative powers of the cosmos, learning to wield the tools of conscious creation in service of personal and collective transformation.

Ptah's domain encompasses the realms of innovation, problem-solving, and the actualization of visionary ideas into concrete form.

Quantum Field

The quantum field is a fundamental concept in quantum physics that describes the underlying fabric of reality. At the deepest levels of existence, this quantum field is seen as a vast, interconnected matrix of pure potentiality, where all possible states and outcomes exist simultaneously in a superposition. It is the formless, energetic substratum from which the tangible, manifested world emerges. In the context of ancient Egyptian spirituality, the quantum field can be likened to the primal waters or "chaos" that precedes creation - the infinite sea of possibilities from which all forms eventually take shape. By accessing and aligning with the quantum field, individuals are said to tap into the wellspring of cosmic creativity, allowing them to transcend the limitations of the physical realm and engage with the deeper, unseen currents of existence. This quantum perspective points to the fundamental unity and interconnectedness that lies at the heart of the universe, where the boundaries between mind, matter, and spirit dissolve into a seamless, undifferentiated whole.

Quantum Entanglement

Quantum entanglement is a principle in quantum physics that describes the profound interconnection between subatomic particles, even when they are separated by great distances. When particles become entangled, their quantum states become inextricably linked, such that the behavior and properties of one particle instantly influence the other, regardless of the physical space between them. This phenomenon is often used as a metaphor for the spiritual interconnectedness that underlies the fabric of existence. Just as quantum particles are able to communicate and influence each other instantaneously across space, the ancient Egyptian worldview suggests that all beings and manifestations in the universe are fundamentally intertwined at the level of consciousness. This concept of "quantum entanglement" points to the notion that we are not isolated, autonomous individuals, but rather aspects of a greater, unified whole. By embracing this perspective, individuals can cultivate a deeper sense of kinship with all of creation, recognizing the sacred web of relationships that binds us together and the profound ways in which we are continuously affecting and being affected by the world around us.

Ra (Egyptian: Rʿ)

Ra is the ancient Egyptian sun god, considered the supreme creator deity who travels across the sky by day and through the underworld by night. As the embodiment of the sun's light and eternal renewal, Ra represents the divine principle of illumination, both in the physical and spiritual realms. Ra's daily journey across the heavens and descent into the depths of the underworld symbolizes the cyclical nature of existence, where death and rebirth are intricately woven into the fabric of creation. Ra is often depicted with a falcon head and the solar disk, or as a solar barque carrying the sun across the sky. His cult was centered in the city of Heliopolis, which was regarded as the primordial mound from which the world emerged. By honoring Ra, the ancient Egyptians sought to attune themselves to the rhythms of the cosmos, aligning their own lives with the perpetual regeneration and enlightenment represented by the sun. Ra's guiding light was seen as essential for navigating both the material and metaphysical aspects of existence, empowering individuals to transcend the limitations of the mortal sphere.

Radiant Blossoming

The "Radiant Blossoming" represents the fourth of the "Lotus-Born Heart" process, where the inner light and spiritual energies that have been cultivated and nurtured throughout the previous stages fully emerge and express themselves in the physical world. This stage signifies a profound alchemical transformation, where the seeker's essence radiates outward with luminous clarity, catalyzing positive change and uplifting the collective consciousness. The Radiant Blossoming is akin to the lotus flower fully opening its petals, revealing the golden heart at its center. It is a state of exquisite balance, where the spiritual and material dimensions of the self are seamlessly integrated, allowing the individual to embody their highest potential and serve as a beacon of light for others. This phase represents the culmination of the inner work, where the seeker's newfound gifts, wisdom, and creative power can be shared unconditionally with the world. The Radiant Blossoming marks the flowering of the Lotus-Born Heart, where the divine spark within each person ignites the path of service, healing, and transcendent joy.

Sacred Geometry

Sacred geometry refers to the mathematical patterns, shapes, and proportions that are believed to underlie the fabric of creation. These divine principles, expressed through form, are seen as the building blocks of the manifest world and the doorways to higher consciousness. In ancient Egyptian spirituality, sacred geometry was deeply revered and incorporated into temple architecture, ritual practices, and sacred texts. Geometric shapes like the circle, triangle, and hexagon were imbued with profound symbolic meaning, representing fundamental forces and energetic archetypes that govern the universe. The intersection of these geometric forms, such as the Flower of Life or the Merkaba, were understood to be portals to expanded states of awareness, facilitating transformation and the integration of spirit and matter. By studying and engaging with sacred geometry, individuals could attune themselves to the harmonic principles that pattern the cosmos, unlocking the mystical secrets of creation and aligning their consciousness with the divine blueprint underlying all of existence.

Sacred Seeding

The "Sacred Seeding" represents the final phase of the spiritual emergence process depicted in the "Lotus-Born Heart" process. In this culminating stage, the individual's inner light and creative potential have fully blossomed, empowering them to sow the seeds of new possibilities in the world. The Sacred Seeding marks a point of transcendent fruition, where the seeker's transformed consciousness radiates outward, catalyzing positive change and uplifting the collective. This phase is analogous to the lotus flower fully opening its petals and releasing its fertile seeds, which then disperse and take root in new places. Similarly, the individual in the Sacred Seeding stage is compelled to share their gifts, wisdom, and visionary insights in service of the greater good. They become a generative, life-giving force, planting the seeds of awakening, healing, and evolutionary growth in the consciousness of others. The Sacred Seeding represents the ultimate flowering of the Lotus-Born Heart, where the individual's spiritual attainment directly manifests in tangible ways that ripple outward, transforming the world.

Scarab Beetle

The scarab beetle was a sacred symbol in ancient Egyptian spirituality, associated with the god Khepri and the principle of transformation and rebirth. The scarab was observed to roll balls of dung across the earth, an action that was likened to the sun's daily journey across the sky. This celestial connection led the Egyptians to revere the scarab as an emblem of the rising sun and the cyclical regeneration of life. The scarab was seen to "push" the sun into the sky each morning, mirroring the soul's journey through the underworld and its eventual rebirth. Additionally, the scarab's ability to emerge from its egg-like larval form as a fully-formed adult was interpreted as a metaphor for spiritual resurrection and the alchemical process of transformation. Images and amulets of the scarab were widely used in Egyptian funerary rites and temple practices, inviting the deceased and the living alike to embrace the eternal cycles of death and renewal that are woven into the fabric of existence.

Seeking Light

The "Seeking Light" represents the second phase of the "Lotus-Born Heart" process, where the seeker actively engages in the journey of spiritual awakening and enlightenment. In this stage, the individual becomes increasingly aware of the need to transcend the limitations of the ego-driven self and align with higher frequencies of consciousness. The Seeking Light phase is characterized by a growing yearning for truth, deeper understanding, and connection to the divine. It involves dedicated practices, study, and ritual immersion that help the seeker to kindle the inner flame of illumination and clear away the obscurations that veil their true nature. During this stage, the individual may experience moments of insight, synchronicity, and expanded awareness that propel them forward on the path of transformation. The Seeking Light represents a crucial pivot point, where the seeker moves from passive contemplation to active engagement in the alchemical process of self-realization and the integration of their divine potential.

Sekhem

Sekhem is an ancient Egyptian concept that refers to the divine life force energy or sacred power that animates all of creation. It is considered the essential vitality that flows through the cosmos, sustaining manifest reality and linking the physical and spiritual realms. Sekhem is associated with deities like Ra, Ptah, and Sekhmet, who were believed to embody and channel this primordial force. In Egyptian temple rituals and mystical practices, practitioners would seek to cultivate, circulate, and direct Sekhem energy within their own bodies and energy fields, using it to catalyze healing, empowerment, and spiritual evolution. Sekhem was seen as the wellspring of divine creativity and the sacred fire that fuels transformation. By attuning to the Sekhem current, individuals could align themselves with the fundamental life force that permeates the universe, tapping into an inexhaustible source of vitality, wisdom, and creative potential. The concept of Sekhem points to the interconnected, energetic fabric of existence that underpins the Egyptian worldview.

Sekhmet (Egyptian: Sbḫmt)

Sekhmet is the ancient Egyptian lion-headed goddess of divine power, healing, and righteous destruction. As the daughter of the sun god Ra, Sekhmet embodies the fierce and purifying aspects of the solar force. She is often depicted with the solar disk above her head, underscoring her connection to the elemental powers of fire, light, and divine inspiration. Sekhmet's leonine features symbolize her strength, courage, and protective nature, as well as her capacity for both nurturing and devastating wrath. In Egyptian mythology, Sekhmet was originally sent by Ra to punish and destroy humanity, but was eventually pacified and transformed into a goddess of healing and regeneration through the intervention of the goddess Isis. This narrative arc represents the idea that Sekhmet's seemingly destructive forces are in fact expressions of a profound, transformative love - a love that consumes the ego's limitations in order to facilitate the emergence of the divine self. By invoking Sekhmet, devotees sought to harness her sacred fire to burn away impurities, ignite spiritual passion, and catalyze profound inner alchemy and rebirth.

Tehuti (Thoth Egyptian: T̠hwty)

Tehuti, also known as Thoth, is the ancient Egyptian god of wisdom, writing, magic, and the keeper of cosmic order. Depicted with the head of an ibis or a baboon, Tehuti is revered as the divine scribe and the inventor of hieroglyphic script. As the patron of knowledge, Tehuti was believed to have recorded the laws and principles that govern the universe, maintaining the delicate balance between all things. Tehuti's domain encompassed mathematics, astronomy, alchemy, and the recording of history - spheres of activity that were seen as integral to upholding the sacred order of creation.

In Egyptian mythology, Tehuti acted as the intermediary between the human and divine realms, translating the will of the gods and ensuring harmonious alignment between the celestial and earthly planes. Through his mastery of language, Tehuti was understood to wield the power of the spoken and written word, using the creative force of the divine logos to shape reality. By aligning with Tehuti's energies, devotees sought to cultivate their own intuitive wisdom, divine intelligence, and capacity for creative manifestation. Tehuti's presence reminded the ancient Egyptians of the vital role that consciousness, cognition, and communication play in the unfolding of the cosmos.

Temple Guardian

The Temple Guardian was a sacred role in ancient Egyptian spirituality, charged with the responsibility of protecting the energetic integrity and sanctity of temple spaces. As the caretakers of these hallowed sites, Temple Guardians were tasked with maintaining the delicate balance of frequencies, powers, and spiritual forces that permeated the temples. Through rituals, invocations, and the deployment of sacred objects and symbols, the Guardians ensured that the temples remained inviolable sanctuaries - places where the veils between the physical and metaphysical realms thinned, and where the initiates could safely commune with the divine.

Beyond the physical guardianship of the temples, the Temple Guardians were also seen as the custodians of the esoteric knowledge and mystical teachings associated with each site. They were responsible for preserving the integrity of the sacred traditions and transmitting them to worthy seekers. In this way, the Temple Guardians upheld the alchemical and transformative potentials inherent within the temples, protecting the portals through which the human and cosmic worlds could interface. Their role was essential in maintaining the sacred spaces as fertile grounds for spiritual awakening, ritual empowerment, and the realization of divine consciousness.

Third Eye Awakening

The "Third Eye Awakening" refers to the activation and development of spiritual vision and intuitive perception in ancient Egyptian mysticism. Also known as the "Eye of Horus," the third eye represents the faculty of extrasensory awareness that transcends the limitations of the physical senses. When this innate spiritual sight is cultivated and brought into full expression, it enables the individual to perceive the subtle energetic realms, divine archetypes, and esoteric patterns that underlie the manifested world.

The third eye awakening was a crucial aspect of the Egyptian initiatory path, facilitating direct communion with the gods, the akashic records, and the greater cosmic intelligence. Through dedicated practices, rituals, and alchemical transmissions, seekers would activate and hone their intuitive capacities, gaining access to realms of visionary insight, prophetic knowing, and mystical revelation. This expanded consciousness allowed initiates to apprehend the deeper, unseen currents of reality and align themselves with the universal principles governing creation.

The opening of the third eye was seen as an essential step in the expansion of human awareness, empowering individuals to transcend the illusions of the physical senses and directly experience the interconnected, multidimensional nature of existence. By awakening this spiritual sight, the ancient Egyptians could more fully embody their divine potential and serve as conduits for the transmission of sacred wisdom.

Underworld Journey

The "Underworld Journey" refers to the symbolic or actual descent into the depths of the subconscious and spiritual realms in ancient Egyptian mysticism, closely associated with the myths and mysteries surrounding Osiris. This descent represented a necessary phase of death, dissolution, and transformation, where the seeker could confront the shadows and hidden aspects of the self to ultimately emerge reborn and spiritually empowered.

Unity Consciousness

Unity Consciousness refers to the state of awareness in which the illusion of separation dissolves, and the fundamental oneness underlying all of existence is directly experienced. This expanded state of consciousness transcends the ego-driven identification with a separate self, recognizing the interconnected, interdependent nature of all phenomena as expressions of a single, undifferentiated field of consciousness.

Universal Field

The Universal Field, in the context of ancient Egyptian spirituality, refers to the underlying matrix of consciousness and energy that connects all beings, phenomena, and dimensions of existence - the primordial ground of being from which the manifested world emerges and into which it ultimately dissolves.

Universal Mind

The Universal Mind refers to the cosmic consciousness or divine intelligence that permeates and sustains all of existence, the infinitely wise, all-knowing source from which the manifested world arises and into which it ultimately dissolves. Aligning with the Universal Mind was seen as the pinnacle of Egyptian mystical experience, conferring spiritual gifts of transcendent vision and conscious co-creation.

Uraeus

The uraeus is a sacred Egyptian symbol depicted as a rearing cobra, often worn on the forehead of pharaohs and deities. The uraeus represents divine protection, royal authority, and the awakening of kundalini energy - the potent, primordial force coiled at the base of the spine that, when activated, rises up the central channel to illuminate consciousness. As a symbol of the sun god Ra, the uraeus was believed to project the fiery, transformative power of the solar deity, warding off enemies and evil influences. Pharaohs and high priests would wear the uraeus crown or headdress as a visible sign of their connection to the divine, their elevated spiritual status, and their role as mediators between the earthly and celestial realms. The uraeus emblem was understood to activate the "third eye" of intuitive, mystical vision, granting the wearer enhanced perceptual faculties and empowering them to maintain the sacred order of creation.

Valley of the Kings

The Valley of the Kings was an ancient Egyptian burial ground that housed the elaborate tombs of pharaohs, filled with sacred texts, imagery, and treasures intended to aid the ruler's journey through the afterlife. This hallowed valley was seen as a portal to the underworld, where the deceased monarch could undergo transformation and rebirth under the protection of the gods.

Valley Temple

The Valley Temple was a sacred structure located at the base of Egyptian pyramids, where initial purification rituals were performed to prepare initiates for the rites and mysteries to be enacted within the main temple complex. These transitional spaces served as thresholds between the earthly and spiritual realms, facilitating the seeker's journey of transcendence.

Void State

The "Void State" represents the sacred emptiness or primordial waters from which new creation emerges in ancient Egyptian cosmology. Associated with the deity Nun, this state of pure potentiality was revered as the wellspring of all manifestation, containing the infinite possibilities that would eventually take form. Accessing the Void State was considered a gateway to profound spiritual insights and the mastery of divine creative powers.

Voice Activation

"Voice Activation" refers to the awakening of one's ability to transmit divine frequencies and sacred energies through sound and speech in Egyptian mysticism. By aligning their voice with the cosmic intelligence, initiates could activate subtle vibrational fields, invoke the presence of deities, and channel healing or transformative energies - tapping into the creative power of the divine logos.

Wadjet (Uatchet Egyptian: W³ḍty)

Wadjet, also known as Uatchet, was the serpent goddess who, together with her sister Nekhbet, formed the Nebty or "Two Ladies" who protected ancient Egypt. As the Eye of Horus, Wadjet represented divine protection, wholeness, and healing power. Her uraeus symbol, the raised cobra emblem, was worn on royal crowns, signifying divine authority and the channeling of kundalini energy for spiritual awakening.

Was-Ankh-Djed

The Was-Ankh-Djed scepter is Ptah's sacred tool, combining three distinct Egyptian symbols: the Was (a staff topped with a cobra head representing divine power), the Ankh (the loop-shaped symbol of eternal life force), and the Djed (a pillar marked with four sacred rings that bridges earth and stars). This tripartite scepter embodies Ptah's role as master builder and architect of manifestation, uniting serpentine power, life force, and cosmic connection into a single instrument of divine creation.

Wings of Isis

The "Wings of Isis" refer to the protective and transformative energy of the divine mother goddess, often visualized as wings of light that embrace and enfold the initiate. This imagery symbolized Isis's role as a nurturing, sheltering presence who guides the seeker through the process of spiritual rebirth and ascension, keeping them safe under the mantle of the sacred feminine.

Wisdom Keeper

A "Wisdom Keeper" was one who maintained and transmitted the sacred knowledge and mystical teachings of ancient Egypt through the generations. These guardians of esoteric wisdom were responsible for preserving the integrity of the traditions and ensuring their continuity, facilitating the unbroken lineage of initiation and spiritual illumination.

Word of Power (Heka)

"Words of Power," or Heka in ancient Egyptian, were sacred sounds, incantations, and phrases that were believed to activate specific spiritual frequencies and effects. These potent linguistic tools were viewed as conduits for divine energies, capable of invoking, directing, and transforming the fabric of reality through the creative force of consciousness expressed through speech.

Zep Tepi

"Zep Tepi" refers to the "First Time" in ancient Egyptian mythology - the primordial golden age when the gods were said to have walked the earth, establishing the fundamental principles and sacred orders that would govern creation. This mythic period of divine presence and harmonious alignment was revered as a template for the restoration of cosmic balance and the return to an enlightened state of being.

Zero Point

The "Zero Point" represents the state of pure potential in quantum physics, where all possibilities exist simultaneously in a field of undifferentiated consciousness. This point of absolute stillness and receptivity was seen as the wellspring from which manifested reality emerges, containing the infinite creative capacities that could be accessed and directed through various spiritual practices and modes of awareness.

ABOUT THE AUTHOR

 Iman Kamel transforms everyday magic into revolutionary awakening through film and writing. Her debut solo book "Quantum Leaps and Lost Socks" emerged from an extraordinary life journey - from climbing forbidden lemon trees in her grandmother's Cairo garden to creating award-winning films that illuminate untold stories.

An acclaimed filmmaker, Iman's documentaries have garnered international recognition, screening at major festivals worldwide. Her film "Nomad's Home" captured the spirit of Bedouin women artisans over seven years, while "Egyptian Jeanne d'Arc" explored themes of revolution and feminine power. Through her lens, ancient wisdom finds contemporary relevance, bridging cultures and bridging consciousness.

A graduate of the Fletcher School of Law and Diplomacy and the Berlin University of Arts, Iman's storytelling weaves together quantum physics and temple mysteries with surprising playfulness. Her work found new depths after a profound initiation with Egyptian Neteru at the Dendera Temple, inspiring her to develop the five-phase Lotus-Born Heart Process shared in this book.

Recognized by the World Economic Forum as an "Iconic Woman Creating a Better World for All," Iman's films and writing invite audiences into a revolution of consciousness that begins in their sock drawers and ends in the infinite. Through vivid adventures - surviving transformative fever dreams in remote China, dancing with dolphins in the Red Sea, and gathering with thirteen women for moonlit ceremonies on the Nile - she shows how life's greatest breakthroughs often arrive disguised as ordinary moments.

When not behind the camera or writing her next book, Iman guides global leaders and creatives through transformative experiences that bridge science and soul.

DANCE WITH THE EXTRAORDINARY

Where Lemon Trees Meet Quantum Dreams

Ready to discover the cosmic secrets in your sock drawer and the ancient wisdom in your morning coffee? Join Iman Kamel and a global community of playful visionaries as we transform the ordinary into the extraordinary through the Lotus-Born Heart Process.

At HolographicBeing.com, unlock:

- Sacred Adventures: From midnight ceremonies in Egyptian temples to dolphin dances in the Red Sea
- Quantum Play Sessions: Where science meets soul in delightful ways
- Creative Crucibles: Art-making that ignites transformation
- Global Gatherings: Connect with fellow seekers wearing mismatched socks
- Leadership Alchemy: Where boardroom meets temple wisdom

UPCOMING JOURNEYS INTO WONDER

→ "Dancing with Sekhmet": Temple Ceremonies in Egypt → "Quantum Coffee & Cosmic Tea": Morning Practice Retreats → "The Art of Sacred Mischief": Global Creativity Workshops → "Weaving Dreams into Reality": Collaborative Projects → "Leading from the Lotus Heart": Revolutionary Leadership Programs

Join us at HolographicBeing.com where every moment becomes a gateway to transformation.

Because the most profound revolutions begin with a single climb up a lemon tree...

Transform Your World by Remembering Your Magic

www.ingramcontent.com/pod-product-compliance
Lightning Source LLC
Chambersburg PA
CBHW071709120626
46550CB00001B/158